FROMMER'S

DE TO ROME

by Darwin Porter

Published by Frommer/Pasmantier Publishers
A Division of Simon & Schuster, Inc.
1230 Avenue of the Americas
New York, NY 10020

ISBN 0-671-52428-3

Manufactured in the United States of America

Motif Drawings by Paul Berkow

Although every effort was made to ensure the accuracy of price information appearing in this book, it should be kept in mind that prices can and do fluctuate in the course of time.

CONTENTS

MAPS

Inflation Alert!!!

Italy has witnessed some of the worst inflation in Europe. Although the hotel and restaurant shopper will still find many bargains, know that some overeager hoteliers, in their leap forward, have been known to increase prices more than 100% within a one- to two-year period. Of course, they are the exception rather than the rule.

Most hotels and restaurants in this guide will probably raise their tariffs during the lifetime of this edition (particularly during its second year, 1986), but perhaps by no more than 20% to 30%—painful enough. If you use this guide in planning your budget for a trip, you would be wise to take into account the probable increases.

The author of this book has spent laborious hours of research trying to ensure the accuracy of prices appearing in this guide. As we go to press, I believe we have obtained the most reliable data possible—but I cannot predict in these uncertain times just how long these prices will hold. However, the recommendations in this book will still represent the best values for your money.

Chapter I

ROME TODAY—BASIC ORIENTATION

YOUR FEET will probably first touch Roman soil at **Leonardo da Vinci International Airport,** alternatively called **Fiumicino** in honor of the town whose location is adjacent. It's a big sparkling glass structure near the mouth of the Tiber River, some 20 miles from downtown Rome.

A taxi into town will cost about 35,000 lire ($21.35) and up, so it's recommended that you take the airlines bus that runs from the front of the terminal building (see Chapter XI). The cost is only a fraction of the taxi fare, and you'll be let off in a good part of town to start your hotel hunt.

The drive in is rather uneventful until you pass through the city wall. The Great Aurelian Wall, started in A.D. 271 to calm Rome's barbarian jitters, is still remarkably intact.

Suddenly, ruins of imperial baths loom on one side, great monuments can be seen in the middle of blocks, and you have the shock of recognition that you're really in Rome—and not simply looking at pictures.

And inside these walls, you'll find a city designed for a population that walked where it was going. Parts of Rome actually look and feel more like an oversize village than the former imperial capital of the Western world.

The bus deposits you on Via Giolitti, right next to the **Stazione Termini,** or Terminal Station. The station faces a huge piazza, the **Piazza dei Cinquecento** (of the 500), which in many ways is an embodiment of the city. It's named after 500 Italians who died heroically in a 19th-century battle in Africa. There are certainly many more attractive sites in Rome, but this piazza has several noteworthy aspects. First, it is flanked by the ultramodern railroad station. And immediately next to the sculptured-cement, cantilevered roof of the station facade is a remnant of the **Servian**

Wall, built nearly six centuries before the birth of Christ by an ancient Roman king.

If that isn't contrast enough, the far side of the piazza is bordered by the ruins of the **Baths of Diocletian,** a former bastion of imperial luxury whose crumbling brick walls were once covered with the rarest of colored marbles, and even now enclose marble and bronze statuary.

Mapping the City

Most of the old city and its monuments lie on the east side of the Tiber (Fiume Tevere), which meanders through town between 19th-century stone embankments. However, several exceptionally important monuments are on the other side, to wit: **St. Peter's Basilica** and the **Vatican,** the **Castel Sant' Angelo** (formerly the tomb of the emperor Hadrian), and the colorful section of town known as **Trastevere.**

The bulk of ancient Rome, and Renaissance and baroque Rome too, lies across the Tiber from St. Peter's on the same side as Terminal Station. The various quarters of the city are linked together by large boulevards (large at least in some places) that have mostly been laid out since the late 19th century. For the 2½ millennia before that, the citizens had to make their way through narrow byways and curves that defeated all but the best senses of direction.

These streets—and they are among the most charming aspects of the city—still exist in large quantities, unspoiled in the main by the advances of modern construction. However, this tangled street plan has one troublesome element: automobiles. The traffic in Rome is awful. Snarls of Fiats and angry buses elbow for room on the Corso, or snake impatiently around the Pantheon. Every so often, the claustrophobic street plans of the Dark Ages open unexpectedly onto a vast piazza, and every driver accelerates full tilt for the distant horizon, while groups of peripatetic tourists and Romans flatten against marble fountains for protection, or stride with firm jaws right into the thick of the howling traffic. The traffic problem in Rome is nothing new; Julius Caesar was so exasperated by it that he banned all vehicular traffic during the daylight hours. Sometimes it's actually faster to walk than take a bus, especially during any one of Rome's four daily rush hours (that's right, *four:* to work, home for lunch/siesta, back to work, home in the evening). The hectic crush of urban Rome is considerably less during the month of August, when many Romans are out of town on holiday. If you visit at any other time of year, however, be prepared for the general frenzy that characterizes your average Roman street.

If you draw a squarish sort of circle with the Tiber River cutting down through the left side, you have a rough idea of the Rome we'll be concerning ourselves with—the section within the ancient walls. In the upper left-hand area, west of the Tiber, is **St. Peter's** and the fabulous museums of Vatican City. In the lower left-hand area, also across the Tiber, is **Trastevere,** which for simplicity's sake you can think of as the equivalent of New York's Greenwich Village. Lots of restaurants are found here, plus *very* old streets and a population (called Trasteverini) that doesn't consider you one of them until your family has lived there for six or seven generations.

The entire bottom flank of our circle is the seat of ancient Rome: the **Palatine Hill,** the **Capitoline Hill,** and the **Roman Forum** in the low area between them. Also in this area are scattered those monuments we've all seen so many pictures of: the **Colosseum,** the **Baths of Caracalla,** the **Arch of Constantine** (standing incongruously in the middle of a traffic island), and the stray pillars and pediments of the **Roman Forum,** and the later **Imperial Forums** built by the emperors better to carry on the trade of the day.

In center left, where the Tiber bulges out between St. Peter's and Trastevere, is the **Campo Marzio,** a former low-lying swampy area that was the heart of Papal Rome. This is where the most twisty streets and ancient-looking buildings (as opposed to ruins) are to be found. The section was sparsely populated by the Romans, who found it too low-lying for their tastes. It was only after the invading barbarians cut the aqueducts that supplied fresh water to the hills that the population (greatly diminished during those trying times from well over a million to a few thousand) moved down to the banks of the river.

Of the many landmarks in the area, the most impressive is the **Pantheon,** more than 2000 years old and still structurally intact. Also in this area, in fact just a few minutes' walk from the Pantheon, is the **Piazza Navona,** a charming baroque square built on the ruins of, and still maintaining the outline of, the Stadium of the emperor Domitian. There are two splendid fountains by Bernini here (the *Fountain of the Four Rivers,* each personified by a statue—check out the Nile, whose head is covered by a shroud since the source of the river was unknown when the fountain was built) and a third fountain by Borromini. On this spot ancient chariot races were held; later the popes flooded it and staged mock naval battles. Today it sees countless summer sidewalk art shows and is an ideal spot to savor a cappuccino at one of the outdoor cafés, and watch the sunlight play through the cascading waters of the Renaissance fountains. Herein lies the true appreciation of Rome, that sense of the endless continuity of life, and all the people who have lived in this city.

At the center of our simplified map is the **Monument to Victor Emmanuel,** a highly controversial pile of snow-white Brescian marble whose construction and quarrying must have employed whole cities. The prime minister at the time of construction was from Brescia, and we assume that had something to do with the choice of marble, since stone of this sort is not found anywhere near Rome. Victor Emmanuel was the first king of Italy after the unification of 1870, the first of the Italian House of Savoy which was to produce only four monarchs before its end at the close of World War II. We have to remember that the Italian peninsula consisted of a maze of independent states for more than a thousand years, between the fall of the Western Empire of Rome and the unification of Garibaldi in the late 19th century. Perhaps the newly unified government needed a monument of this scale to convince themselves they were really unified. You'll hear visitors make all sorts of comments about it—some assume it's a work of art and wax properly enthusiastic; some feel obligated to make snide and cynical remarks about its overwhelming gaucheness; others simply accept it as somehow a part of the Italian character, a character at once charming and lacking in subtlety.

Along the top of our "circle" is the **Villa Borghese,** called also the Borghese Gardens. This is a park that lies outside the ancient wall, entered from the Via Veneto through a gate built by Belisarius around 550. The Villa was laid out as a summer retreat in the 17th century by Cardinal Scipio Borghese. Today it's a beautiful park, containing an exquisite lake, long lanes with fountains and formal plantings, the Galleria Borghese (which contains Canova's celebrated statue of Pauline Borghese, the sister of Napoleon and quite a woman about town in early 19th-century Rome), and acres of eerie *Juliet of the Spirits*–type pine trees that are bound to delight the Fellini in you.

In the area between the Villa Borghese and the Victor Emmanuel monument are the **Spanish Steps,** the **Quirinal Palace** (successive home of popes, kings, and currently presidents), the **Piazza Barberini** (where there's a famous fountain by Bernini), and the **Via Veneto,** former haunt of the beautiful people. About the only part of our map not yet filled in is the right-hand side, and this is the area dominated by **Terminal Station,** and the aforementioned Piazza dei Cinquecento. It's a rather commercial area and, with several notable exceptions, most of our hotel selections are in the more graceful, more aesthetically appealing parts of the city.

THE MOST IMPORTANT STREETS: The sections of Rome are held together by what amounts to a mere handful of major arteries, which you'll keep crossing over and over again. Starting from the Victor Emmanuel monument, in the geographic center of our simplified map, there's a street running practically due north to the Piazza del Popolo and the city wall. This is the **Via del Corso,** one of the main streets of Rome, noisy, congested, always crowded with buses and afternoon shoppers, called simply "the Corso."

Again from the Victor Emmanuel monument, the major artery that goes west (and ultimately across the Tiber to St. Peter's) is the **Corso Vittorio Emanuele.** To go in the other direction, toward the Colosseum, you would take the **Via dei Fori Imperiali,** named after the excavated ruins of the imperial forums that flank this magnificent avenue. This road was laid out in the '30s by Mussolini, who was responsible for much of the fine archeological work in Rome, if perhaps for the wrong reasons.

Yet another central conduit is the **Via Nazionale,** running from the Piazza della Repubblica (also called the Piazza Esedra), ending again right by the Victor Emmanuel Monument, at the Piazza Venezia which lies in front of it.

GETTING AROUND: Getting around within the city isn't hard at all, once you have some idea of the geography before you set out, and the best way to do that is by purchasing a map. Be warned in advance *not* to depend on simplified maps, since too many streets are inevitably eliminated. Go to a newsstand and buy a copy of the *Nuovissima Pianta di Roma* (New Plan of Rome), published by several different outfits, in several different colors, and priced according to how chic the neighborhood is around the newsstand. In the ABCs chapter (XI) you'll find the details on getting into town from the airports, and getting around the city.

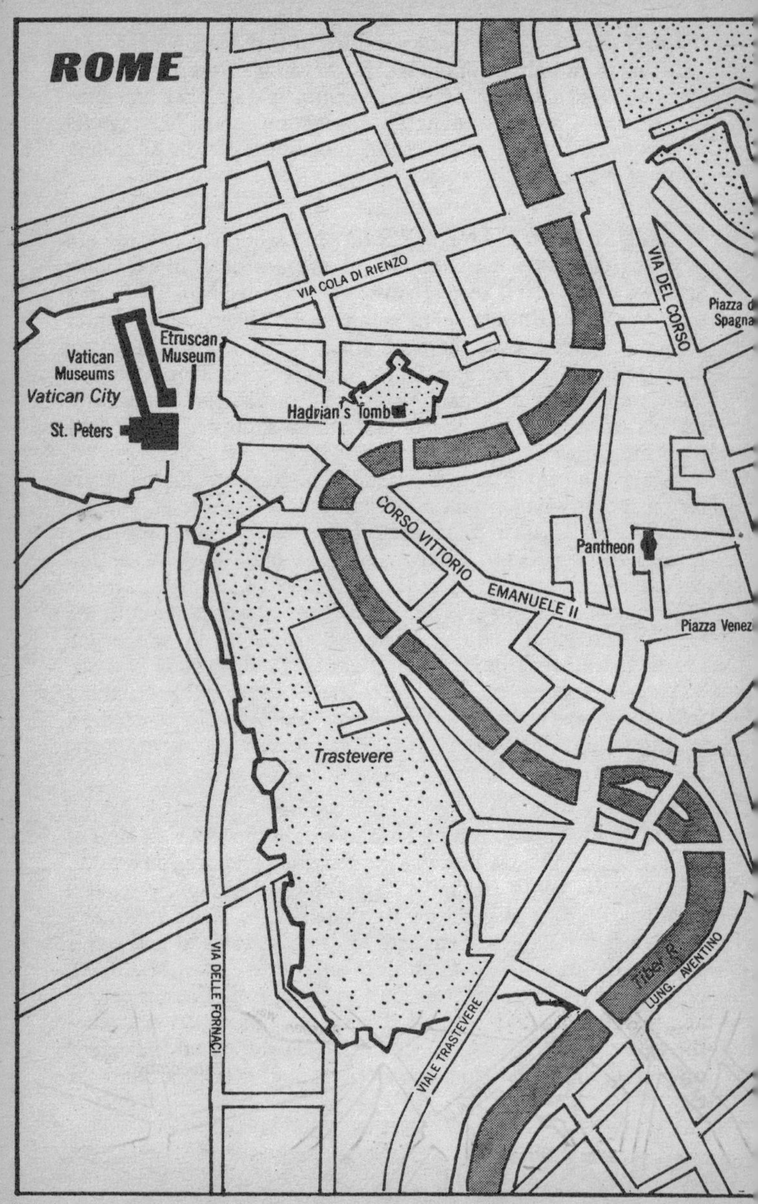
ROME
VIA COLA DI RIENZO
VIA DEL CORSO
Piazza d
Spagna
Etruscan
Museum
Vatican
Museums
Vatican City
St. Peters
Hadrian's Tomb
CORSO VITTORIO
EMANUELE II
Pantheon
Piazza Venez
Trastevere
VIA DELLE FORNACI
VIALE TRASTEVERE
Tiber R.
LUNG. AVENTINO

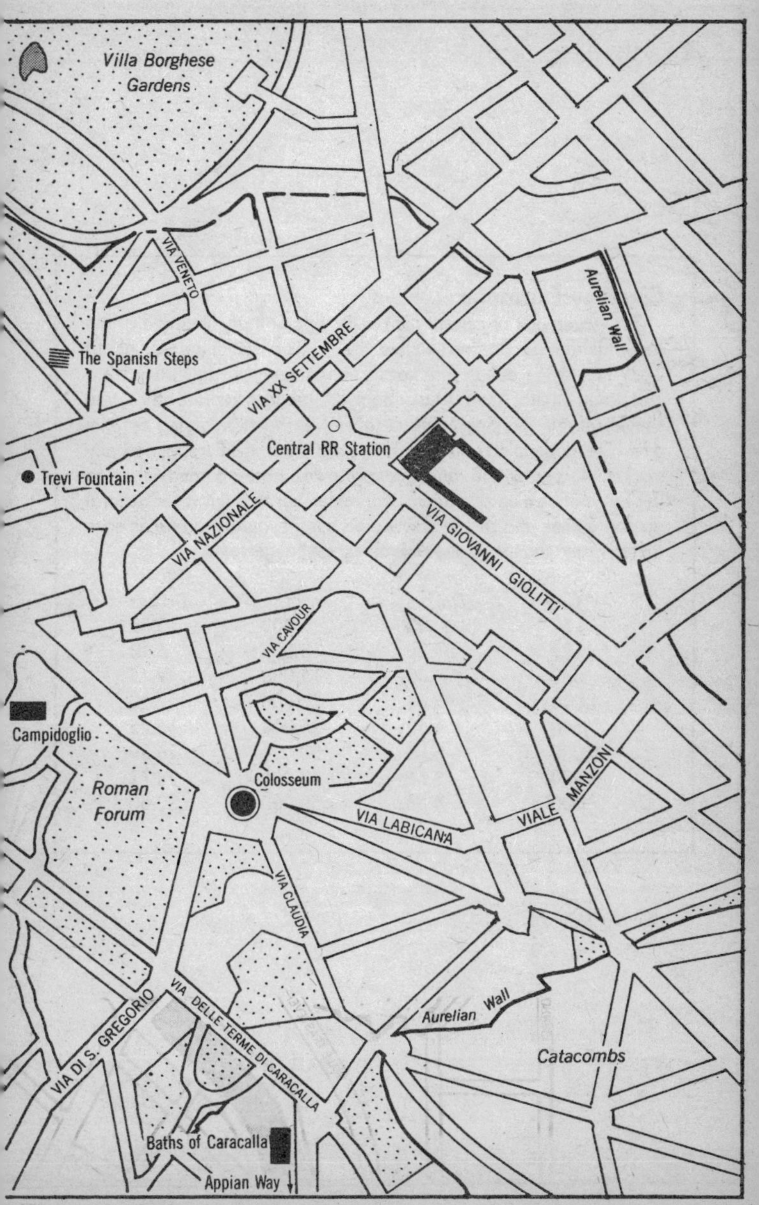
Villa Borghese
Gardens
VIA VENETO
The Spanish Steps
VIA XX SETTEMBRE
Central RR Station
Trevi Fountain
VIA NAZIONALE
Aurelian Wall
VIA GIOVANNI GIOLITTI
VIA CAVOUR
Campidoglio
Roman
Forum
Colosseum
VIA LABICANA
VIALE MANZONI
VIA CLAUDIA
VIA DI S. GREGORIO
VIA DELLE TERME DI CARACALLA
Aurelian Wall
Catacombs
Baths of Caracalla
Appian Way

Currency Exchange

The Italian unit of currency is the lira (plural form, lire), and at the time this edition was researched the rate of exchange was about 1639 lire to the dollar. The conversions throughout this book were calculated on that basis. At any bank or American Express office, you should receive this approximate rate of exchange, varying by only a few lire, depending on the daily fluctuations of the European money market. At a hotel, the rate is usually lower. Here's a handy chart to use for your own computations, but remember that this is for general guidance only, and should be checked before your departure, in case there is any change in the prevailing exchange rates.

Lire	*Dollars*	*Lire*	*Dollars*
50	$ .03	9,000	$5.49
325	.20	10,000	6.10
650	.40	15,000	9.15
1,000	.61	20,000	12.20
2,500	1.53	25,000	15.25
5,000	3.05	30,000	18.30
6,000	3.66	40,000	24.71
7,500	4.58	50,000	30.50

Chapter II

WHERE TO STAY

AFTER A LONG and careful process of elimination, I offer this list of recommended hotels. And although they come in several different price categories, they all share something in common: style. I've looked for places with architectural grace and a relaxed ambience, establishments where the management is alert and understanding, where the facilities provide all necessary comforts. But more specifically, I've sought out those hotels with personality, hotels that treat you like a guest instead of a walking travelers check.

HOTELS BY COST: My selections have been divided into three major categories: deluxe and first-class hotels, moderately priced hotels, and low-cost hotels. Rome's poshest hotels, while no bargain, are the equal of the poshest in Europe. The bulk of this chapter, however, concerns hotels in the medium-priced range, where you'll find rooms with private baths. The final group is low-cost hotels, and a charming group they are. They're not just for students, but for anyone with an eye to conserving hard-earned cash. Each one of them has been adjudged clean and cheerful, and they offer surprisingly more in services and facilities than one would expect from the prices they charge. In this latter category, you'll find a few pensions.

The pension is hard to describe if you've never seen one. Undoubtedly, the earliest ones were run by persons who had large apartments and simply rented out a room or two. Today, some pensions are actually hotels for all intents and purposes, and the appellation "pension" seems archaic. In general, they do tend to have a more personal touch, and most of them are still situated in parts of apartment buildings (as opposed to occupying an entire building). Some are quite elegant, located in swank parts of the city, and others are homey; it depends on the personality of the owner, whom you'll probably meet during your stay.

ROME: AVERAGE MONTHLY TEMPERATURES

Month	Temp.	Month	Temp.
January	49	July	82
February	52	August	78
March	57	September	73
April	62	October	65
May	70	November	56
June	77	December	47

All the hotels of Rome are rated by the government in various classifications from deluxe on down to fourth class. These classifications are dispensed with little or no regard for aesthetics or location, so it's quite possible to find a hotel (one such is listed in this chapter) with gilt furniture, ultramodern private baths for each of the rooms, antiques in the bar, located just a block from the Spanish Steps, but rated second class because there is no dining room. Second- and third-class hotels are frequently fashionable with international travelers, so it's no reflection on your social standing to stay in one.

WORDS TO THE WISE: Before I begin describing my choices, I'm going to warn you about some customs and situations in Italian hotels that you won't find in the States. Number one is that rooms vary substantially in the same hotel, even though the prices wouldn't seem to indicate it. It is perfectly acceptable to ask to see the room first, before you check in. Often you'll be sent up with a bellboy who has several keys, and you can choose the room that suits you best—unless, of course, only one room is vacant. Second, Rome tends to be noisy and so, unfortunately, are its hotel rooms. Accommodations facing outside are invariably noisy—so be prepared.

As for hotel bills, everything is "à la carte," as it were. You have a bathless room? Then be prepared to pay extra for a shower. It's hot outside? Then that air conditioner in your room will probably cost quite a bit *extra* on top of the room price. It's cold outside? Sometimes even heat is charged for, although rarely these days. The next thing you should know is that some hotels have off-season rates; if you're traveling between November and Easter, ask at the desk and you may be in for a nice surprise. As for tipping, far too many Americans think that because "service and tax" are added onto their bills, the chambermaid has been taken care of. Not entirely true. In all but deluxe hotels, the service charge covers only pension funds and the like, and gives nothing to the maid for herself.

The Reservation Question

It's always a good idea to make reservations before you go, and this can be done through a travel agent or else by writing directly to the hotel (some establishments require deposits, and this takes a great deal of time, especially considering how slow the Italian mails are). It's invariably easy to obtain an expensive room at any time of the year, but low-cost accommodations are generally heavily booked.

In case, however, you haven't made reservations—and quite a few travelers never seem to get around to doing so—you're bound to find some place that can put you up, for the *first night.* My advice, in that event, is to get up at the earliest possible time in the morning (say, 8 a.m.), get yourself together, and head straight for your first choice of hotels, timing your arrival for shortly before 9 a.m. At this hour of the morning, desk clerks usually know who will be leaving, but no arrivals will be there yet. If there is any space to be had, you'll be assured of getting first chance at it.

A Word about Taxes

All Italian hotels impose an I.V.A. (Imposta sul Valore Aggiunto) tax. This tax is in effect throughout the other Common Market countries. It applies only to the "value added" to products and services as they progress from source to consumer. It replaces some 20 other taxes and is an effort to streamline the tax structure.

What that means for you is an actual increase in the price you'll pay for a hotel room. Deluxe hotels will slap you with a whopping tax of 18%, while first-class, second-class, whatever, hotels will impose 9%. Most hotels will quote you an inclusive rate, covering this tax. However, other establishments prefer to add it on when you go to pay the bill. To know exactly what you're going to pay for a room, ask to be quoted an inclusive rate—that is, service, even a continental breakfast (which is often obligatory)—when you check in. It will avoid unpleasant surprises later.

Deluxe Choices

The **Grand,** 3 Via Vittorio Emanuele Orlando (tel. 4709), just off the Piazza della Repubblica, is one of the great hotels of Europe. When it was inaugurated by its creator, César Ritz, in 1894, Escoffier presided over a lavish banquet, and the note of grandeur struck then has never died away. The hotel has been likened to a gracious and aristocratic dowager who doesn't get older, just better. Its roster of guests has included some of the greatest names in European history, including royalty of course, and such new-world moguls as Henry Ford and J. P. Morgan. Only a few minutes from the Via Veneto, the Grand has long been popular with both international and Roman elite and a favorite of the diplomatic corps.

It looks like a large, late Renaissance palace, its five-floor facade covered with handsomely carved loggias, lintels, guoins, and cornices. Inside are the kind of lounges and lobbies in which you can rejoice. The floors are covered with marble and thick Oriental rugs. The walls are a riot of baroque plasterwork painted in soft hues of gray. Huge crystal chandeliers, Louis XVI-style furniture, lush potted palms, and antique clocks and wall sconces complete the picture. One opulent room leads to another, and thanks to upholsterers and painters and considerable spending by the CIGA chain, the Grand is still the most elegant hotel in Rome.

The personal service rendered to occupants of the 175 bedrooms, directed by Renzo Chiaranda, concierge and one of the greatest problem solvers of all time, is impeccable. As for the bedrooms, they are lavishly decorated with matching curtains and carpets and equipped with TVs, small bars, telephones, dressing rooms, and fully tiled baths. Every accommodation is different—while most are traditional, with antique headboards and Venetian chandeliers, some are ultramodern. The regular singles and doubles are quite spacious, costing from 200,000 lire ($122) to 300,000 lire ($183) in a single from 280,000 lire ($170.80) to 390,000 lire ($237.90) in a double, plus I.V.A. and city tax. Every guest room is soundproofed, and the housekeeping is immaculate.

There is a snackbar called Le Pavillon where you can enjoy snacks amid potted plants. Le Rallye is the bar and grill room, and the decor includes plaid carpets and soft lighting from wall sconces that are actually small horns for fox hunts (or facsimiles). Meals are à la carte. Dietetic and kosher foods can be arranged with advance notice.

The hotel has a beauty salon and babysitting service, and you can make arrangements to have your car parked in a garage.

Cavalieri Hilton International, 101 Via Cadlolo (tel. 31-51), combines all the advantages of a resort hotel with the convenience of being within a few minutes' drive from the center of town. With imperial stature, it overlooks Rome and the Alban Hills from its perch on top of Monte Mario. Its design includes carefully patterned masonry, sweeping expanses of aluminum, glass, and travertine, and the kind of intensely cultivated landscaping that, combined with the sparkling air and the wide vistas over Rome, make you feel refreshingly removed from the congestion of the city below.

It is set in Eden-like gardens, a total of 15 acres of carefully placed trees, flowering shrubs, and stonework. The facilities are so complete that many visitors (obviously not first-timers to Rome) never leave the hotel grounds. A view from the window of one of the tastefully contemporary bedrooms might include the waters of the big outdoor pool and sundeck, the verdant umbrella pines and palm trees of the garden, and the sparkling lights of the city just at the bottom of the hill. There are tennis courts a few steps away, a jogging path for getting rid of jet lag, a sauna with massage facilities, two highly accommodating bars, and one of the best restaurants and nightlife attractions in Rome, the Pergola (more about this later).

The entrance to the hotel leads you past a uniformed doorman (who's always eager to summon one of the waiting taxis) into the marble lobby, whose imaginative sculpture and dramatic, winding stairwells are usually flooded with sunlight from the massive windows. A lower level contains a marble fountain whose waters swirl into a circular channel down an almost interminable vortex, chiseled into the white stone.

On the premises is an indoor arcade of elegant shops, a garden-style restaurant—the Trattoria del Cavalieri—serving well-prepared meals of almost any degree of formality, and a constantly changing international clientele that is usually only about 25% American. A 24-hour concierge service is there to provide you with solutions to "whatever your problems," including a free hotel bus that makes frequent runs to the Via Veneto and the Spanish Steps.

Each of the spacious rooms contains a large, well-appointed bath, a tiled sun balcony, color TV, phone, well-stocked mini-bar, spacious closets, and access to 24-hour room service. Single rooms range from 175,000 lire ($106.75) to 250,000 lire

($152.50) daily, while doubles go from 275,000 lire ($167.75) to 350,000 lire ($213.50).

Excelsior, 125 Via Vittorio Veneto (tel. 4708), is among the best known of Rome's luxury hotels. Pronounced "Ess-shell-see-or," it is a limestone palace whose baroque corner tower (which looks right over the U.S. Embassy) is a landmark in Rome. A handsome entrance, complete with flocks of big Fiat Flaminias and Mercedes limousines, as well as trees in pots and elegant wrought-iron gates, leads to a string of cavernous reception rooms of the same design school as the Grand a few blocks away. There are more thick rugs, marble floors and chandeliers, more gilded garlands and pilasters on the walls. However, amid the profusion of gilded wall decorations and Empire furniture (supported by winged lions and the like), you'll notice a quite different atmosphere.

There are 234 double rooms here, 96 singles, and 37 suites, all air-conditioned with thermostatic control and with direct phone lines. The place clicks like a well-oiled machine. The rooms come in two basic varieties: new (the result of a major renovation program) and traditional. Doubles are spacious and elegantly furnished, often with antiques, and with silk curtains. The furnishings in singles are also of high quality. Most of the bedrooms are different, many with sumptuous Hollywood-style baths, marble walled with separate baths and showers, sinks, bidets, and mountains of fresh towels. Singles rent for 195,000 lire ($118.95) to 280,000 lire ($170.80) and doubles for 280,000 lire ($170.80) to 410,000 lire ($246.10), the higher prices charged for superior deluxe rooms. The city tax and I.V.A. are added to all charges.

The Excelsior Bar is perhaps the most famous on the Via Veneto, and La Cupola restaurant is celebrated for its national and regional cuisine, with dietetic and kosher food being prepared on request. Among the amenities at the Excelsior are continuous room service, a beauty salon, a barber, a sauna, and babysitting service. This is one of the more prestigious members of the CIGA chain.

The palatial hotel, near the American Embassy, once attracted some of the stellar lights of the "Hollywood on the Tiber" era—notably Shelley Winters, Vittorio Gassman, Ingrid Bergman, and Roberto Rossellini. Nowadays, you're more likely to bump into international financiers and Arab princesses.

Hassler Villa Medici, 6 Trinità dei Monti (tel. 679-2651), has an ambience of the 1930s, and the overall effect is highly successful. First, a few preliminaries: The location is superb, right at the top of the Spanish Steps, at the hub of Rome. The clientele is swank too. Kings and queens have been known to keep suites here, and everybody from Eisenhower to Kennedy to Nixon has checked in. The lobbies and public rooms sport curved and gilded, indirectly lit ceilings supported by forests of square marble pillars. Shimmery blue-velvet chairs and Oriental carpets together with silk curtains and freshly cut flowers give an aura of hushed smartness. The Hassler has but 100 rooms, furnished with wall-to-wall carpets, antique-painted beds, Oriental runner rugs, and usually matching bedspreads and curtains. Some rooms have balconies with breathtaking views of Rome; all accommodations contain private bath, usually with two sinks and a bidet. And while the rooms aren't as large as those in the Grand, they're every bit as comfortable. With tax included, singles rent for about 250,000 lire ($152.50), doubles for about 350,000 lire ($213.50). In summer, breakfast and lunch are served in a charming, flower-bedecked courtyard. On the top floor is the Hassler Roof Restaurant, a great favorite with visitors and Romans alike for its fine cuisine and lovely view.

Eden, 49 Via Ludovisi (tel. 474-3551), stands in an enviable position at the entrance to the Borghese Gardens and the Via Veneto. Actually the hotel was built before the turn of the century, but it has been so completely renovated you'd never know it. While not exactly a baroque palace, it still has rich trappings to give it distinction. In the chic Ludovisi district, it is surrounded by the gardens of the Villa Ludovisi, the old Convent of S. Isidoro, and the Villa Medici. The carpeting and lavish use of marble in the entrance hall is befitting such a deluxe hotel. The rooms are good size, furnished in a way that is conservative and dignified, but attractive. A few have been given a completely modern look with built-in pieces. All contain private baths or showers. Singles range in price from 200,000 lire ($122) to 230,000 lire ($140.30); doubles from 250,000 lire ($152.50) to 300,000 lire ($183)—including service, tax, heating, or air conditioning.

The most spectacular feature of the Eden is its penthouse restaurant and bar, offering one of the most panoramic views of Rome. Called Charles, the restaurant was named for the maître d', Giancarlo Castrucci. You might begin with rigatoni with ricotta and pepper, then follow with filet of beef alla Charles. You can dine well here for about 100,000 lire ($61) per person, including wine. Arrive early for dinner so you can enjoy a drink in the bar, with its tufted sofas and armchairs in black leather.

Quirinale, 7 Via Nazionale (tel. 479-901), is for opera buffs. In that sort of no-man's-land between a deluxe hotel and a superior first-class contender, it was built by the same architect who designed Rome's Teatro dell'Opera. In fact, you can walk right through the lobby into the opera house. The hotel has had a long and illustrious history, having housed many stars who appeared in the theater. As a historical footnote, Giuseppe Verdi stayed here on April 13, 1893, during the première of *Falstaff.* Most of the bedrooms have been refurbished and are well maintained. Doubles rent for 250,000 lire ($152.50); singles from 175,000 lire ($106.75)—all tariffs including service and tax. The rooms overlooking the garden are grabbed first. Even if you're not staying at the Quirinale, you might want to drop in before the opera and have a drink in the hotel bar, with its decorative motif of vintage car prints and medallions of leading automobile clubs throughout the world.

OTHER LEADERS: Grand Hotel Leonardo da Vinci, 324 Via Dei Gracchi (tel. 063-9680), lies across the bridge from the Piazza del Popolo in the Quartiere Prati on the Vatican side of the Tiber. Recently built, it has the aura of a modern art museum. Original lithographs, paintings, and watercolors decorate the public rooms (even the hair salon has a work of art). The irregularly shaped bedrooms vary in decoration, but all are equipped with private baths and air conditioning. Free-form molded white-plastic furnishings give an avant-garde look to some of the rooms. All this luxury is not without its price tag: singles cost 150,000 lire ($91.50); doubles, 200,000 lire ($122). Full board is 85,000 lire ($51.85) per person daily in addition to the room rate. Dining is in a grill, a snackbar, or a restaurant.

Cardinal Hotel, 62 Via Giula (tel. 654-2719). Like many of the constructions in this part of town, this particular building has had a long and complicated history. Built by Bramante in the 1400s with stones hauled from the Roman Forum, it was intended as a courthouse but later became the center of the Armenian church in Rome. It stands on the city's most beautiful Renaissance street. Today, clients get a glimpse of the original stonework in the exposed walls of both the bar and the breakfast room, as well as the chiseled inscription of a Sabine tomb built into the red walls of one of the sitting areas. About a block from the Tiber, the hotel includes two inner courtyards dotted with statues, comfortable leather couches, and an interior decor almost entirely done in shades of scarlet.

The sunny bedrooms are clean, well furnished, and from the upper floors, offer interesting views of Renaissance Rome. Double rooms rent for around 175,000 lire ($106.75), while singles cost around 110,000 lire ($67.10). Each, of course, has a private bath, and a continental breakfast is included.

Boston, 47 Via Lombardia (tel. 473-951), is an old place that's been completely renovated and now basks in a first-class rating. The location is excellent—three blocks from the Via Veneto, five minutes on foot to the Spanish Steps, and across the street from the Villa Borghese. It's a bustling place, with 130 rooms and multileveled lobbies glistening with brown marble and velvet. The guest rooms are comfortably fitted with new furniture, much of it reproductions of Victorian pieces. Rates include service, tax, and a continental breakfast. The single cost is 130,000 lire ($79.30), increasing to 210,000 lire ($128.10) in a double. Air conditioning is included as well. The bar downstairs is all carved wood and smoked mirrors, with an adjoining room where drinkers can relax on velvet chairs. The restaurant is a mammoth place filled with red plush chairs and crisp white cloths.

Hotel Lord Byron, 5 Via G. de Notaris (tel. 360-9541), is an art deco villa set on a residential hilltop in Parioli, an area of embassies and exclusive town houses at the edge of the Villa Borghese. From the moment you climb the gently curving entrance steps from the staffed parking lot in front, you'll see the kinds of design accessories that would attract what might be among the most discreetly sophisticated clientele in Italy.

An oval Renaissance urn in finely chiseled marble fills a niche especially created for it in the strikingly simple reception area, whose walls are covered with top-quality burled paneling, finished to a dull sheen with successive coats of plasticized lacquer. In the evening, a piano provides live music near the angular lobby bar, where vintage antiques have been covered with unusual fabrics and what might be considered among the best of modern Italian design. Masses of flowers are everywhere, the lighting is discreet, and everything is on the kind of intensely cultivated small scale that usually makes such a place seem more like a well-staffed (and extremely expensive) private home than a hotel.

Each of the 40 rooms is different, most often with lots of mirrors, upholstered walls, spacious bathrooms with gray marble accessories, big dressing rooms/closets, and all the amenities needed. Singles cost around 260,000 lire ($158.60), while doubles go for around 320,000 lire ($195.20), breakfast not included. On the premises is one of Rome's best restaurants, covered separately in the dining section.

Flora, 191 Via Vittorio Veneto (tel. 497-821), is a "grand hotel" styled like a palazzo. For many years it has stood at the top of the Via Veneto at the gateway to the Borghese Gardens. The public rooms are furnished with well-selected reproductions and antiques, with Oriental carpets and crystal chandeliers. The accommodations are well furnished and well maintained, each with a private bath. In high season, a double costs 180,000 lire ($109.80); a single, 110,000 lire ($67.10)—including a continental breakfast. Air conditioning is optional, but it will cost an extra 6000 lire ($3.66). A focal point of social get-togethers is the Empire Bar.

Jolly, 1 Corso d'Italia (tel. 8495). Jolly hotels used to be built in remote parts of Italy lacking suitable tourist accommodations. That policy, long ago rescinded, utterly disappeared with the opening of the chain's showcase hostelry, between the Villa Borghese gardens and the Via Veneto. Totally ignoring the traditional, the hotel's architects opted for avant-garde modern in metal and concrete, distinguished by bronze-tinted windows. Try to get one of the accommodations with garden views. To register, you descend a grand staircase, arriving at a sunken lobby. The rooms here are bold in concept, compact in space, and contemporary in furnishings. For a room and a buffet breakfast, the single tariff is 170,000 lire ($103.70), increasing to about 220,000 lire ($134.20) in a double. These rates include tax, a continental breakfast, and service. You can take your Campari on one of the panoramic terraces or else sneak away for a cozy rendezvous in the American bar.

Hotel Raphaël, 2 Largo Febo (tel. 656-9051), is known to the discerning who prefer a palace buried in the heart of Old Rome. A tasteful place, its facade draped in ivy, furnished with fine old Italian pieces, it lures with its sophisticated and restful atmosphere. International celebrities check in and out unobtrusively. All of its air-conditioned bedrooms have private baths or showers, and a few have their own terraces. A single rents for 105,000 lire ($64.05), a double for 175,000 lire ($106.75), all tariffs including a continental breakfast, service, and taxes. The bedrooms are individually decorated, simply done with wood-grained built-ins. The hotel is air-conditioned. In the lounges are fine antiques, excellent art objects, ornate gilt mirrors, and high-backed chairs. The dining room has a log fire-

Life in a Belle-Époque Palace

Giulio Cesare, 287 Via degli Scipioni (tel. 310-244), is a palace built in the closing days of the pre–World War I "belle époque." Many years ago, it was the private residence of the Countess of Solari, and judging from its size, one can just imagine the entertaining that once went on here. The baroque stone building stands in a neighborhood of palaces on a quiet tree-lined street. You enter the reception area via a short flight of wide stairs. Note the ceiling fresco of the boy playing the pipes for two maidens. The elevator runs up the old stairwell, and once upstairs there are long, hushed corridors with thick carpets—a different color for each floor. Your room will be completely carpeted in a pale pastel, the chairs will be needlepoint or plush, light will come from an antique chandelier, and the walls are papered. The baths are ultramodern, and your balcony (more than half the rooms have one) will probably be shaded by one of the old trees that grow in the garden. With an American breakfast buffet, a single in high season rents for 170,000 lire ($103.70), a double for 200,000 lire ($122). Other facilities include a lovely garden where breakfast is served, a snackbar, a piano bar, and a garage.

place, and the bar carries its liquor inside a gilded baroque cabinet. But the special delight is the rooftop terrace, with its many levels. You can have drinks here, enjoying the vista of tile rooftops on nearby buildings.

Grand Hotel de la Ville, 67–71 Via Sistina (tel. 6733), looks deluxe, even though it's officially rated first class, from the minute you walk through the revolving door, whose swing is initiated by a smartly uniformed doorman. At the hotel, which was a palace built in the 19th century on the site of the ancient Lucullo's Gardens, the eye is greeted with Oriental rugs, marble tables, brocade furniture, and a smiling staff that speaks English in correctly hushed tones. There are endless corridors leading to what seems, at first, a maze of ornamental lounges, all elegantly upholstered and hung with their quota of crystal lighting fixtures. Some of the public rooms have a sort of '30s elegance to them, others are strictly baroque, and in the middle of it all is a lovely open courtyard. The Patio Restaurant on the second floor overlooks the garden and serves both Italian and international cuisine. The hotel has an American piano bar presided over by a resident pianist.

The 194 bedrooms, all with private baths, are quite pleasant, some streamlined and functional, furnished with sleek Formica pieces; others a bit larger and more comfortably old-fashioned. The higher rooms with balconies have one of the most spectacular views of Rome to be found anywhere, but of course all guests are free to use the roof terrace with the same view. Doubles with private bath go for 250,000 lire ($152.50); singles, 185,000 lire ($112.85); these tariffs include a continental breakfast, service, air conditioning, and tax.

Grand Hotel Plaza, 126 Via del Corso (tel. 672-101). The Empress Carlotta of Mexico received Pope Pius IX here in 1866, and in 1933 Pietro Mascagni composed his opera *Nerone* here. Today Vincent Price views this as his favorite hotel in Rome (he admits that he always stayed here while making "all those bad movies"), and when you see the slightly faded but very grand decor, you'll understand why. The public rooms are vintage 19th century and contain stained-glass skylights, massive crystal chandeliers, potted palms, inlaid marble floors, and a life-size stone lion guarding the entrance to the ornate stairway leading upstairs. If you decide to have a drink at the bar, which seems an almost interminable distance across the parquet floor of the opulent ballroom, you might spend more time staring at the ceiling than at whomever you happen to be with. Single rooms rent for around 110,000 lire ($67.10), while doubles go for 160,000 lire ($97.60). Extra beds can be set up in any of the spacious bedrooms for an additional 40,000 lire ($24.40).

Hotel Mediterraneo, 15 Via Cavour (tel. 464-051). You'll quickly get a feeling of expanded space and Italian style when you enter the high-ceilinged lobby of this quality hotel near the railway station. The public rooms are covered from top to bottom with light-gray marble and accented throughout with busts of Roman statesmen, marquetry mosaics (*Prometheus Bound* is patterned above the green marble fireplace), and comfortable reading chairs. Considered the flagship hotel of the family-run Bettoja chain, the establishment contains a well-recommended restaurant, the 21, and a friendly and efficient personnel, plus a series of well-appointed bedrooms in either a new or a slightly older wing. Each of the 274 units has all the modern conveniences, including air conditioning, and rents for around 170,000 lire ($103.70) in a single, for around 210,000 lire ($128.10) in a double, with a continental breakfast included.

Hotel Massimo d'Azeglio, 18 Via Cavour (tel. 463-288), is the up-to-date hotel near the train station that was established as a small restaurant by one of the founders of an Italian hotel dynasty more than a century ago. Today, this once-great hotel is less appealing than it was in its heyday, but it still offers clean and comfortable accommodations in a central part of town. Its facade is one of the most elegant neoclassical structures in the area, although its lobby has been renovated into a low-ceilinged structure with light paneling, plus an adjacent bar and a well-trained staff. This oldest member of the Bettoja chain charges 120,000 lire ($67.10) for a single and 190,000 lire ($115.90) for a double. Each accommodation has a private bath and air conditioning, and the rates include a continental breakfast. The restaurant is covered separately in the dining chapter.

Hotel d'Inghilterra, 14 Via Bocca di Leone (tel. 672-161), is a truly elegant little hotel, two blocks from the foot of the Spanish Steps, just off Via Condotti. It stands on its own little piazza, surrounded with ancient-looking buildings that match or harmonize with its ochre color. It looks rather like a small palace, and it's been a home in Rome to such notables as Ernest Hemingway, Sir Alec Guinness, and Anatole France, among others. In the 19th century, the King of Portugal met here with the pope. The entrance rooms are small, done in marble and gilt, and to the left is a sumptuous Victorian lounge. Beyond the desk area, crisply uniformed maids pad unobtrusively up and down the marble stairs, bearing silver breakfast trays to the rooms above. Accommodations have the same discreetly refined air you feel in the lobby, and the decor frequently includes quality antiques made of dark, heavy wood. Rooms with bath cost 190,000 lire ($115.90) in a double, 150,000 lire ($91.50) in a single. An English-style bar on the premises is an ideal spot for a drink and a snack.

Hotel Forum, 25–30 Via Tor dei Conti (tel. 679-2446), off the Fori Imperiali, offers an elegance that savors the drama of Old Rome, as well as tasteful, sometimes opulent, accommodations. It's a medium-size nugget (90 rooms, all with bath or shower), whose units and dining roof terrace look out on the sights of the ancient city, the Colosseum or Forum. The hotel is built around a medieval bell tower, incorporating it happily. The bedrooms are exquisitely appointed with fine antiques, mirrors, marquetry, and Oriental rugs. In high season, the Forum charges an inclusive 225,000 lire ($137.25) in a double, 175,000 lire ($106.75) in a single. Reserve well in advance. The hotel's lounges are conservatively conceived as a country estate, with paneled walls and furnishings that combine Italian and French provincial. Dining is an event, either sitting on tapestry-covered chairs in front of picture windows, or on the spacious terrace. You can enjoy an *aperitivo* at the hotel's bar on the roof, surveying the timeless Roman Forum.

Hotel Atlante, 34 Via Vitelleschi (tel. 654-4738), is a first-class hotel a short distance from St. Peter's Basilica and the Vatican. The tastefully renovated lobby is covered with dark marble, chrome trim, and lots of exposed wood, while the upper floors somehow give the impression of being inside a luxuriously appointed ocean liner. This stems partly from the lavish use of curved and lacquered surfaces and an intensely cultivated decor that includes walls upholstered in freshly colored printed fabrics, streamlined modern bathrooms, and plush wall-to-wall carpeting. Even the door handles are art deco–inspired brass. These open into small but posh accommodations outfitted with all the modern comforts, such as frigo bar, phone, color TV, and air conditioning.

For 120,000 lire ($73.20) per person, including breakfast, you can stay here in a twin or double room, with tax and service included. Singles pay 185,000 lire ($112.85) per night. The most attractive feature of the hotel is its roof-garden restaurant and solarium, with one of the most striking views of St. Peter's of any hotel in Rome. The restaurant has double rows of windows, planting, and terracotta floors along with white-painted garden furniture. A meal here costs from 35,000 lire ($21.35). If there is no room at this inn, the owner, Mr. Menucci, will try to get you a room at his nearby Atlante Garden.

Incidentally, Mr. Mencucci is the only hotel owner in central Rome to offer a free pickup service at the airport upon your arrival. Naturally, you must notify him of your flight number and arrival time.

Hotel Atlante Garden, 78 Via Crescenzio (tel. 359-8884), is a recently renovated inner-city hotel on a tree-lined street near the Vatican. The entrance takes you through a garden-style tunnel lined with potted plants that eventually leads into a warmly appointed series of public rooms decorated with sunflower-colored, burlap-textured wallpaper, midnight-blue carpeting, and white lacquer trim. More classical in its decor than its sister under the same management (the Hotel Atlante), the Atlante Garden offers 19th-century bedrooms that have been freshly papered and painted, which contain tastefully conservative furniture. The renovated baths are tiled and open into rooms filled with all the modern accessories. The hotel will pick you up at the airport if you arrange for it in advance. Singles cost 182,000 lire ($111.02), while doubles rent for around 238,000 lire ($145.18), breakfast included. An extra bed can be set up in any room for another 56,000 lire ($34.16).

The Moderate Range

Fontana Hotel, 96 Piazza di Trevi (tel. 678-6113), has rapidly become one of the chic little hotels of Rome. It stands directly across from the Trevi Fountain, although it is much older than the fountain. The hotel was once a monastery in the 13th century. Now it has been completely renovated and restored. To provide enough room, two former monks' cells have been joined to make one accommodation. One is the bedroom, the other the bathroom with ingeniously designed built-in areas. The decorative theme is the same throughout the bedrooms—the walls and ceiling covered with soft blue and white flowers. There are muted draperies and window seats with soft pads. About ten rooms overlook the fountain, and these are assigned on a first-come, first-served basis. In a double, the rate is 130,000 lire ($79.30), dropping to 80,000 lire ($48.80) in a single, these tariffs including a continental breakfast served in an enclosed rooftop loggia where a rustic decor has been tastefully combined with a stark black-and-white modern theme.

Albergo Nazionale, 131 Piazza Montecitorio (tel. 6789-251), occupies a central location adjacent to the Piazza Colonna and next to the Parliament buildings. The exterior is the color of burnt umber, and the facade is severely simple with only the shuttered windows breaking the expanse of stone. Inside you'll see the results of a major renovation program. The management has installed wood-paneled lobbies, but preserved the fine antiques that give the hotel its character. For the most part, rooms are large, either carpeted in muted gray or sometimes floored with marble. Often, in addition to the substantial old-fashioned furnishings, you'll find a small icebox—a thoughtful extra. A spacious double with private bath costs 160,000 lire ($97.60), while a single with similar amenities is priced at 110,000 lire ($67.10). Your continental breakfast is included in the rates quoted. But if you want air conditioning, an extra 6000 lire ($3.66) will be added.

Columbus, 33 Via della Conciliazione (tel. 656-4874). Remember the film (and book) *The Agony and the Ecstasy,* with Pope Julius II driving Charlton Heston (as Michelangelo) into a frenzy over the Sistine Chapel? Well, the *real* Pope Julius once lived here. Of course, he was a cardinal then, and it was his private palace, but the building looks much as it must have those long centuries ago—a severe time-stained facade, small windows, and heavy wooden doors from the street to the courtyard. The cobbled entranceway leads to a reception hall with castle-like furniture, then on to a series of baronial public rooms, remarkable for their size as well as general appointments. Note especially the main salon with its walk-in fireplace, oil portraits, battle scenes, and Oriental rugs. The hotel enjoys a convenient location a block from St. Peter's on Via della Conciliazione, the triumphal boulevard built by Mussolini in the 1930s to "open up" the Vatican after the Lateran Treaty of 1929 (which created the Vatican State).

As for the rooms, they're considerably simpler than the tiled and tapestried salons, done up in soft beiges and furnished with comfortable and serviceable modern pieces. All accommodations are spacious, but a few are enormous and still have some original details, like decorated wood ceilings and frescoed walls. Rates at the Columbus, which was built some 12 years before its namesake set off for America, are 52,000 lire ($31.72) to 90,000 lire ($54.90) in a single, and 85,000 lire ($51.85) to 130,000 lire ($79.30) in a double.

Napoleon, 105 Piazza Vittorio Emanuele (tel. 737-646), is a first-class hotel conveniently located in a central area, but quiet nevertheless. Just off the main railway station and air terminal, it offers 82 rooms, each traditionally furnished, all with bath or shower, air conditioning, phone, and radio. Rates, inclusive of taxes and service, in a single room are 76,000 lire ($46.36), rising in a double room to 130,000 lire ($79.30). A buffet-style breakfast costs extra. Dinner is from 22,000 lire ($13.42).

Hotel Oxford, 93 Via Boncompagni, off the Via Veneto (tel. 474-0805), is centrally located, not only near the smartest street in Rome, but also adjacent to Borghese Park. The Oxford has recently been renovated, and it is air-conditioned throughout, as well as centrally heated and fully carpeted. There is a pleasant lounge, a cozy bar (which serves snacks), plus a dining room offering a good Italian cuisine. The hotel is on the American embassy's preferred list of moderately priced hotels in Rome that can be confidently recommended to U.S. visitors. In a twin-bedded room, the charge is 140,000 lire ($85.40), dropping to 85,000 lire ($51.85) in a single, including a continental breakfast.

Hotel Gregoriana, 18 Via Gregoriana (tel. 679-4269), is a small, elite hotel favored by members of the Italian fashion industry who tend to book rooms here for visiting friends from out of town. The ruling matriarch of an aristocratic family left the building to an order of nuns in the 19th century, but they eventually retreated to other quarters. Today, there might be a slightly more elevated spirituality in Room C than in the rest of the hotel, as it used to be a chapel. However, throughout the establishment, the smallish rooms provide a maximum of comfort and an imaginative Italian design. The elevator cage is a black-and-gold art deco fantasy, while the door to each accommodation is indicated with a reproduction of an Erté print whose fanciful characters in some way indicate the letter designating that particular room. You'll pay the bill in the tiny, rattan-covered lobby where a member of the staff is happy to tell you all about the neighborhood. The rooms, all with air conditioning and private baths, rent for 90,000 lire ($54.90) in a single, 155,000 lire ($94.55) in a double, and 200,000 lire ($122) in a triple, with breakfast included.

Sitea, 90 Via Vittorio Orlando (tel. 475-4696), is a case of a pension starting out on the top floor and becoming so successfull that it eventually gobbled up the whole building and became a hotel. That success was engineered by Gianni de Luca, who has spent more than a quarter of a century enlarging and refining the Sitea. The result is an exceptional small hotel (37 rooms, 32 with private bath) priced reasonably and located superbly.

A tiny ground-floor lobby is furnished with a hand-painted wooden antique reception desk and a fine crystal chandelier overhead. The seven floors of rooms are reached by elevator. Most of the accommodations are furnished with antiques—17th-century armoires, Florentine console tables, hand-painted headboards, Oriental rugs—and are equipped with decorated tile baths. A smattering of rooms contain no baths. Air-conditioned doubles with bath rent for 146,400 lire ($89.30); singles with bath, 102,000 lire ($62.22). These tariffs include a continental breakfast taken at the rooftop bar, which, with the snackbar, reflects the management's good taste.

Internazionale, 79 Via Sistina (tel. 679-3047), resulted from the combination of several old palaces, and traces of their past splendor can be seen in a few of the public rooms. Just half a block from the top of the Spanish Steps, the Internazionale has been a favorite of knowledgeable travelers since the 1920s. You'll find the atmosphere of a small inn here, and service both friendly and efficient. Rooms are furnished with old wooden pieces that couldn't really be called antiques, yet are substantial and comfortable. Doubles with private bath rent for 190,000 lire ($115.90), and similarly equipped singles cost 150,000 lire ($91.50). All prices include a continental breakfast and air conditioning. Accommodations facing the narrow and often noisy Via Sistina now have double windows. Bits and pieces of former elegance remain, especially in the dining room or Salon de Pranzo, whose ceiling is charmingly paneled.

Valadier, 15 Via della Fontanella (tel. 361-0592), might amaze its former occupants. A published report maintained that it was once what the French call a *maison de tolérance* (and what we call a brothel). However, its former inhabitants and their patrons have long ago abandoned the site. The transformation into one of the best small hotels in Rome has been remarkable. The hotel is first class, but its tariffs remain moderate for the category. Between the Spanish Steps and the Piazza del Popolo, it charges 73,000 lire ($44.53) for a single, increasing that to 105,000 lire ($64.05) for a double, these tariffs including a continental breakfast, service, tax, and air conditioning. Accommodations are attractive, with matching inlaid wood pieces, gilt mirrors at dressing tables, and, of course, such amenities as private baths and showers, telephones, and radios. All its public salons have fruitwood and gilt antiques. Its own restaurant, Le Renoir, serves a savory Roman cuisine.

Carriage, 36 Via della Carrozze (tel. 679-5166), a few blocks from the Spanish Steps, is rated second class by the government, but the lobby contains gilded mirrors and chandeliers. From the outside it looks somber and plain in the true Roman tradition, but inside, the 24 rooms are decked out every bit as tastefully as the lobby and adjoining Renaissance bar. Thick wall-to-wall carpets, elegant wallpaper, antique reproductions, and modern baths with bidets make you comfortable. Even the single rooms aren't neglected, fitted out with the same matching fabrics and coordinated color schemes. Tariffs are 75,000 lire ($45.75) in a single, 105,000 lire ($64.05) in a double. Service and taxes are included, and the continental breakfast is served at no extra charge. Some rooms are equipped with air conditioning, at a cost of 5000 lire ($3.05) per person. And why is it rated second class? There is no dining room.

Anglo-Americano, 12 Via Quattro Fontane (tel. 472-941), is immediately next door to the Barberini Palace, half a block from the Piazza Barberini, and half a dozen blocks from the Fontana di Trevi. A total renovation converted this 1888 hotel into an ultramodern hostelry by means of upholstering the entire interior. Walls are in blue, floors are done in red, chairs and couches in the lobby are covered with black leatherette, and the rooms are covered from floor to ceiling in pastel-colored fabrics. The overall effect is hushed and smart—probably some of the best rooms (albeit somewhat small) in Rome. Then there are the extras, items like wall-to-wall carpeting, telephone, air conditioning, refrigerator, private bath, and even color television in each of the compact and functional modern rooms. The inclusive single rate is 105,000 lire ($64.05), increasing to 135,000 lire ($82.35) in a double. A continental breakfast is included.

Quattro Fontane, 149 Via Quattro Fontane (tel. 475-4936), is a delightful little place just up the street from the Anglo-Americano—hence, with many of the same advantages. The building is small (only 40 guest rooms), but surprisingly lavish in appointments. In the lobby are thick carpets, elegantly decorated ceilings, chandeliers, and a minuscule bar dispensing libations in the evening. Upstairs the rooms are not large, but nicely done with upholstered headboards, color-coordinated curtains and bedspreads, even indirect lighting. The private tile baths are sleek and efficient. A bathless single costs 32,000 lire ($19.52), increasing to 45,000 lire ($27.45) in a single with bath. Bathless doubles go for 62,000 lire ($37.52), peaking at 70,000 lire ($42.70) with bath, these tariffs including a continental breakfast, service, and tax.

Colosseum, 10 Via Sforza (tel. 475-1228), is on a small, quiet street running parallel to Via Cavour, not far past the Santa Maria Maggiore Basilica. The exterior, as is often the case in Rome, is unprepossessing—but not the interior. Inside it's updated Renaissance, resembling a hacienda. There are red tiles on the floor, heavy, masculine wood furniture, wrought-iron chandeliers hanging from an arched ceiling, and dark sconces on starkly white stucco walls. Upstairs, you'll find glistening marble floors and paneled doors with numbers set in lucky horseshoes. The room decor is as handsome as the lobby would lead you to expect: antique reproductions in carved wood, iron wall fixtures, brightly colored curtains and spreads, baths with shower and bidet. Rates include a continental breakfast. Singles pay 65,000 lire ($39.65); doubles, 94,000 lire ($57.34).

Alexandra, 18 Via Veneto (tel. 461-943), is a fine medium-priced choice for those who want to stay on the Via Veneto. It's a narrow stone building with baroque detail work on the windows and a white lobby with red carpeting and a scattering of antiques. Fifty rooms are reached via a postage-stamp elevator. The accommodations are usually spacious (the biggest are the doubles in the rear), sometimes with fascinating views of the action on the Via Veneto. All are equipped with phones, faded print chairs, and blond furniture. Some of the doubles have fine old beds and plaster detail work on the ceiling. All are quite comfortable and have private baths or showers. For the privilege of the address, high-season (Easter to the middle of November) guests will pay 125,000 lire ($76.25) in a double, 85,000 lire ($51.85) in a single.

Hotel Dinesen, 18 Via di Porta Pinciana (tel. 460-932). Across from the Borghese Gardens, right near the top of the Via Veneto, the Dinesen occupies a choice piece of real estate but is one of the most moderately priced hotels in this high-rent district. In summer, doubles rent for 62,000 lire ($37.82) to 90,000 lire ($54.90); singles, 35,000 lire ($21.35) to 45,000 lire ($27.45). These tariffs include service and taxes. The bedrooms have been pleasantly and traditionally decorated; they are of good size and are immaculately kept. All of the accommodations contain private baths or showers. From some of the rooms you can look out on the Borghese Gardens. Others open onto an inner courtyard filled with pots of plants and shrubbery, like a Spanish parador. The elegant public rooms are spacious and contain unusual Mediterranean-style antiques, including a scattering of oil paintings and an antique printing press skillfully converted into a planter. A grandly proportioned, gently sloping stairwell leads to the bedrooms upstairs.

Hotel Sole al Pantheon, 63 Piazza del Pantheon (tel. 679-3329), is a complete restoration of a former run-down inn, opening directly onto the facade of the landmark Pantheon, deep in the heart of Old Rome. The building is venerated, having housed many composers and artists, such as Pietro Mascagni who wrote several of his compositions here. The inn dates from 1496, making it one of the oldest hotels in the Eternal City. The taste level of the restoration has been fine. Shower baths and other creature comforts have been installed. Doubles with shower facing the square rent for 110,000 lire ($67.10), although the charge for the rooms in the rear is slightly cheaper for those who don't mind depriving themselves of the view. Singles go for 55,000 lire ($33.55) with rear views.

Fiamma, 61 Via Gaeta (tel. 475-8912), is on the far side of the Baths of Diocletian. It's a renovated old building, with five floors of shuttered windows and a ground floor faced with marble and plate-glass windows. The lobby is long and bright, filled to the brim with a varied collection of furnishings, including overstuffed chairs upholstered in aggressive prints, a blue urn mounted on a winged dragon, blue enamel railings, and indirect lighting (all of which sounds absurd, but doesn't look bad at all). On the same floor (made of marble, no less) is a monk-like breakfast room with splashy tablecloths. All rooms have private baths or showers: doubles rent for 108,000 lire ($65.88); singles, 78,000 lire ($47.58). These quotations include a continental breakfast, tax, and service. Air conditioning will cost another 8000 lire ($4.88) per person.

Hotel Tiziano, 110 Corso Vittorio Emanuele (tel. 655-087), is a former palace that fronts on the main thoroughfare between the Piazza Venezia and St. Peter's. The Tiziano is a fine building whose lobby has been subjected to one of those odd periodless renovations that combines crystal chandeliers with indirect lighting and marble columns with modern furniture. The overall effect, however, is not unpleasant. Rooms upstairs are quiet and unpretentious, furnished with plain pieces for the most part, and rather homey in a way. The inclusive rate for a double room with private bath and continental breakfast is 110,000 lire ($67.10); a single with bath and breakfast costs 70,000 lire ($42.70). Singles without bath go for 45,000 lire ($27.45), bathless doubles for 90,000 lire ($54.90).

Hotel Pavia, 83 Via Gaeta (tel. 475-9090), is my favorite hotel on this quiet street near the gardens of the Baths of Diocletian and the railway station. You'll pass through a wisteria-covered passageway that leads to the recently modernized reception area of what used to be a private villa. The public rooms are tastefully covered in light-grained paneling with white lacquer accents and plush blue carpeting. The staff is friendly and attentive, and if you're lucky enough to be there when he is, you'll hear the whistles and chirps of a talking bird from India, whose cage has been placed near the bar area. Each room is unusually quiet, often with a good view, and attractively furnished with simple, modern wood furniture and calming colors. Double units, with breakfast included, range from 75,000 lire ($45.75) to 100,000 lire ($61).

Hotel Madrid, 93–95 Via Mario dei Fiori (tel. 679-1243), evokes fin-de-siècle Roma. The interior has been redone, and many modern comforts have been added. The hotel appeals to the individual traveler who wants a good standard of service. Guests often take their breakfast amid ivy and blossoming plants on the roof terrace. The view of the rooftops and the distant dome of St. Peter's is beautiful. Some of the doubles are really quite large, equipped with telephones, small scatter rugs, veneer armoires, and shuttered windows. All of the accommodations contain private baths, air conditioning, refrigerated bars, telephones, radios, and TV sets. There are 17 doubles and seven suites in all. A double rented as a single goes for 110,000 lire ($67.10); as a double, 140,000 lire ($85.40). One of the suites costs 170,000 lire ($103.70). These rates are inclusive of service, tax, and a continental breakfast. The hotel is an ochre-colored building with a shuttered facade on a narrow street practically in the heart of the boutique area centering around Via Frattina, near the Spanish Steps.

King, 131 Via Sistina (tel. 460-878), is a rather regal name to describe what is a modestly furnished, although comfortable, accommodation. However, the location is ideal, right on this boutique-lined narrow street that leads to the Spanish Steps. This older, sedate hotel offers many rooms with private bath and shower, plus phones. Many repeat visitors speak of the King as their "oasis in the heart of Rome." The most expensive doubles rent with bath for 110,000 lire ($67.10), and singles with bath cost 75,000 lire ($45.75). The continental breakfast, included in the tariffs, is the only meal served. On the rooftop is an open terrace with sheltered garden benches, tables, and flower boxes, and from the perch you'll have a sweeping vista of the Eternal City.

Albergo Venezia, 18 Via Varese, near the intersection of Via Marghera (tel. 494-0101), is the type of place that restores one's faith in moderately priced hotels. The location is good—three blocks from the railroad station, in a part-business, part-residential area dotted with a few old villas and palm trees. The Venezia received a total renovation some years ago, transforming it into a good-looking and cheerful hostelry. There are 65 rooms, served by a charming collection of lobby-sitting rooms furnished with blue velvet chairs and loveseats. The floors are brown marble, and every wall has been freshly papered. The rooms are bright, furnished with light wood pieces, equipped with telephones, and papered in stripes or floral patterns. Some accommodations have balconies for surveying the action on the street below. The housekeeping is superb—the management really cares. The rate in a double room with shower is 95,000 lire ($57.95). Some of the rooms accommodate three at a charge of 130,000 lire ($79.30) with shower. Some four-bedded units are also rented at a cost of 152,000 lire ($92.72). Some economy specials without shower are also available. These tariffs include service, a continental breakfast, and tax.

Albergo Alicorni, 11 Via Scossacavalli (tel. 565-786), is about as close as you can get to sleeping in St. Peter's. This 16th-century mansion with a private courtyard is only a minute or so away. In 1950 it underwent a major renovation to transform it into a hotel. However, its cobbled courtyard with a graceful colonnade and an upper open loggia are well preserved. The interior has been renovated, although the latter-day furnishings are nondescript. The entire "albergo" is orderly, well kept, and clean. (Be warned: I have had complaints about "sad" breakfasts and "tepid" water here.) In a time of inflationary tariffs, it keeps its prices fairly low: from 35,000 lire ($21.35) in a single without bath to 42,000 lire ($25.62) in a single with bath. A bathless double is 60,000 lire ($36.60), rising to 70,000 lire ($42.70) with bath. A continental breakfast, tax, and service are included. The Alicorni is family owned and operated.

Albergo Cesàri, 89A Via di Pietra (tel. 679-2386), on a quiet street in the old quarter of Rome, has been around since 1787. Its overnight guests have included Garibaldi, Mazzini, and Stendhal. Its exterior is still well preserved, and harmonious with the Temple of Neptune and many little antique shops nearby. Completely renovated, the interior has mostly functional modern pieces, although there are a few traditional trappings as well to maintain character. No meals, other than breakfast, are available. In a bathless single, the charge is 45,000 lire ($27.45), rising to 72,000 lire ($43.92) with bath. Bathless doubles go for 75,000 lire ($45.75), but the tariff is 90,000 lire ($54.90) with bath. These rates include taxes and service. The bar here, incidentally, can be a lively social center.

The **Rex,** 149 Via Torino (tel. 462-743), was built by a Spanish duke for entertaining in Rome. It's an old palace, whose entrance has made some concessions to modernity. The lobby, reached by a flight of green marble stairs, is very much in its original condition, richly paneled and coffered, and hung with crystal chandeliers. Accommodations are divided into two wings, one occupying the palace proper, the other in a new and modest structure that probably stands where the late duke's garden once bloomed. Of the 55 rooms, about 70% are equipped with private baths. Rooms in the new wing are smallish, with 1950s motel-type furniture, but they're neat as a pin, blessedly quiet, and brightened by cheerful prints and random antiques. I'll confess that the older rooms suit my fancy much more, due largely to 14-foot plaster relief-work ceilings and furniture of uncertain origin but substantial presence. Some of these older rooms are so large they even possess couches and chairs in addition to the beds and armoires. No matter which wing you're in, a room with bath will cost 53,000 lire ($32.33) in a single, 92,000 lire ($56.12) in a double.

Hotel Margutta, 34 Via Laurina (tel. 679-8440), on a cobblestone street near the Piazza del Popolo, offers attractively decorated rooms, often in a riot of contrasting fabrics and patterns, and friendly staff. You'll register in a paneled lobby with a black stone floor, off of which is a simple breakfast room covered with framed lithographs. The 25 rooms have private baths and phones. Doubles rent for around 75,000 lire ($45.75), while singles cost around 60,000 lire ($36.60), with a continental breakfast included.

Hotel Miami, 230 Via Nazionale (tel. 475-7180), is squarely and conveniently situated in the heart of a major shopping artery. This is a fifth-floor pension done over nicely with warmly tinted marble floors, olive-green wall coverings, and comfortable, low-slung chairs in the conservatively elegant sitting room. From the high-ceilinged street-level lobby, you'll ride an elevator up to the reception area. The spacious and simple bedrooms are filled with lots of sunlight, warm colors, and chrome accents, each with a handsomely tiled bath. This former duchess's palace offers some 20 units for 95,000 lire ($57.95) in a double, around 70,000 lire ($42.70) in a single, with breakfast included. The quieter rooms get a little less sunlight, as they look out on a courtyard. Air conditioning is available in the rooms for an additional 6000 lire ($3.66) per person. A garage (not connected with the hotel) is conveniently nearby in the Via Napoli.

Condotti, 37 Via Mario dei Fiori (tel. 674-769), is a little hotel about two or three blocks from the foot of the Spanish Steps. It's a narrow, four-story affair on an old cobbled street. The lobby, furnished with pleasant antique furniture and fresh-cut flowers in vases, looks rather distinguished. The recently furnished accommodations are clean and functional, equipped with padded headboards and phones. Of the 21 rooms, a few have private baths, the others containing showers. The rate in a double is 70,000 lire ($42.70), dropping to 35,000 lire ($21.35) in a single. Some of the rooms have little terraces, with charming views of the narrow streets and the constant parade of fruit vendors, tourists, and knowledgeable Romans headed for the many excellent restaurants in the area. Breakfast is extra.

Hotel Homs, 71 Via della Vite (tel. 679-2976), is a modest, 100-bedroom hotel, just around the corner from the Piazza Mignanelli, in the vicinity of the Spanish Steps. The rooms have no great style or flair, but they are pleasantly proportioned, light, and airy. Most of the accommodations are bathless doubles, going at a rate of 60,000 lire ($36.60) per night. However, a double with private bath costs 70,000 lire ($42.70). Singles, bathless only, are tabbed at 35,000 lire ($21.35). Included in these quotations are taxes, service, and a continental breakfast.

Memphis, 36A Via degli Avignonesi (tel. 475-1955), is two blocks from the Piazza Barberini and four blocks from the Trevi Fountain. It's in an ancient little building, snuggling with its sisters along a tiny street. English is spoken fluently. The sparkling-clean lobby is furnished modestly, with small chairs, vinyl couches, and a bar. Upstairs are 17 rooms, each with a tile floor, private bath or shower with bidet, wardrobe, and good beds with reading lights attached to the headboards. The rates include service, tax, and a continental breakfast taken in a cheery room on tables covered with plastic cloths. Singles cost 37,000 lire ($22.57); doubles, 62,000 lire ($37.52).

The Best of the Pensions

Scalinata di Spagna, 17 Trinità dei Monti (tel. 679-3006), is the most appealing pension in the area of the Spanish Steps. In fact, it's right at the top of the steps, directly across the small piazza from the deluxe Hassler. This is a delightful little building —only two floors are visible from the outside—done up in mustard yellow and burgundy red paint and nestled between much larger structures. You'll recognize the four relief columns across the facade and the window boxes with their bright blossoms, which themselves look as if they should be out in the country somewhere instead of in the center of Rome. The interior is like an old inn—the public rooms are small with bright print slipcovers, old clocks, and low ceilings. Each of the 14 guest rooms has a frigobar. The decorations vary radically from one room to the next, and some have low, beamed ceilings and ancient-looking wood furniture, while others have loftier-looking ceilings and more average appointments. Everything is spotless and most pleasing to the eye.

In a single with bath, the tariff is 50,000 lire ($30.50). A double with shower or bath rents for 80,000 lire ($48.80). Tariffs include taxes and a continental breakfast. In season, breakfast is served on the roof garden terrace with its sweeping view of the dome of St. Peter's across the Tiber. Reserve well in advance.

Pensione Orsini, 4 Via Virginio Orsini (tel. 312-829), is on a street of fanciful Gothic villas. Ring the bell outside and, when you hear the buzzer, push the gate and you'll be in a luxuriant private garden of hanging vines, flowering plants, and palm trees. Inside the old mansion is a high-ceilinged living room and 11 comfortable guest rooms (eight with bath), that are spacious and airy, furnished with occasional antiques. And is it *quiet* here. Rates are most reasonable and include a continental breakfast. Doubles range from 60,000 lire ($36.60). Singles go from 45,000 lire ($27.45). Taxes, service, and a continental breakfast are included.

Leda Mainoldi and her aging mother, Bianca, are the owners of this warmhearted place. Ably assisted by their housekeeper, Theresa, they run an establishment loaded not only with charm but with a scattering of baroque sculpture and antique engravings as well.

Forti's Guest House, 2 Via Fornova (tel. 382-431), is a fine bargain on the Vatican side of the Tiber. The neighborhood is a peaceful residential one, a block from the river, and the parking is free and ample. Bus transportation to just about everywhere is a few steps away, and the Piazza del Popolo is within walking distance. Better yet are the rooms, the home-cooked meals, the easy ambience, and the advice of owner-manager Charles Cabell, an American married to an Italian (she cooks; he advises). Prices are 25,000 lire ($15.25) in a single, 42,000 lire ($25.62) in a double, with breakfast but without bath. Best is Cabell's "budget special": 50,000 lire ($30.50) per person for bed, breakfast, a box lunch, and a four-course dinner. Via Cosseria runs parallel to Viale Giulio Cesare and Viale delle Milizie, just one block from the Tiber. A private entrance from Via Fornova allows you to avoid going through the Via Cosseria condominium. The pension is on the A line subway route to the Statione Termini (Lepanto stop).

Amati, 155 Via Vittorio Veneto (tel. 493-651), comes as a surprise—a moderately priced place to stay right in the middle of the Via Veneto. It's on the second floor of a substantial elevator building, offering 35 bedrooms, all with private baths or showers. Rates are 70,000 lire ($42.70) in a double, dropping to 50,000 lire ($30.50) in a single. The long corridors are decorated with pictures and enlarged prints of rare postage stamps. You'll register at a reception area covered with light-grained paneling before proceeding into the high-ceilinged lounge area, one end of which is graced with a baronial oak stairwell leading to many of the bedrooms. The more quiet rooms, of course, face an inner courtyard rather than the noisy Via Veneto. The small bedrooms are equipped with Italian modern furniture. All is colorful and compact, including the very compressed private baths. Breakfast is offered family style in a corner room which is furnished with antique chairs.

Pension Suisse, 56 Via Gregoriana (tel. 678-3649), is excellent, although small. It's run with efficiency and panache by Sig. Jole Ciucci, who has been in the business for about 50 years, the last 30 of which have been here on Via Gregoriana. The Suisse is a simple, sparkling-clean affair, with 35 rooms spread out over the fourth and fifth floors of an old building. Halls and lobbies are in muted beige, with high ceilings, leather chairs, and occasional throw rugs on glistening tile floors. There's also a charming writing room with parquet floors, overstuffed leather easy chairs, and a Victorian chandelier. The rooms are big, simple, and comfortable. Furnished either in blond-tone modern pieces or antiques, they all have sinks, and about 14 contain private baths. A single rents for 32,000 lire ($19.52) without bath. Bathless doubles cost 28,000 lire ($17.08) per person, increasing to 40,000 lire ($24.40) per person with bath. All these tariffs include a continental breakfast taken in a pleasant rooftop room.

The **Pensione Esedra,** 47 Piazza Esedra (also known as the Piazza della Repubblica; tel. 463-912), is one of the best of the many low-cost pensions that abound in Rome. Mrs. Moretti offers eight attractive rooms, charging 30,000 lire ($18.30) in a two-bedded unit and 25,000 lire ($15.25) in a one-bedded accommodation. Use of the shower costs 2000 lire ($1.22) extra. Reached either by a grand staircase or a creaking elevator, the Esedra's third-floor rooms open onto a wide hall. The preferred rooms are in the front—they're quite large, at least 30 feet long, and have high ceilings, old-fashioned wooden furniture, and wide windows with a view of the Fountain of the Naiads out front. The smaller rooms are pleasant as well, furnished with the same heavy wood pieces, and sometimes including little beflowered balconies overlooking a jumble of rooftops and courtyards. None of the accommodations has a private bath, but the public facilities are kept clean.

Hotel Pension Elide, 50 Via Firenze (tel. 463-977), just off the

Via Nazionale near the Opera House, is a simple and attractive 18-room pension whose entrance is one floor above ground level. It's surprisingly quiet for an establishment so close to the center of town, with an added calm for rooms facing the inner courtyard. You'll register in what you might consider a depressingly plain lobby, but then you proceed down freshly papered hallways to clean, well-maintained bedrooms scattered over three floors of the 19th-century building. The rooms with private baths are close to quite-adequate facilities a few steps away, and the three floors are connected by a winding marble staircase. Room 16 has what may be the most elaborately gilded ceiling of any pension in Rome. Its design is repeated in the ceiling of the unpretentious breakfast room, whose workaday furniture provides an amusing contrast to the opulence of another era. Singles without bath rent for 30,000 lire ($18.30), and doubles with bath go for 50,000 lire ($30.50). Doubles with private bath cost around 60,000 lire ($36.60). The owner is Roma Giovanni.

Chapter III

WHERE TO EAT

ROME IS ONE of the world's greatest capitals for dining. From elegant, deluxe palaces with lavish trappings, to the little trattoria opening onto a hidden piazza deep in the heart of Old Rome, the city abounds with good restaurants in all price ranges.

The better known restaurants have menus printed in English. Even some of the lesser known establishments have at least one person on the staff who speaks English a bit to help you get through the menu.

Many visitors from North America erroneously think of the Italian cuisine as limited. Of course, everybody's heard of minestrone, spaghetti, chicken cacciatore, and spumoni ice cream. But the chefs of Italy hardly confine themselves to such a limited repertoire.

Throughout your Roman holiday, you'll encounter such savory viands as **zuppa di pesce** (a soup or stew of various fish, cooked in white wine and herb flavored); **cannelloni** (tube-shaped pasta baked with any number of stuffings); **riso col gamberi** (rice with shrimp, peas, and mushrooms, flavored with white wine and garlic); **scampi alla griglia** (grilled prawns, one of the best-tasting, albeit expensive, dishes in the city); **quaglie col risotto e tartufi** (quail with rice and truffles); **lepre alla cacciatore** (hare flavored with white wine and herbs); **zabaglione** (a cream made with sugar, egg yolks, and Marsala); **gnocchi alla Romana** (potato-flour dumplings with a sauce made with meat and covered with grated cheese); **stracciatella** (chicken broth with eggs and grated cheese); **abbacchio** (baby spring lamb, often roasted over an open fire); **saltimbocca alla Romana** (literally "jump-in-your-mouth"—thin slices of veal with cheese, ham, and sage); **fritto alla Romana** (a mixed fry that's likely to include everything from brains to artichokes); **carciofi alla Romana** (tender artichokes cooked with such herbs as mint and garlic, and flavored with white wine); **fettuccine all'uovo** (egg noodles served with butter and cheese); **zuppa di cozze** (a hearty bowl of mussels cooked in broth); **fritta di scampi e calamaretti** (baby squid and prawns fast fried); **fragoline** (wild strawberries, in this case from the Alban Hills); and **finocchio** (a celery-like raw vegetable, the flavor of licorice, often eaten as a dessert).

Incidentally, except in the south, Italians do not use as much garlic in their food as most foreigners seem to believe. Most Italian dishes are butter based. Spaghetti and meatballs, by the way, is not an Italian dish, although certain restaurants throughout the country have taken to serving it "for homesick Americans."

Rome also has many specialty restaurants, representing every major region of the country. The dishes they serve carry such designations as alla Genovese, alla Milanese, alla Napolitana, alla Fiorentina, and alla Bolognese.

RESTAURANTS BY COST: My restaurant chapter is divided into three basic parts: some top restaurants, specialty restaurants, and moderately priced and budget restaurants (further divided according to location). The major emphasis, however, is on those establishments in the medium-priced category. There are quite a lot of restaurants in this latter category. Naturally, I couldn't include all of them, but the ones presented here represent a good sampling.

The deluxe restaurants are a happy surprise. You can eat with the elite of Rome in elegant surroundings for much less than you'd expect. And the food is what can only be described as memorable. So try at least a few if your budget will allow for it.

The medium-priced restaurants represent a sampling of places to eat for those who must keep their costs trimmed. But many of them are worth a visit even if you aren't trying to save money.

RANDOM THOUGHTS ON ROMAN RESTAURANTS: A popular way to keep meal expenditures under control is to ask for the **menu turistico,** which describes the fixed-price meal offered by some restaurants. Such a meal might be accompanied by a quarter-liter of either white or red wine, and include a pasta dish (spaghetti perhaps), a meat dish (veal al Marsala or the like), and end with some fresh fruit or ice cream. The beauty of it is that the single price you see at the top of the menu turistico includes all the extra charges that are normally tacked onto the bill: service charge, bread, and cover charge. The main drawback is that the food, while quite good, seldom includes the specialty of the house. Also, many resturants, even though they offer it, don't want to serve you the tourist menu. The à la carte menu is much more rewarding.

A **prezzo fisso** is another type of menu turistico—but be prepared for a number of extra charges. There is, first, the cover charge (usually 800 lire—49¢—and up), which is sometimes combined with the bread charge (but sometimes bread will be extra). On top of that, there's a service charge of usually 10% to 15%, and after everything is paid, it's bad form not to leave a tip on the change plate. Altogether, these little charges can certainly add up. As for the extra tip on top of the service charge, there are two points to keep in mind: the first is that this additional tip is really small in relation to the bill; the second is that Europeans are among the world's best tippers, and this extra bit of change will be appreciated and almost expected by your waiter.

Meal hours are rather confining in Italy. In the rare event that you're not required to take a continental breakfast at your hotel, you can have coffee and sweets at any of the countless **tavola caldas** all over town. The name literally means "hot table," and they're stand-up snackbar-type arrangements, open all day long. Lunch is served between 1 and 3 in the afternoon, dinner between about 7:30 and 11 p.m.; at all other times, restaurants are closed for business. Dinner, by the way, is taken late in Rome, so while the restaurant may open at 7:30, even if you get there at 8 p.m., you'll frequently be the only one in the place.

A few random thoughts and observations: Tip the strolling musicians (it doesn't have to be a lot; 200 lire is fine). . . . Roman meals customarily include at least three separate courses: pasta, meat, and dessert. But if you're not that hungry, it's perfectly all right to order just the pasta à la carte and skip the meat course (even though the waiter may feign surprise). . . . Meats, while tasty, are definitely secondary to the pasta dishes, which are much more generous and filling. . . . The wine is so good (especially the white Frascati wine from the nearby Castelli Romani), and moderate in price, that I strongly recommend you adopt a European custom and have it with every meal. Soon enough you'll appreciate why it's a European custom.

An Italian restaurant is either called a **trattoria,** or a **ristorante.** Supposedly there's a difference, but I've yet to discern one. Trattorie presumably are smaller and less formal, but sometimes in a kind of reverse snobbism, the management will call an elegant place a trattoria. A ristorante is supposed to be more substantial, but often the opposite is true.

Further, I'd recommend that you leave a few hours free—and go to a different part of town for dinner each night. It's a great way to see Rome.

A final word: All Roman restaurants are closed at least one day a week (usually Sunday or Monday, but it varies). Also, beware of August, the month when most Romans go on their holidays. Scores of restaurants close down, displaying only a lonely *chiuso per ferie* sign.

Some Top Restaurants

Upper-bracket dining in Rome is a thoroughly pleasant experience, if you can afford it. What follows is a random sampling of some of Rome's best restaurants—best from the standpoint of cuisine, ambience, and chic.

The **Pergola,** Cavalieri Hilton International, 101 Via Cadlolo (tel. 31-51). You'll enjoy a view of all of Renaissance and ancient Rome from the panoramic windows of the world-renowned restaurant set on the uppermost level of this deluxe hotel. It's considered by some cuisine critics as one of the four or five best restaurants in Europe, but with its glamorous clientele, superb service, and relaxing ambience, it would still be a sought-after rendezvous even if the food were not as good as it is.

You'll ride to the dramatically lit entrance vestibule in the hotel elevator and emerge face to face with porcelain renditions of two snarling panthers. Guido Angelini or his assistant will give you a warm but formal greeting before escorting you amid window-walls of glass, intimate lighting, unusual modern paintings, and a stylish decor consisting of easy-on-the-eyes accents of glittering brass, silver, and black. Clients have included virtually all the political leaders of Italy, as well as film stars such as Marcello Mastroianni, and members of the international diplomatic community.

The restaurant offers a frequently changing list of seasonal specialties, as well as the popular carpaccio with slivers of parmesan and country salad, risotto with shrimp and filets of chicken, giant prawns in white wine sauce, roast rack of lamb in black pepper sauce, and tenderloin of beef in red wine with bone marrow. There's an adjoining disco (see the nightlife chapter) for after-dinner entertainment. Its entrance is free for restaurant guests. Expect to pay from 65,000 lire ($39.65) to 80,000 lire

($48.80) per person. Reservations are important, and it is closed Sunday.

Sans Souci, 20 Via Sicilia (tel. 493-504), is gorgeous and impressive, drawing patrician Romans and a host of international visitors, including the biggest movie star (whoever that is) in the Eternal City for a visit. In the neighborhood of the swank Excelsior Hotel, it is right off the Via Veneto—and serves dinner only (starting at 7:30 p.m. every day except Monday; reserve ahead). You descend into a dimly lit bar at the bottom of the stairs. There you're presented with a menu—both classically Italian dishes and international specialties—by a maître d'. Selections are made as you admire yourself in one of the glittering mirrors. A good number of the specialties deserve distinguished compliments. I endorse the espadon, a mixed grill served with pilaf rice and a green peppercorn sauce, or the duck in orange sauce. The staff loves to indulge in flambé fireworks. I'd recommend, if you're so inclined, mazzancolle flambée Danilo. Good as well is the cheese soufflé, prepared only for two persons. Expect to pay a tab ranging from 55,000 lire ($33.55) to 70,000 lire ($42.70).The waiters pay special attention to the very chic clientele, including well-known models. In all, Sans Souci is the most elegant spot in Rome for a late-night supper.

El Toulà, 29 Via Della Lupa (tel. 678-1196), is one of the finest links in a chain that stretches from Cortina to Sardinia. Its Roman showcase dispenses the haute cuisine, and does so superbly well, attracting some of the favorite flowers of the international set, along with your visiting film star. The place is elegant, with vaulted ceilings and large archways dividing the rooms. After you're let in, you can stop in the charming bar, enjoying a drink while perusing the menu. I'd suggest that you begin your meal with soffiatelli con fonduta ai formaggi, a savory cream puff that has been stuffed with fonduta cheese and baked with a cheese fondue topping it. The tagliolini verdi consists of slender green noodles that have been tossed with a heavenly blend of prosciutto, cream, and freshly grated cheese. Numbered among my celestial dining delights in the Roman capital is a salad, called insalata Toula. Served in a stemware glass, it consists of cold corn kernels, hearts of palm (in season only, otherwise wedges of avocado), romaine lettuce, slivers of parmesan cheese, and a perfectly blended and spiced vinaigrette sauce. For your main course, I'd suggest a plate of scampi, well flavored and grilled just right. For the same price, you can also order squab that has been grilled and served with a pungent and well-seasoned sauce of crushed green peppercorns. At certain times of year a filet of beef is offered. It has been roasted in a bag with fresh Roman artichokes. For dessert, try one of the sherbets of the season. The cantaloupe is excellent, as is one made of fresh strawberries, but these are seasonal. The lemon is an all-year favorite. If you request it, your waiter will serve you a mixed selection. Expect to spend from 50,000 lire ($30.50) to 70,000 lire ($42.70). Always make a reservation, as you'll have to compete with Roman society in the evening for a table, although you shouldn't have trouble at all at lunch. Closed Sunday and in August.

Le Rallye, Grand Hotel, 3 Via Vittorio Emanuele Orlando (tel. 47-09). Dining at "Le Grand" has been an aristocratic Roman tradition since 1894 when César Ritz opened the hotel. Escoffier was on hand to prepare the first lavish dinners to delight the elegantly attired clientele made up of *tout Roma.* Dining at this leading hotel of Rome has undergone many changes over the decades. Today the classic cuisine is impeccably maintained at Le Rallye. It's decorated with Scottish plaid carpeting and a hunting motif. You sit in supremely comfortable red chairs at a table of immaculate napery and fine china.

Chef Adelio Pagani is one of the finest in Rome, and he's accustomed to pleasing a wide range of diners, from visiting kings from the Middle East to American rock stars. To begin your meal, you may choose one of several delectable antipasti. Or perhaps you'll begin instead with some of the finest pasta dishes in the city. (They are made by a woman called a *sfoglina,* in the way grandmother did—that is, by hand.) For a main course, you might try the young spring lamb served with fresh spinach, cooked perfectly. My recent "classic trout" was one of the finest I've ever enjoyed. A filet of sole, also sampled recently, came stuffed with beets and presented in a tomato sauce. If you're here for lunch, you might be tempted by the chicken salad, made with, among other ingredients, fresh basil and raw mushrooms. For dessert, try the tart, which is made with some of the best fresh fruits of sunny Italy along with a sweet-tasting ricotta.

The restaurant has an excellent wine cellar. Some of its contents is made of grapes grown in the hotel's own courtyard. The vines were planted by much earlier Romans, and the method of making this wine is centuries old. The charge for dinner here is about 66,000 lire ($40.26) and up. Always reserve a table. La Rallye is closed Saturday, Sunday, and in August.

La Cupola, Excelsior Hotel, 125 Via Vittorio Veneto (tel. 47-08). The merits of the hotel in which this deluxe restaurant is housed have already been extolled in the hotel chapter. A CIGA property, La Cupola is now one of the finest restaurants in Rome, attracting many of those who heretofore shunned hotel dining rooms. The late Luigi Barzini, in a survey of the rebirth of elegance in the dining rooms of Italy's grand hotels, suggested that "the maître d' is once again what his grandfather was before 1914."

Since 1907 the Excelsior has led several lives and lavishly fed many of the celebrities of the world. Restaurant critics have suggested that La Cupola, under its executive chef Vittorio Sacconi, is better now than ever. The dining room is stunning architecturally in the white and gold Empire style, and the service is impeccable, as are the napery and china.

Only the finest ingredients are used in the preparation of the cuisine, and they are brought in fresh daily. Many of the dishes in the chef's repertoire are classic; others are nouvelle variations that may surprise and delight. For example, your pasta salad might be made with fresh stringbeans (the Italians like everything fresh and in season), matchstick slices of baby spring lamb (which has been roasted), olive oil, a sweet raw onion from the south, and green peppers, along with the actual pasta. More classic is homemade tagliolini with lemon or fettuccine in the style of the chef (that is, in a cream sauce that has been considerably enlivened with salmon from Scotland and fresh tomato). The beef and fish dishes are invariably excellent. Dinner is from 66,000 lire ($40.26) per person up.

George's, 7 Via Marche (tel. 484-575), is one of the finest restaurants in Rome. It's not run by George, as many diners seem to think, but by Enrica Jarratt, the widow of its founder, who has maintained the high standards that have given this establishment an international reputation. Originally, her late husband was with the British embassy until he decided to devote all his time to his real love, gourmet food. Mrs. Jarratt is a principal of the Cordon Bleu schools of Italy, and together with a time-tested staff (many have been there for a quarter of a century), they continue to offer a cuisine prepared with the best of ingredients. Of course, this uncompromising attitude of quality costs money, and you pay, and pay quite a bit, at this temple of gastronomy. Soups are velvety smooth, as exemplified by the vichyssoise. The chef also makes the best gazpacho in town, at the same price. From a varied and imaginative menu, you can order such main dishes as roast duck or planked steak for two persons. A touch of medieval England is sounded in the dessert specialty—it's syllabub (a frothy cream dessert, flavored with wine). Meals begin at 70,000 lire ($42.70).

The dining room is quiet and dignified, decorated with prints, photographs, and *New Yorker* cartoons. However, in summer you may prefer the garden. In the evening, diners enjoy soft piano music. In the neighborhood of the Via Veneto, behind the swanky Excelsior Hotel, the restaurant is closed in August. Telephone in advance for a reservation.

L'Eau Vive, 85 Via Monterone (tel. 654-1095), enjoys a vogue among Roman society. A French restaurant opened in 1965 on the first and second floors of a palace, it is between Largo Argentina and the Piazza Navona, near the Pantheon. It's unique—run by a missionary family. Waitresses aren't dressed in habits, but rather in national dress or discreet European clothing. They seat you and serve you with friendliness and courtesy in either of two large rooms with antique frescoes and lofty, vaulted ceilings, decorated with modern, gray-stained oak paneling. The soft lighting is from crystal wall fixtures, and fresh flowers (usually roses) brighten each table.

Dining here is an unusual experience for many people. In this formal atmosphere the waitresses, at 10 o'clock each evening, chant a religious hymn and recite a prayer. Your gratuity for service will be turned over for religious purposes. Pope John Paul II used to dine here when he was still archbishop of Cracow, and it's a popular place with overseas monsignors on a visit to the Vatican. There is piped-in music, most likely works of Mozart.

Specialties include hors d'oeuvres, French style, crêpes, and frog legs. An "international dish" is featured daily. The restaurant's cellar is well stocked with French wines. Your bill is likely to run from 25,000 lire ($15.25) to 40,000 lire ($24.40). Fellow diners represent a broad cross section of the European continent —French spoken at one table, German at another, Italian at another. The place is highly recommendable, but closed Sunday.

Le Jardin, Hotel Lord Byron, 5 Via dei Notaris (tel. 360-9541), is one of the best places to go within Rome for *la nuova cucina.* On the ground floor of one of the most elite small hotels of the capital (see the hotel chapter), the decor is almost aggressively lighthearted, combining white lattice with cheerful pastel colors, red carpeting, a purely decorative brass-trimmed fireplace, many meters of white lacquer trim, and massive bouquets of fresh flowers. A grouping of early 20th-century portraits and a pair of large Japanese vases are almost lost amid the contrasting colors of this intensely planned room, although since many of the well-known diners here have often been photographed by the media, you might quickly forget everything except the company, the polite service, and the well-prepared food. Many of the cooks and service personnel were trained at foreign embassies or diplomatic residences abroad.

Today, classified as a *Relais et Château,* the establishment serves a frequently changing array of dishes that might include seafood crêpes, noodle pie with salmon and asparagus, rabbit fricassée, tangerine-flavored beef filet, or fresh salmon with asparagus. Dessert may be a charlotte kiwi royal or "the chef's fancy." Expect to pay from 50,000 lire ($30.50) to 75,000 lire ($45.75) per person for dinner. Reserve in advance. It is closed on Sunday.

Ristorante G. Ranieri, 26 Via Mario dei Fiori (tel. 679-1592), just off the Via Condotti, was founded in 1843, and it's always maintained its high standards. Everything here bespeaks old European quality. From the minute you pass through the red curtains at the front door, you'll be struck by the unpretentious graciousness of the place. There are several small dining rooms, with brocaded walls of yellow, red, or green (a different color for each room). There are old fireplaces, antique-white woodwork, chandeliers, and mirrored wall sconces with little pleated shades. Waiters hustle back and forth wheeling trolleys laden with pastries or pasta. In this latter category, the house specialty is lasagne verdi (green noodles). Fish and meat entrees are usually delectable. The dessert specialty is zabaglione, a feathery-light treat made here with pineapple. The average meal ranges from 30,000 lire ($18.30) to 55,000 lire ($33.55). The patrons are mostly knowledgeable Romans, and the atmosphere is subdued and congenial. Closed Sunday.

Passetto, 14 Via Giuseppe Zanardelli (tel. 654-3696), is dramatically positioned at the north end of the landmark Piazza Navona. Not the decor, but its reputation for excellent Italian food brings people there. The surroundings are quite pleasant—three rooms, one long and narrow, lined with banquettes and lit with 1940s-looking frosted-glass cylinder chandeliers. Another is a bit more traditional and baroque looking. However, one of the outside tables is preferred in summer. Formally dressed waiters, crisp white linen, and heavy silverware add a touch of luxury. Pastas are exceptional. Recommendable main courses include fonduta alla Piemontesa with truffles and two roast quail. Meals range in price from 35,000 lire ($21.35) to 50,000 lire ($30.50). Closed Sunday.

Massimo d'Azeglio, 18 Via Cavour (tel. 46-06-46), in a hotel but with a separate entrance, serves a Roman cuisine that has been popular since 1875. Angelo Bettoja is the guiding light behind its present sparkle. His great-great-grandfather was the founder of the restaurant. Don't be put off by its location in the Terminal area. The cognoscenti of Rome, to whom it has traditionally appealed, certainly aren't. The average trattoria can't even begin to match the food served here. For example, Mr. Bettoja was once inspired by a piece of gastronomic prose written by Alexandre Dumas to create "pheasant Porthos." This was a boned pheasant stuffed with partridge breast that was lined with thrush breast. Buried in this treasure was a ball of foie gras. The game birds came from Mr. Bettoja's estate near Orvieto. Meats from the spit are featured nowadays. You can also have risotto with seafood, stuffed green peppers, or veal medallions with artichokes. A set meal cost 23,000 lire ($14.03), while an à la carte dinner may tally from 30,000 lire ($18.30) up. Closed Sunday.

Ristorante dal Bolognese, 1–2 Piazza del Popolo (tel. 361-1426), has pleasant tables set outside on a deck, carpeted with squashy fake grass, and shaded by big, blue awnings. The view is of the magnificent Piazza del Popolo, the formal gardens of the Pincio, and the goings and comings of the beautiful people at Rosati next door. Diners sit amid blooming plants in cement pots and order from an à la carte menu that specializes in dishes prepared with meat. Many of the dishes are rich in cream and cheese, as befits the gastronomic capital, Bologna, for which the restaurant is named. Specialties of the house include lasagne verdi. However, you may want to try the more typical tagliatelle alla Bolognese. The most recommendable main course is cotolette alla Bolognese. Expect to spend from 50,000 lire ($30.50), plus wine, per person. Dal Bolognese is closed for Sunday dinner and Monday.

Taverna Flavia di Mimmo, 9 Via Flavia (tel. 474-5214), is just a block from Via XX Settembre. It is a robustly Italian restaurant where movie people and society folk meet over tasty dishes. In true Roman fashion there are tables out front, and a collection of dining rooms inside grouped around a corridor whose sideboard is laden with fresh fruit, vegetables, meat, and poultry. The atmosphere is theatrical—autographed pictures of such stars as Marlon Brando, Rock Hudson, and Gloria Swanson literally cover every patch of wall space. Between them are poster blowups of beautiful women, curtained windows, and hanging lanterns. Everything is à la carte. An excellent opener is the risotto with scampi, although for curiosity you may want to try spaghetti al whisky. Each day a specialty dish is featured. On Saturday it's Roman tripe. Roaming the menu, I'd suggest prosciutto, osso buco with peas, seafood salad, and fondue with truffles. Desserts are rich tasting and well prepared. For a complete meal the cost is from 25,000 lire ($15.25) to 35,000 lire ($21.35), plus another 15% for service. The restaurant is closed Sunday.

Ristorante Ulpia, 2 Foro Traiano (tel. 678-9980), is one of the most unusual dining rooms in Rome, built into the ruins of an old Roman basilica, near Trajan's Forum. Director Joseph Sinigaglia maintains—and rightly so—that Ulpia is "the most aristocratic and distinguished place in the heart of Imperial Rome." As such, it has been dispensing hearty meals and solid drink for nearly two centuries. The kitchen is well known for its opening specialty, fettuccine Ulpia. However, you may prefer a tempting array of varied hors d'oeuvres—called "antipasti" in Italy. The main-dish specialty is chicken "fiamma sacra." Everything tastes better with a bottle of Chianti. The average bill will range in price from 25,000 lire ($15.25) to 35,000 lire ($21.35). In this tavern, filled with Roman museum pieces, music is played for dancing in the evenings. Treat the restaurant like a nightclub, and plan to make an evening of it any time except Sunday.

Alfredo alla Scrofa, 104 Via della Scrofa (tel. 654-163). In both Europe and America you see the word "Alfredo" listed after many dishes in Italian restaurants. When visitors reach Rome, they ask their hotels to direct them to Alfredo's restaurant, some of which even claim to be the original and authentic one. Once, there really was an Alfredo. He was given a gold fork and spoon by two noted travelers to Rome, Mary Pickford and Douglas Fairbanks. That Alfredo crowned himself *Il Re delle Fettuccine* (king of the noodles), but eventually he sold his business and retired. Since the Pickford-Fairbanks incident, there has been much dispute about which Alfredo's owns that gold fork and spoon (as if it really mattered).

One of the leading claimants is Alfredo alla Sorofa. The premises have been entirely redone, with oak panels on the walls that contain gold-framed photographs of famous personages who have visited the restaurant. Look for photographs of Gregory

Peck and Audrey Hepburn, who visited in the 1950s during the filming of *Roman Holiday.* The flooring is parquet,, and the chairs are Viennese style. Of course, all first-time visitors order maestose fettuccine al triplo burro. The owner, Massimo Mozzetti, makes choreography out of whipping butter and cheese into this dish. The main-course specialty is filetto di tacchino dorato. This is breast of turkey, delicately sauteed in batter and covered with thin slices of Piemontese white truffles. Some of the chef's newer specialties include filetto di bue al pepe, costolette di abbacchio alla Villeroy with Roman-style artichokes, and new desserts, crêpe all'Alfredo and profiterol cake. You might finish with an Irish coffee. The bill will reach 30,000 lire ($18.30) to 45,000 lire ($27.45), plus 13% service. Strolling musicians entertain you at night. Closed Tuesday.

La Fontanella, 86 Largo Fontanella Borghese (tel. 678-3849). Everyone from the Kennedys to movie stars has dined at this "little fountain" since 1953. It is one of the leading Tuscan restaurants in the city. It stands on a famous old square, across from the Palazzo Borghese, which was built in the shape of a harpsichord for Pope Paul V.

As in all Florentine restaurants, beefsteak is the specialty. The beefsteak is grilled over charcoal and served rare if that's how you like it. The real Florentine orders it with a plate of white beans, which are delicate in flavor, seasoned with sage and olive oil.

You might begin with the house's pasta specialty, pappardella al sugo di caccia, a wide-noodle dish in a rich hare sauce. Or perhaps you'll sample finocciona, a Tuscan sausage studded with peppercorns and pistachio nuts. From October to December, Roman gourmets flock here to order ovoli, an exquisite mushroom, golden orange in color, which grows in the Italian woods. It is tossed into a salad with matchstick strips of gruyère and celery. Over the top the delicate white Italian truffle is sprinkled. The cost of this salad is fantastico, recommended for dedicated gourmets only. (It's never on the menu anyway. You have to make a special request for it.) For a regular meal, expect to pay between 35,000 lire ($21.35) and 45,000 lire ($27.35). This highly recommendable restaurant is closed on Monday.

The Specialty Restaurants

Girarrosoto Toscano, 29 Via Campania (tel. 493-759), is right off the Via Veneto, facing the walls of the Borghese Gardens. It attracts a fashionable crowd, both foreign and domestic. The setting is subterranean, under vaulted ceilings. Because of the mass popularity of this establishment, you must often wait in line, a chore eased by having an apértif at the stand-up bar. While waiting, you can watch the fresh meats placed on the open charcoal grill. The room is lined with wine bottles. The chef does a medley of Florentine or Tuscan specialties. You can begin with homemade fettuccine or pasta e fagioli (beans and pasta) alla Fiorentina. Another fine opener is Tuscan salami. For a main course, the true Florentine might order boiled fowl from the Arno Valley, served in a green sauce. However, I much prefer the bistecca alla Fiorentina, a grilled steak seasoned with pepper, salt, and oil, priced according to weight, often 35,000 lire ($21.35) for a large serving. For dessert, try a bouquet of gelati (ice cream) misti, an assortment of different flavors. Expect to pay about 45,000 lire ($27.45) to 55,000 lire ($33.55) per person for a complete meal (not beefsteak), including wine. Closed Wednesday.

Il Drappo, 9 Vicolo del Malpasso (tel. 657-365), on a hard-to-find, narrow street off a square near the Tiber, is a Sardinian restaurant operated by an attractive brother-sister team named Paolo and Valentine. The facade is graced with a modernized trompe l'oeil painting above the stone entrance, which is flanked with potted plants. Inside, you'll have your choice of two tastefully decorated dining rooms festooned with yards of patterned cotton draped from supports on the ceiling. Flowers and candles are everywhere. Dinner, which will be partially selected by the host if you wish his assistance, may include a wafer-thin appetizer called carte di musica (sheet music), which is topped with tomatoes, green peppers, parsley, and olive oil, followed by fresh spring lamb in season, a fish stew made with tuna caviar, or a changing selection of strongly flavored regional specialties that are otherwise difficult to find in Rome. Service is friendly and personal, and meals, with wine included, usually cost around 25,000 lire ($15.25) per person. This restaurant is best appreciated at night, although lunch is served as well. It is closed Sunday and during part of August.

Scoglio di Frisio, 256 Via Merulana (tel. 734-619), is such a fine example of the Neapolitan cuisine, I only wish Naples had something as good. Frankly, the decor is corny, with strolling tenors and weeping violins. The decorator was carried away with a grotto-like effect, with droopy fish nets and crustacean art. Every night Americans so pack the joint that you're ready to expect a tourist trap—but don't be put off. Scoglio di Frisio serves some of the finest food in the city, at remarkably low prices. For example, try the heavenly cannelloni or the Neapolitan pizza with clams and mussels. You may then settle for chicken cacciatore, hunter's style, or the house specialty, veal scaloppine alla Frisio, with mushrooms, peas, and melted cheese. Meals range from 25,000 lire ($15.25) to 40,000 lire ($24.40) and up. Scoglio di Frisio also has entertainment. The restaurant is open evenings only from 7 p.m. It's closed Monday from November 1 to April 30 and Sunday from May 1 to October 31. It is on a broad street, south of the railroad station.

La Cantinella, 19 Via Francesco Crispi (tel. 679-5069), is one of the rarest restaurants in Rome in that it specializes in island dishes from Sardinia. A delightful little family-run place, it is just off the Via del Tritone (which runs into Piazza Barberini). The restaurant consists of two small rooms—the kitchen is in between them—decorated with cheerful pink tablecloths and small pictures on the walls. The food is good and reasonably priced. Pasta specialties include culuxionis (cheese-filled ravioli), malloreddus (tiny pasta with a special meat sauce), and homemade fettuccine. By all means, ask for pane frattau (a kind of Sardinian bread, prepared with eggs and a tomato sauce). Meat dishes feature porceddu (suckling pig) and prosciutto di cinghaile alla Nuraghe (wild boar, with cannonau red wine, Sardinian style). A perfect dessert, by the way, is macedonia con gelato, a fresh fruit cup with vanilla ice cream, or the Seadas (cheesecake fried with honey and sugar on top). Meals range from 20,000 lire ($12.20) to 32,000 lire ($19.52), including a service charge of 12%. Closed Wednesday and in August.

Ambasciata d'Abruzzo, 26 Via Pietro Tacchini (tel. 878-256), is somewhat hard to find, lying out in the Parioli sector, but it's well worth the search. Plan to make an evening of it—and don't eat for days. For a blanket price of about 25,000 lire ($15.25), including wine, you can eat all you want all night. When you sit down, a basket of sausages is placed on your table, even a herb-flavored ham from which you can cut as much as you wish. Next, you can make a selection from the antipasti table near the entrance. I'd recommend that you sample the pasta misti, a selection of three pastas served on an oval-shaped platter, which are the specialties of the chef. The food is typical of the Abruzzo section of Italy. This is a land with a tasty and rich cuisine, although most of its dishes are simple and healthy, based on good, country produce. Featured are the fresh and tasty meats of the sheep and cattle raised in high pastures on aromatic grasses, the farm poultry, the cheeses, the sweet and salty pork sausages, and the salad greens extolled by the Latin Sulmona writer, Ovid. At the end of your gargantuan repast, bottles of liqueur are placed on your table. Try to avoid crowded Saturday afternoons, and expect to wait in line unless you arrive early. Closed Sunday.

Lon Fon, 46 Via Firenze (tel. 475-5261), has been acclaimed as the best Chinese restaurant in Italy. The food is authentic, as are the ingredients, and the service is fine as well. This delightful cuisine is not low budget, but it's not prohibitively expensive either, unless you select one of the chef's proud specialties such as Pekinese duck for two persons, or "beggar's chicken" for two. Recommendable are large meatballs with a Chinese sauce, squirrel shredded chicken, and, as an appetizer, hot-and-sour soup. Many of Rome's Chinese colony come here for a meal, and they're not only hearty eaters, but they take their food seriously. The average meal will cost 30,000 lire ($18.30) and up, service included. The restaurant is open from noon to 3 p.m. and from 7:30 to 11:30 p.m. Closed Wednesdays.

Budget to Moderate Dining

MIDTOWN—VIA VENETO TO THE COLOSSEUM: Ristorante Abruzzi, 1 Via de Vaccaro (tel. 679-3897), is my first choice, just a block and a half from Piazza Venezia, at the end of Piazza SS. Apostoli. Abruzzi is known for its antipasto, a series of delectable cold appetizers chosen from a trolley and briskly served by efficient, white-jacketed waiters. The combination of tastes is great. My last meal there consisted of a liter of white wine; the already-mentioned antipasto; stracciatella (a full-bodied Roman soup made with egg, Parmesan cheese, and seasonings in a chicken broth), saltimbocca alla Romana (those wonderfully seasoned slices of veal), cheese, and a macedonia congelato (fruit compote with ice cream). Meals cost from 19,000 lire ($11.59) to 30,000 lire ($18.30). The food is good and the atmosphere—cozy and bright in simple rooms with small, white-clothed tables—is relaxing and agreeable. Closed Saturday and for part of August.

Quirino, 84 Via della Murate (tel. 679-4108), just around the corner from the Trevi Fountain, specializes in a Roman cuisine. For an opener, try spaghetti with clams or risotto, Milanese style. Main dishes include fried squid and shrimp, brains in butter, and mussels, sailor style. For dessert, fresh fruit makes for a soothing finish. The atmosphere is relaxed, with a decor highlighted by a beamed ceiling, muraled walls, and an abundance of Chianti bottles hanging from the rafters. It's a great favorite with Italian families who live and work in the area and who spend from 22,000 lire ($13.42), including service, for an average meal. The place is closed on Saturday.

Er Tartufo, 59 Vicolo Sciarra (tel. 678-0226), is on a tiny street just off the Corso, not far from the Piazza Colonna. Well insulated from the roar of nearby traffic, the "Truffle" has a string of outdoor tables under awnings, numerous potted plants along the walls, and a simple indoor dining room whose decor includes a wine keg set in the wall. The restauranteur, Signor Cesaretti, is most hospitable. A specialty of the house is a plate of truffles, an expensive treat. You might want to try the fried squid or Roman tripe, although you can't go wrong with the baked lamb or excellent sole. Dinner will cost about 20,000 lire ($12.20) per person. It's quiet, informal, and reasonably priced, in a charming location on a quaintly crooked street. Closed Sunday.

Trattoria l'Albanese, 148 Via dei Serpenti (tel. 474-0777), has a fine kitchen. Its sun-dappled rear garden is a delight for lunch, especially after sightseeing at the nearby Colosseum. Besides the garden, there are a series of cheerful rooms connected by arches and fitted out with small tables in intimate corners. The food is inexpensive. The tourist menu, for example, is priced at 12,000 lire ($7.32). A few sample meat items would be pollo alla Romana (Roman-style chicken), a nicely seasoned entrecôte, and various fresh fish dishes, such as scallops. In the evening, pizzas are served. Closed Tuesday.

NEAR THE SPANISH STEPS: **Trattoria alla Otello Concordia,** 81 Via della Croce (tel. 679-1178), is about two blocks from the Piazza di Spagna, near its northern end. The Otello serves good food under a leafy canopy in an enclosed courtyard. You enter through a stone corridor that leads from the street. The courtyard tables with their fresh white cloths are divided by rows of potted plants into two areas. There are two small rooms inside, but in fair weather you'll want to sit outside. A few golden rays of sunshine penetrate the greenery above, perhaps at one of the tables near the ornamental fountain, usually banked with fresh fruit from the Roman campagna. If you're planning to order à la carte, and plan on having a pasta dish, the fettuccine is excellent. Main dishes include breast of turkey with mushrooms and eggplant parmigiana. You can order most fish dishes sauteed, boiled, or broiled. A fruit salad rounds out the meal nicely, along with white Frascati wine. The dry white wine is well chilled, and is a nice companion with any meal, which is likely to range in cost between 16,000 lire ($9.76) and 28,000 lire ($17.08), plus 15% for service. The trattoria is closed on Sunday and from Christmas until the first week in January.

Nino, 11 Via Borgognona (tel. 679-5676), is no longer with us, but his daughter, Anna, continues on in the fine tradition. Her late father Gioacchino (Nino) Guarnacci became quite celebrated with Roman society for transporting those big Florentine or T-bone steaks down from Tuscany where the best cattle are raised. Each night you could see—and still can—models from the nearby high-fashion houses devouring one on a strictly high-protein diet. Those not on a diet can begin their meals with Tuscan salami, penne all'arrabbiata, or perhaps the cannelloni. Main dishes other than steak include two deviled quail, zampone, fagioli cotti al fiasco, baccalà alla Livornese (only on Friday), and grilled veal. Expect to spend from 35,000 lire ($21.35) for a complete meal. Closed Sunday and from July 25 to September 1.

Osteria Margutta, 82 Via Margutta (tel. 679-8190), enjoys an enviable position on a street that houses many of the finest art galleries in Rome. Some of the city's most successful painters occupy upper-story apartments along this colorful street that enjoyed a brief reign in the early '70s as a center of mod culture and hip paraphernalia. Now it has returned to its traditional role. Inside, a softly lit tavern atmosphere prevails, and walls are decorated with artwork. As you enter, an array of antipasti—hors d'oeuvres—is there to greet you, priced according to your choice. The chef specializes in, of all things, Hungarian goulash. Another good local dish is Roman-style tripe. A pasta specialty is rigatoni Margutta. A good meal here will cost from 35,000 lire ($21.35).

Ristorante Mario, 55–56 Via della Vite (tel. 678-3818), is a good-size trattoria featuring some excellent Florentine and game specialties, a complete meal costing from 25,000 lire ($15.25) to 30,000 lire ($18.30), including service. Mario can seat about 80 in air-conditioned comfort on the street level, although many prefer to descend to the cellar. He does an interesting pasta—pappardelle, served with caccia (a game sauce). The classic Florentine beefsteak for two is also a menu highlight, but if you're the experimental type, you may prefer Florentine tripe. Hare (in season) is served here with polenta (made with cornmeal cooked in butter with thin slices of cheese). Mario also offers some good Tuscan cheese, which might provide a proper finish for your meal. A liter of Chianti goes well with about everything. Closed Sunday and for the entire month of August.

RENAISSANCE ROME: Cave di San Ignazio, 169 Piazza San Ignazio (tel. 679-7821), is a block off the Corso, near the Piazza Colonna. The interior is inn-like, but outside is a collection of tables and umbrellas—plus a superb view of an unspoiled square. This is the sort of restaurant where they bring wine (after first inquiring if you'd prefer red or white) before you even order. The chef specializes in fresh fish and scampi, which the waiter taking your order seems inclined to push a bit—but maybe that's because they don't have a very good command of English here, and those dishes may be more understandable to the person serving you. I can also recommend the filet steak in cognac sauce, and the Florentine beefsteak is good too. You're likely to spend more than 25,000 lire ($15.25) if you order the scampi or a fresh fish dish. Closed Sunday.

Mastrostefano, 93–96 Piazza Navona (tel. 654-1669), has an ambience that is high Renaissance, with the magnificent sculpture of the Piazza Navona outside. This restaurant is on the east side of the piazza, a shock of brightly colored umbrellas against the sun-washed ochre buildings. Directly in front is Bernini's *Fountain of the Four Rivers,* whose cool cascades are like music. I'd suggest you begin with spaghetti carbonara. Two main-dish favorites are osso buco (the veal knucklebone stew) and curried rice with seafood. Your tab is likely to run up to 30,000 lire ($18.30) to 45,000 lire ($27.45), plus 15% for service. Closed Monday, for most of January, and from mid-August until the first of September.

For dessert, why not walk across the square to **Tre Scalini,** 28–32 Piazza Navona (tel. 654-1996), and order a famous tartufo at 2200 lire ($1.34) to take out, 3500 lire ($2.14) at a sidewalk table.

Il Domiziano, 88 Piazza Navona (tel. 659-647), is a pizzeria and beer cellar, serving all types of antipasti and pizzas daily except Monday. It faces a little street called Corsia Agonale, leading right into the square where you can admire the statuary in the piazza. Reasonably priced and well-prepared antipasti and pizzas are taken in an atmosphere evoking the past. The original pillar dating back to the emperor Domitian has been left totally intact. The name "Domiziano" commemorates the Piazza Navona's former use—it was once the stadium of the emperor Domitian, and used for chariot races. The approximate cost of an antipasto and pizza is 10,000 lire ($6.10).

Hostaria Angoletto, 51 Piazza Rondanini (tel. 656-8019), is the best restaurant in the vicinity of the Pantheon. It is only two blocks from the Pantheon—with your back to the colonnade, it's one block beyond the Piazza della Rotondo, and one block to the left—but unless you're lucky, you'll have to ask directions. When you get to the Piazza Rondanini, you'll see the Angoletto in the far corner, occupying a portion of an old palace. Outside is a wood-floored terrace with a roof instead of the usual umbrellas or awnings. An average meal might consist of stracciatella, a hearty soup with egg and cheese in chicken broth, followed by saltimbocca alla Romana (veal with ham and cheese) or perhaps tripe and ravioli con ricotta. For dessert, I'd recommend the ice cream with whisky. A complete meal will cost from 18,000 lire ($10.98) to 30,000 lire ($18.30). The clientele seems to know the waiters pretty well. It's rather more chic than you'd expect. Unstinting praise is usually dispensed to the chef, who deserves it.

Il Barroccio, 13–14 Via dei Pastini (tel. 679-3797), is a popular moderately priced restaurant right near the Pantheon serving traditional Roman food. It's thronged with patrons sitting cheek by jowl in the several small rooms. Decorations include racks of wine, graffiti, and lucky horseshoes on the walls, brick arches, wagon-wheel lights, bronze lanterns, and lots of festive-looking dried corn. You probably will eat to the strains of whatever itinerant musicians happen to be wandering through at the moment. A set meal costs 18,000 lire ($10.98), but if you order à la carte, expect to spend from 25,000 ($15.25), plus service. Most diners begin with one of the pasta dishes. A seafood antipasto is especially delectable, and you might follow with bollitto misto (an assortment of boiled meats). Baked lasagne and Florentine beefsteak are well prepared and served. At night, pizzas are a specialty. Closed Monday and in August.

THE OLD GHETTO: Down in the old ghetto of Rome, south of Corso Vittorio Emanuele and adjacent to the Victor Emmanuel Monument, are several superb little restaurants. The atmosphere in this part of town is characterized by ancient buildings, quiet streets, and charming piazzas.

Angelino a TorMargana, 37 Piazza Margana (tel. 678-3328), is about three blocks from the Piazza Venezia. You eat by candlelight on this Renaissance piazza, all the time listening to the inevitable strolling guitarists. There are the usual potted bushes (quite lush here), interspersed with lanterns and umbrellas. Some sample items from the menu include rigatoni alla carbonara and chicken alla peperonata. In addition, tonnarelli all' Angelino is a spectacular spaghetti dish with a sauce of mushrooms, peas, and cheese. Also recommended is melanzane (eggplant) alla parmigiana. Expect your tab to be in the neighborhood of 25,000 lire ($15.25) or a lot more. Add 15% for service. Angelino, by the way, seems to enjoy a rather elegant international patronage. Closed Sunday.

Piperno Monte Cenci, 9 Via Monte de Cenci (tel. 654-0629), reigns as the Artichoke Capital of the World in Rome's old Jewish Ghetto. The restaurant is nonkosher. It is known for its carciofi alla giudia. These are opened and flattened artichokes, sliced crosswise. In an unknown batter recipe, they are deep-fried until crisp and golden. The Roman carciofi are not like the types grown in America and France. Many diners go here just to sample this unique gastronomic experience. Also good, and you can request them as a side dish, are the mixed vegetables, fried a deep golden brown. A table of antipasti awaits you as you enter the precincts of this fairly simple family dining room. As a main course, another typically Roman dish is filetti di baccalà, strips of codfish, batter fried, also a golden brown. Main dishes include baked lamb and Roman tripe. The dessert specialty is le palle di nonno fritte. This is a deep-fried, flaky pastry that has previously been stuffed with homemade fruit preserves and cream. Expect to pay from 40,000 lire ($24.40) to 50,000 lire ($30.50), including service. The restaurant is closed every Sunday night and Monday, in August, and from December 23 to January 2.

da Giggetto, 21A Via del Portico d'Ottavia (tel. 656-1105), is a modest little trattoria renowned for honest Italian cooking, "old ghetto" style. On any given night, it's likely to be the most bustling establishment in town—and in Rome that's saying a lot. Everyone from movie stars to papa, mama, and all the bambini patronize this colorful establishment. The one dish that's a "must" here is carciofi alla giudia: these are the tender fried artichokes for which the chefs of the ghetto are noted. Another typical dish is filetti di baccalà, slender strips of codfish filets which are rolled in batter, then deep-fried in oil. Main dishes include osso buco, scampi in a wine sauce, little milk lamb roast, and rolled veal with mozzarella and ham inside, in wine sauce. For dessert (in season), order the fresh strawberries from Nemi, a Roman hill town. Meals begin at 22,000 lire ($13.42) and go up. Closed Monday.

Vecchia Roma, 18 Piazza Campitelli (tel. 656-4604), has an inviting decor: canvas umbrellas in bright colors, ivy-covered walls, great iron grills on the windows, candles in wrought-iron holders, and ubiquitous cats from the ruins of the nearby Theater of Marcellus. Giuseppe and Toninno cook what looked good at the market that day. They're known for their "fruits of the sea." Their antipasti marini with fresh sardines and anchovies is exceptional, and you may get tiny octopus, shrimp, mussels, and sea snails. In the true Jewish ghetto tradition of Rome, they offer batter-dipped, deep-fried artichokes. If you want meat, try the veal kidneys or veal chop, or perhaps you'd enjoy another specialty, roasted goat. Meals begin at 25,000 lire ($15.25). The restaurant is closed for the first three weeks of August.

IN THE PARIOLI DISTRICT: **Al Ceppo,** 2 Via Panama, near Piazza Ungheria (tel. 844-9696), greets you with a glittering antipasto tray, including such delectable suggestions as stuffed yellow and red peppers, finely minced cold spinach blended with ricotta, unpeeled eggplant with a topping of tomato, mozzarella, and anchovy, and at least two dozen other dishes, many of which taste good either hot or cold. Because of its somewhat hidden location (although it's only two blocks from the Villa Borghese), the clientele is likely to be Roman rather than foreign. "The Log" features an open fireplace that is fed with wood. On it, the chef does lamb chops, even quail, liver, and bacon, to charcoal perfection. The beefsteak, which hails from Tuscany, is also succulent. If you can order both a pasta and the hors d'oeuvres, I'd suggest linguine con peperoni. These are thin noodles blended with green peppers cut thin like matchsticks. Expect to pay from 25,000 lire ($15.25) to 35,000 lire ($21.35), plus 13% service, for a really filling repast, including a carafe of the house wine. Closed Monday and in August.

NEAR ST. PETER'S: **Il Matriciano,** 55 Via dei Gracchi (tel. 359-5247). Between treks through St. Peter's and the vast museums of the Vatican, a person can get hungry. But finding a good restaurant in that precinct takes talent. Il Matriciano, at Via Silla, is the exception to the rule. It's not fancy, rather specializing in well-prepared Roman fare served in ample portions at moderate prices, a complete meal costing from 30,000 lire ($18.30) to 45,000 lire ($27.45), service included. In fair weather you can try to get one of the sidewalk tables behind the hedge and under a canopy. However, the faithful list of year-round habitués is likely to grab these choice spots. Instead, you may retreat to one of the two family-style dining rooms where you can order such fare as abbacchio al forno. This is baked baby lamb, and it's especially good when served with a crisp green salad. Very typical is trippa alla Romano, although many North Americans don't like this dish. For a good beginning, try the tagliolini con tartufi. The restaurant is closed on Wednesday in winter and on Saturday in summer.

NEAR THE PIAZZA DI CAMPO DEI FIORI: **Ristorante da Pancrazio,** 92 Piazza del Biscione (tel. 656-1246), occupies the ruins of Pompey's ancient theater. Surrounded by medieval and Renaissance buildings, it offers a series of colorfully decorated dining rooms on the ground floor, although most diners prefer the "buca" or cellar, the actual ruins. Typical Italian specialties are featured, including risotto alla pescatora (that is, rice simmered in a rich stock, then laced with fruits of the sea), cannelloni alla Pancrazio, a veal scaloppine with mushrooms, prosciutto, and tomato sauce, as well as the celebrated saltimbocca alla Romana. In season, you can get roasted baby quail. The mixed fish fry is also good. Expect to pay from 30,000 lire ($18.30) to 40,000 lire ($24.40) for a good meal, including service and tax. Closed Wednesday and from August 10 to 25.

AT THE CIRCUS MAXIMUS: **Alvaro al Circo Massimo,** 53 Via dei Cerchi (tel. 678-6112), is actually right on the edge of the Circus Maximus, by the corner of Via di S. Teodoro. The location isn't really too far out of the way, and the food, the atmosphere, and the simpatico waiters make the place lots of fun for dinner. The ceiling has all manner of hanging items—sausages, garlic, dried corn—amid beams and iron chandeliers. The dining room seems nonetheless airy and spacious, with shining tile floors, rusticated wood paneling, and wine racks. The house antipasto is a fine way to start things off, followed perhaps by tonnarelli fettuccine or any of the other quite good pasta dishes. Meat courses include the likes of bistecca di manzo (beef) or scaloppine al Marsala. For dessert, there's the always-reliable fresh fruit. An average three-course meal will cost 25,000 lire ($15.25). It's a great Roman family favorite. Closed Monday and in August.

NEAR THE TERMINAL STATION: **Peppino,** 70/a Principe Amedeo (tel. 474-5387), is a small, unheralded little trattoria between the Terminal Station (about three blocks from it) and the Basilica of Santa Maria Maggiore, quite close to Via Manin. The pasta here is incomparable—the spaghetti literally melts in your mouth—and the place is bright and cheerfully unpretentious. Multicolored bead curtains separate the street from a series of small, well-lit rooms, half-paneled in a glittery green stone and illuminated with modern chandeliers and recessed mirrors surrounded with neon. The cloths on the tables are crisply white, and the aging wooden chairs hold droves of Italian families sampling the fettuccine with approving nods and complimenting the white-coated waiters, who always bow appreciatively. The menu turistico is a good buy for 14,000 lire ($8.54), and includes a choice of about ten main dishes. If you order à la carte, a meal will cost about 18,000 lire ($10.98). Meat dishes include such items as calf liver with onions and stewed veal, hunter's style. Good service; closed Sunday.

TRASTEVERE: One of the oldest sections of the city, Trastevere is a goldmine of colorful streets and, for our purposes, restaurants with inspired cuisine. Although across the Tiber, it's rather far from St. Peter's—actually it's just adjacent to the old ghetto, whose synagogue can be seen across the river between the spires of the island called Tibertina.

Sabatini I, 13 Piazza Santa Maria in Trastevere (tel. 582-026), owned by the Sabatini brothers, is one of the most popular dining spots in Rome. At night, Piazza Santa Maria—one of the settings used in Fellini's *Roma*—is the center of the liveliest action in Trastavere. Roman Polanski (or whoever) might be your dining companion, as the restaurant is a favorite with celebrities. In summer, tables are placed outside on this charming square, and you can look across at the floodlit golden mosaics of the church on the piazza. It you can't get a table outside, you may be assigned to a room inside under beamed ceilings, with stenciled walls, lots of paneling, and framed oil paintings. So popular is this place that you may have to wait for a table even if you have a reservation.

You can choose from a large table of antipasti, or perhaps you'd like melon with prosciutto, a favorite appetizer here. Fresh fish and shellfish, especially grilled scampi, may tempt you. The spaghetti with "fruits of the sea" is excellent. My most recent selection was pollo con peperoni, chicken cooked with red and green peppers, a savory treat. Meals begin at 35,000 lire ($21.35) but can go much higher if you order grilled fish or the Florentine steaks. For wine, if it goes with what you ordered, try a white Frascati or an Antinori chianti. The wine comes in hand-painted pitchers.

The restaurant is closed Wednesday and for two weeks in August. If you can't get in at Sabatini I, try **Sabatini II,** 18 Viocolo de Santa Maria in Trastevere (tel. 588-307), just around the corner. It is closed Tuesday and for two weeks in in August. However, the August closings of the two Sabatinis are staggered so you can dine at one place if you are there at the wrong time for the other. Both charge the same prices.

When you're ready to leave either place, ask the waiter to call you a cab. Don't try it yourself, as the Sabatini staff seems to have a special code word to get a taxi to pull up to the door.

Trattoria Vincenzo, 173 Via della Lungaretta (tel. 589-2876), is quite close to the Piazza in Piscinula, the first square you'll come to after crossing the bridge from Tibertina. A large, bright dining room is decorated with trompe-l'oeil stone walls and beams, plus coarse tablecloths proudly bearing the word "Vincenzo." Popular with neighborhood people, the restraurant has a varied menu, offering pastas such as spaghetti alla carbonara. Meat items include cotoletta alla Bolognese and scaloppine al Marsala. Fish fanciers won't be disappointed either, especially with the zuppa di pesce. It seemingly consists of everything that was swimming within miles of a fishing boat. For dessert, try the charlotte. Meals cost from 25,000 lire ($15.25). Vincenzo does a thriving lunch business too, when it's packed with Italians engaged in animated conversation. Closed Sunday nights and Monday.

La Cisterna, 13 Via della Cisterna (tel. 582-2543), is a centuries-old tavern in the heart of Trastevere. It's an ancient place efficiently run by the Simmi family for the last half a century. The name comes from an ancient well (in the cellar) that dates from the late Imperial years of Rome. You can dine outside in fair weather—at other times, inside in one of a series of rooms decorated with murals depicting everything from the rape of the Sabine women to Romulus and Remus with their friendly she-wolf. The waiters wear short trousers, with colored sashes and white shirts. Mouthwatering Roman specialties are served in this atmosphere redolent of the past. The antipasti are right out on the street. Fresh fish dishes are particularly outstanding, although the standard Roman meat dishes are also well prepared. Expect to pay from 23,000 lire ($14.03) to 30,000 lire ($18.30), including service.

Romolo, 7 Via Porta Settimiana (tel. 581-8284), is a Trastevere gem. You can sit in a Renaissance garden that once belonged to Raphael's mistress, della Fornarina (the baker's daughter), who posed for some of his madonnas. Now it's known and has been patronized by everybody from celluloid heroes (Kirk Douglas) to political personalities and authors (Clare Boothe Luce and Margaret Truman) to collegians. Favorite dishes offfered? To begin your meal, try the fettuccine with meat sauce, followed by scaloppine al Marsala or deviled chicken. A fresh garden salad is extra. For dessert, try a charlotte (a sponge cake lathered with whipped cream and topped by a decorative motif). Your final bill should be in the neighborhood of 25,000 lire ($15.25) to 40,000 lire ($24.40), plus service. Even if the garden isn't in use, you'll like the cozy interior, with its bric-a-brac of copper, wood, and silver. The restaurant is closed Monday and during most of August.

ON THE TIBERTINA: Sora Lella, 16 Via di Ponte Quattro Capi (tel. 656-1601), is a little beamed inn right on the island of Tibertina. The medieval setting on this little island that looks like a boat, the hanging lanterns and cozy fireplace, and the pasta dishes, make Sora Lella a delight for dinner—especially an intimate one. The owner is the sister of a beloved Roman actor, and the restaurant attracts a theatrical crowd. Spaghetti and most pasta dishes begin your meal, followed by one of the tasty meat or fish specialties. Expect to pay 25,000 lire ($15.25) for an average meal. Closed Sunday.

FOR PIZZAS: Ricci's, 32 Via Genova (tel. 464-412), is a Gemini pizza parlor and trattoria, a renowned place established in 1900 and run by the brothers Gino and Aldo Ricci. They are known for the wine, *Est! Est!! Est!!!*, which is a white wine with a distinctive flavor. The ristorante and pizzeria stare across the street at each other at the end of a cul-de-sac, with sidewalk tables, all of this a block from the Via Nazionale, an easy walk from the railway station. The pizza parlor is unmarred by modern invasion, with a respectable patina on its wood paneling. The food is simple but good, and nearly everybody orders the sizzling hot pizzas, in many varieties. However, you may want to precede that with antipasti, and the desserts here are good, also. Specialties include Napolitana and capricciosa pizza, or you can order calzoni or crostini (small slices of bread covered with various savory ingredients). Count on spending from 18,000 lire ($10.98) for a complete meal, and that includes either the local wine or a couple of mugs of beer. Closed Monday and on holidays.

SELF-SERVICE: Piccadilly, 2–16 Via Barberini (tel. 465-107), is an enormous cafeteria-cum-coffeeshop-cum-restaurant-cum-Cockney-Pub near Bernini's Triton fountain. This veritable restaurant complex is a U.S. turnpike-style place with tile floors and indirect lighting. It's possible to spend more than you intend, although your tab is likely to read from 12,000 lire ($7.32) for a meal. So some good advice is to order a pasta dish, such as spaghetti, and something to drink, then go back later if you're still hungry. Pizzas are featured after 7 p.m. Onion soup is also a good choice, and there's a large selection of omelets, sandwiches, and grilled meats. You'll also be able to order such standard American fare as a milkshake or a banana split.

FOR AMERICAN-STYLE SNACKS: The Cowboy, 68 Via Francesco Crispi (tel. 474-5328), is the place to go when the hamburger withdrawal syndrome becomes too much to take. A Coca-Cola and french fries here will confirm to you that everything is still okay with the world. And you can get Texas-style cooking at fairly reasonable prices. For example, Mexican chili is regularly featured. Or you may prefer a Texasburger or southern style fried chicken. The Italian specialty is cannelloni. For dessert there's mother's homemade apple pie with ice cream, and you can get a good cup of American coffee. This place is popular with Americans, who like the good beer and get a laugh from the satirical western mural inside. Meals cost from 12,000 lire ($7.32), but after midnight prices are raised by 15%. Closed Monday.

FOR VEGETARIANS: **Margutta Vegetariano,** 119 Via Margutta (tel. 678-6033), is one of the few vegetarian restaurants in Rome. The stone detailing of its maroon facade is known to a circle of friends who ignore the riches of traditional Italian cuisine in favor of a simple list of frequently changing high-fiber items whose names are written on a blackboard. Tables and chairs are about as unpretentious as you'll find in Rome, and at one end of the high-ceilinged room there's a remarkable photographic blowup of green and red pappers in all their colorful detail. When I was there, they had an unfortunate lack of vegetarian pasta dishes, although there's almost always a soup, a mixed salad, a melange of fried vegetables, a collection of crudités, risotto, and fresh desserts. Expect to spend around 15,000 lire ($9.15) per person. It shuts down on Sunday.

TIME OUT FOR TEA: **Babington's Tea Rooms,** 23 Piazza di Spagna (tel. 678-6027). Back when Victoria was on the throne in England, an Englishwoman named Amy Mary Babington arrived in Rome and couldn't find a place for a good "cuppa." With stubborn determination, she opened her own tea rooms near the foot of the Spanish Steps. Surprisingly, the rooms are still going strong, with high ceilings, brass and glass star-shaped chandeliers, and straw mat-covered tables. You can order anything from Scottish scones to a club sandwich to Ceylon tea and American coffee. Breakfast of ham and eggs, muffins, and juice is offered for 20,000 lire ($12.20) per person—a price considered very high owing to its location. Tea will cost you from 5000 lire ($3.05). It's open from 9 a.m. to 8:30 p.m. Closed Thursday.

Victor Emmanuel Monument

Chapter IV

SEEING THE MAJOR SIGHTS

Seven Walking Tours of Rome

WHERE ELSE but in Rome could you admire a 17th-century colonnade designed by Bernini, while resting against an Egyptian obelisk carried off from Heliopolis while Christ was still alive? Or stand amid the splendor of Renaissance frescoes in a papal palace built on top of the tomb of a Roman emperor? Where else, for that matter, are there Vestal Virgins buried adjacent to the Ministry of Finance?

Tourists have been sightseeing in Rome for 2000 years. There is, in fact, almost too much to see, at least for visitors on a typical 20th-century timetable. Would that we were traveling around as our 19th-century forebears did, in a coach with tons of luggage, stopping a month here and a month there. Instead, we swoop down from the sky, or roar up at the train station, and expect to see everything in a few days. Those travelers with this approach have met their match in Rome. An absolute minimum of time to see the city with any sort of perspective is five days, and even that's heavy sightseeing. Seven days would be better.

HOW WE'LL SEE ROME: This chapter is organized into a series of do-it-yourself walking tours, five major ones to cover the most important sights, and an additional two tours to pick up a number of secondary sights. I've settled on this approach in the belief that it's the only way to see the city economically, at your own speed, and with reasonable thoroughness—you could, after all, spend years here and not see everything. Let me add that there are numerous organized tours available, and herds of air-cooled

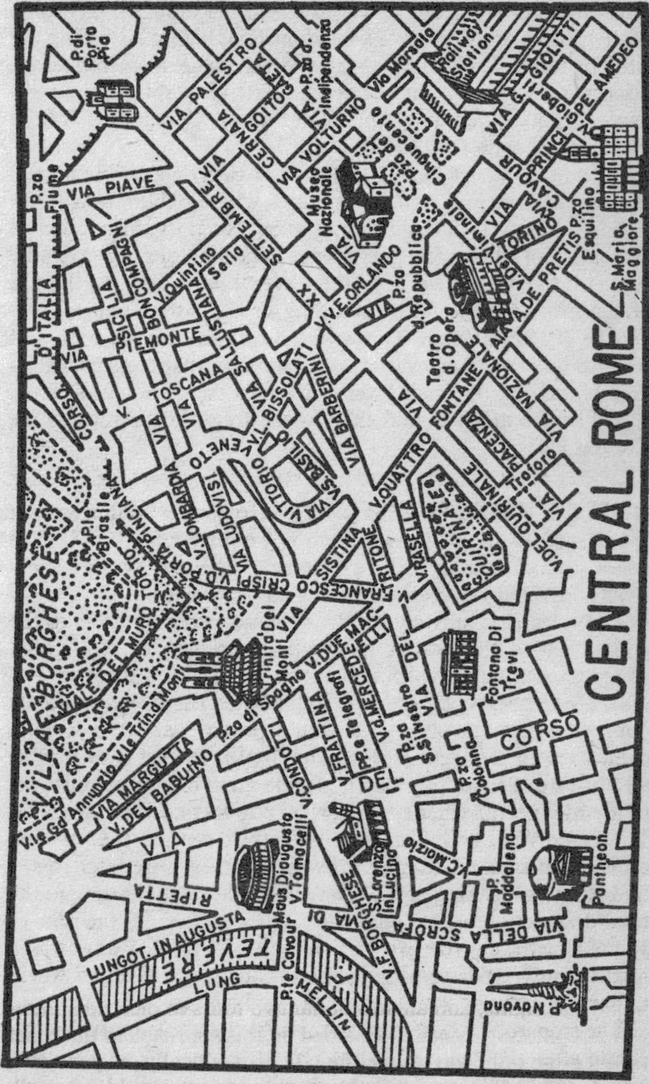
CENTRAL ROME
P. di Porta Pia
P.zo Fiume
VIA PIAVE
VIA PALESTRO
VIA GOITO
VIA GAETA
P.zo d. Indipendenza
VIA VOLTURNO
Via Marsala
Railway Station
VIA G. GIOLITTI
PRINCIPE AMEDEO
VIA CAVOUR
Museo Nazionale
P.zo d. Cinquecento
P.zo Esquilino
S. Maria Maggiore
VIA TORINO
V. d. Viminale
VIA A. DE PRETIS
VIA NAZIONALE
Teatro d. Opera
P.zo d. Repubblica
VIA V.E. ORLANDO
VIA XX SETTEMBRE
VIA CERNAIA
V. Quintino Sella
VIA QUATTRO FONTANE
VIA BARBERINI
VIA L. BISSOLATI
VIA SALLUSTIANA
VIA TOSCANA
PIEMONTE
BONCOMPAGNI
SICILIA
CORSO D'ITALIA
VIA VENETO
VIA VITTORIO
VIA BASILICO
VIA LUDOVISI
V. LOMBARDIA
PORTA PINCIANA
VILLA BORGHESE
VIALE DEL MURO TORTO
V.le Brasile
VIA FRANCESCO CRISPI
SISTINA
TRITONE
V. RASELLA
QUIRINALE
V. DEL QUIRINALE
PIACENZA
Traforo
Fontana Di Trevi
CORSO
VIA DEL CORSO
Trinità Del Monti
P.zo di Spagna
V.le Trin. d. Monti
V.le G. d'Annunzio
VIA MARGUTTA
V. DEL BABUINO
VIA RIPETTA
V. CONDOTTI
V. FRATTINA
V. DUE MACELLI
V. d. MERCEDE
PP. e Telegrafi
P.zo S. Silvestro
P.zo Colonna
Mous Dioguusto
V. Tomacelli
S. Lorenzo In Lucina
VIA DI BORGHESE
V.F. BORGHESE
C. Marzio
P. Maddalena
VIA DELLA SCROFA
Pantheon
P. Novona
LUNGOT. IN AUGUSTA
TEVERE
P.te Cavour
LUNG MELLIN

buses thunder from one end of town to the other all day long. Many people prefer to take a bus tour first, before beginning the walking tours. They claim it's a good way to get an introductory orientation to Rome. There are a number of qualified tour companies around, including American Express Company S.A.I, 38 Piazza di Spagna (tel. 6764).

Each of my tours begins and ends at easily accessible places, usually large streets or major squares where public transportation to other parts of town won't be confusing. I've also followed something of a historical progression. The first tour, for example, begins at the Roman Forum, where everything began. At the end of the fifth tour, you'll be standing in the Sistine Chapel, the apogee of Papal Rome. Those who have time for the sixth and seventh tours can see a variety of sights of perhaps less historical import, ending by tossing their lire into the Fontana di Trevi (just like the movies), and thereby ensuring their return to the Eternal City.

A LITTLE TIME OUT FOR HISTORY: A Roman revolution against the Etruscans toppled them from power around 510 B.C. The result was a republic with two consuls, a senate, and a society strictly divided between patricians and plebeians.

The stern Roman Republic was characterized by belief in the gods, heed to the lessons of the past, strength of the family, education through books and public service, and most important, obedience. R. H. Barrow, in his book *The Romans,* points out that "through obedience comes power," and the Roman dedication to the ideal of a worthy life led to vast empire. The all-powerful Senate presided as Rome grew to become mistress of the Mediterranean, defeating rival powers one after the other. The Punic Wars with Carthage in the third century B.C. cleared a major obstacle to Rome's growth, but men were later to say that Rome's breaking of the treaty with Carthage (leading to the total destruction of that city) put a curse on her. By the time of Julius Caesar, on the eve of the birth of Christ, Rome was a mighty empire whose generals had brought the Western world under the sway of Roman law and civilization.

The emperors, whose succession started with Augustus's principate after the death of Julius Caesar, brought Rome to new, almost giddy heights. Augustus transformed the city from brick to marble—much the way Napoleon III transformed Paris in later years. But success seemed to lead to corruption. The colorful centuries of the emperors witnessed a steady decay in the ideals and traditions that had built the empire in the first place. The army became a fifth column of barbarian mercenaries; the tax collector became the scourge of the countryside; for every good emperor (Augustus, Trajan, Vespasian, Hadrian, to name only a few), there were three or four incredibly corrupt and debased emperors (Caligula, Nero, Domitian, Caracalla, etc., etc.).

The Roman citizen in the capital either lived on the public dole and spent his days at gladiatorial games and imperial baths, or he was a disillusioned patrician at the mercy of emperors who would murder him for his property. The third century A.D. saw so many emperors that it was common, as H. V. Morton tells us, to hear of the election of an emperor in the provinces together with a report on his assassination. The fourth-century reforms of Diocletian held the empire together, but at the expense of its inhabitants, who were reduced to tax units. This was the emperor who split the empire in two—he perceived it as totally ungovernable due to its immense size—and instituted heavy taxes, wage and price controls, and a socioeconomic system that made profession hereditary. In other words, if the father was a basket weaver, woe be to the son who might try to be a silversmith, for to try would be to commit a crime.

In A.D. 330 Constantine moved the imperial capital away from Rome—the menace of possible barbarian attack had increased greatly—and took the best of the artisans, statesmen, and public figures of Rome with him to Constantinople. Rome continued for almost a century, apparently on the sheer momentum derived from a thousand years of power. As the Goths advanced in the early fifth century, they were frequently welcomed by Romans in the provinces, who had grown to hate and fear the cruel bureaucracy that was the legacy of Diocletian. Then the pillage began.

Rome was first sacked by Alaric in August of 410. Several interesting sidelights to this historic event have come down to us. First of all, the populace behaved in the most disgraceful manner —no attempt was made to defend the city (other than trying vainly to buy off the Goth, a tactic that admittedly had worked three years before) and most people simply fled into the hills, or headed to their country estates if they were rich. The feeble Western emperor, Honorius, hid out in Ravenna the entire time.

More than 40 troubled years passed until the siege of Rome by Attila the Hun. Strangely enough, it was the daughter of

Honorius's stepsister Placidia who sent her seal ring to the barbarian and precipitated his march on the city. Attila was, however, dissuaded from attacking thanks largely to a peace mission headed by Pope Leo I. That was in 452, but relief was short-lived, for in 455 Gaiseric the Vandal carried out a two-week sack that was unparalleled in its pure savagery. Whereas Alaric had attacked Rome out of anger stemming from his failure to attain the rank of Roman general, Gaiseric attacked Rome for the sheer pleasure of loot and destruction. The empire of the West lasted for only another 20 years; finally the sacks and chaos ended it in A.D. 476, and Rome was left to the popes, under the nominal auspices of an exarch from Byzantium (Constantinople).

The last would-be caesars to walk the streets of Rome were both barbarians: the first was Theodoric, who established an Ostrogoth kingdom at Ravenna from 493 to 526; and the second was Totilla, who held the last chariot races in the Circus Maximus in 549. Totilla was engaged in a running battle with Belisarius, the general of the Eastern emperor Justinian, who sought to regain Rome for the Eastern empire. The city changed hands several times, recovering some of its ancient pride by a brave resistance to Totilla's forces, finally being entirely depopulated by the continuing battles.

So a ravaged Rome entered the Middle Ages, her once-proud population scattered and unrecognizable in rustic exile. A modest population started life again in the swamps of the Campus Martius, while the seven hills, now without water since the aqueducts were cut, stood abandoned and crumbling. It was Pope Gregory II who renounced Rome's dependence on Constantinople in 731, thereby ending the twilight era of the Greek exarch who nominally ruled Rome in the name of the emperor in Constantinople. Papal Rome turned forever to the Europe she would soon give birth to, and in A.D. 800, a king of the barbarian Franks was crowned Holy Roman Emperor by Pope Leo III. That king's name was Charlemagne.

TOUR ONE
The Roman Forum, The Palatine Hill, The Colosseum, The Arch of Constantine

THE ROMAN FORUM: The entrance to the Forum is off Via dei Fori Imperiali, right at the intersection with Via Cavour. Via dei

Fori Imperiali, built by Mussolini to show off the ancient splendors of Rome, connects Piazza Venezia (with the huge monument of Victor Emmanuel) with the Colosseum, and this street is plied regularly by buses from various parts of town. The entrance to the site is a small cement room. The Forum is open from 9 a.m. until two hours before sunset daily except Tuesday, when it is closed. You must leave no later than an hour before sunset. On holidays, you may visit from 9 a.m. to 1 p.m., exiting no later than 2 p.m. Admission costs 4000 lire ($2.44) for adults, free for children under 12 if accompanied by grownups. On the first and third Saturday and the second and fourth Sunday of the month, admission is free.

The Roman Forum is the literal heart of Roman history. It was at once the center for trade, religion, and politics. From a rude swampy area that lay between the Palatine Hill (where legend has it that Romulus and Remus were suckled by the she-wolf) and the Capitoline Hill (since Etruscan times, the site of the Temple of Jupiter), it grew first into a busy trade area under the Roman kings.

With the overthrow of the ancient kings in 509 B.C., and the establishment of the Roman Republic, the Forum prospered and grew more elaborate. During the heady days of the empire, from the first century B.C. to the second century A.D., the swarm of merchants selling everything from blond barbarian tresses to foodstuffs, and the general throng of often shady characters who hung about the Forum, gradually removed themselves to the more spacious imperial forums, whose remains we see sprouting on either side of Via dei Fori Imperiali.

Although emperors reigned in Rome until A.D. 476, the Roman Forum spent most of the Imperial years as a collection of monuments, used mostly by senators bowing and scraping in the most degrading manner to the whims of the emperors, and Vestal Virgins, that group of extraordinarily privileged ladies who watched the sacred fire, symbolic of the life of Rome. It was essentially a museum of incredible marble temples, roofed with purest gold, surrounded with magnificent columns, and periodically rebuilt (frequently after fires) by one or another of the emperors.

The scattered columns and scarred triumphal arches we see today are the faintest shadow of what the Forum must have been in its balmy days. Sometimes we can see little more than the foundations of this incredible collection of temples that were covered with precious marbles from the far corners of the Roman world and filled with rare treasures.

What happened to it? That string of barbarian invasions and lootings, starting in the early fifth century, did incalculable damage. This combined with a thousand years of neglect and random earthquakes (natural erosion of the surrounding hills plus the settling of virtual mountains of rubble raised the level of the land a good 20 feet). Rome's Renaissance rulers had apparently no qualms whatsoever about ripping off the remaining marbles, even destroying whole monuments (the arch of Claudius, for example, which once stood on the Corso) to get needed building materials at a cheap price. We can only regret that the masterpieces of these years—the Palazzo Farnese, St. John in Lateran, etc.—were created by such shortsightedness.

In time, the Forum reverted to a cowfield, and it was this romantic *campo vaccino* of gentle pastures and quaint ruins that so enchanted Keats and Shelley in the early 1800s. Although excavations were begun as early as the 17th century, the most substantial took place under the Italian government at the end of the 19th century and the beginning of the 20th.

As you walk down the ramp from the entrance, you'll be heading for the Via Sacra, the ancient Roman road that ran through the Forum connecting the Capitoline Hill to your right, with the Arch of Titus (first century A.D.), way off to your left. Back when this was the *campo vaccino,* and all these stones were underground, there was a dual column of elm trees connecting the Arch of Titus, off to your left, with the Arch of Septimius Severus (A.D. 200) to your right.

Arriving at the Via Sacra, we turn right. The random columns on the right as we head toward the arch of Septimius Severus belong to the **Basilica Aemilia,** formerly the site of great meeting halls and shops all maintained for centuries by the noble Roman family who gave it its name. At the corner nearest the Forum entrance are some traces of melted bronze decoration that fused to the marble floor during a great fire set by invading Goths in A.D. 410.

The next important building is the **Curia,** or Senate house—it's the large brick building on the right, that still has its roof. Romans had been meeting on this site for centuries before the first structure was erected, and that was still centuries before Christ. The present building is the fifth (if one counts all the reconstructions and substantial rehabilitations) to stand on the site. Legend has it that the original building was constructed by an ancient king, with the curious name of Tullus Hostilius. The tradition he began was a noble one indeed, and our present legislative system owes much to the Romans who met in this hall. Unfortunately, the high ideals and inviolate morals which characterized the early Republican senators gave way to the boot-licking of Imperial times, when the Senate became little more than a rubberstamp. Caligula, who was only the third emperor, had his horse appointed to the Senate (it was a life appointment), and that pretty much sums up where the Senate was at by the middle of the first century A.D.

The building was a church until 1937, when the Fascist government tore out the baroque interior and revealed what we see today. The original floor of Egyptian marble and the tiers that held the seats of the senators have miraculously survived. In addition, at the far end of the great chamber we can see the stone on which rested the fabled golden statue of Victory. Originally installed by Augustus, it was finally disposed of in the late fourth century by a fiercely divided Senate, whose Christian members convinced the emperor that it was improper to have a pagan statue in such a revered place.

Outside, we head down the Curia stairs to the **Lapis Niger**, the remains of black marble blocks that reputedly mark the tomb of Romulus. They bask today under a corrugated roof. Go downstairs for a look at the excavated tomb. There's a stone here with the oldest Latin inscription in existence, which unfortunately is nearly unintelligible. All that can be safely assumed is that it genuinely dates from Rome of the kings. Remember, they disappeared in a revolution in 509 B.C.

The **Arch of Septimius Severus** was dedicated at the dawn of the troubled third century to the last decent emperor who was to govern Rome for some time. The friezes on the arch depict victories over Arabs and Parthians by the cold but upright Severus and his two dissolute sons, Geta and Caracalla. Severus died on a campaign to subdue the unruly natives of Scotland at the end of the first decade of the third century. Rome unhappily fell into the hands of young Caracalla, chiefly remembered today for his baths in whose ruins the summer opera season is held.

Caracalla became sole emperor when he had his brother Geta slashed to pieces while the latter cringed in their mother's arms. This ominous act set the tone for practically the entire century, a time of plots, mass murders, palace revolts, and civil wars that tore the heart, or what was left of it, out of the Roman empire. The 73 years after the death of Septimius Severus saw 23 emperors, two of whom ruled for only a month before being disposed of. This chaotic period was finally ended by the reforms of Diocletian. When we look at this arch, it really emerges as a sort of signpost of the end of Imperial sanity, which up to that point had been pretty precarious anyway.

Walk around to the back of the Severus arch, face it, and look to your right. There amid the rubble can be discerned a semicircular stair that led to the famous **Rostra,** the podium from which dictators and caesars addressed the throngs of the Forum below. One can just imagine the emperor, shining in his white toga, surrounded by Imperial guards and distinguished senators, gesticulating grandly like one of the statues on a Roman roofline. The motley crowd falls silent, the elegant senators pause and listen, the merchants put down their measures, even the harlots and unruly soldiers lower their voices in such an august presence. Later emperors didn't have much cause to use the Rostra, making their policies known through edict and assassination instead.

You might glance across the high road that separates the Forum from the Capitoline Hill at this point, where lie four ancient monuments that used to be part of the Forum. The road clearly shows how much earth the Forum was buried under before the excavations, as it lies on the former ground level. The **Carcer,** actually rather difficult to see from this angle, was a jail for the most dangerous political prisoners. The **Temple of Concord** is today nothing but a foundation, but once commemorated the conciliation of the patricians and plebeians after the civil war of 367 B.C. Livia, wife of Augustus, pressured her son Tiberius to pay for the construction of this now-vanished monument, an undertaking that nearly bankrupted him. The three standing columns, clearly seen between the road and the Capitoline heights, belong to the **Temple of Vespasian,** a remnant of the first century A.D., while to the left of this is the **Porticus of the Dii Consentes,** which once held magnificent golden statues of the 12 major gods of the pagan pantheon. For now, we'll continue in the part of the Forum not cut off by the modern road.

The great temple whose ruins adjoin the modern road on our side is the **Temple of Saturn,** where once reposed the public treasury. This was undoubtedly the first stop on many a barbarian tour of Rome, and considering that, it's amazing the whole thing wasn't trampled to dust. The beautiful columns date from the fourth-century reconstruction, necessitated, the inscription tells us, by a fire.

Now, facing the colonnade of the Temple of Saturn and going to the left, we come to the ruins of the **Basilica Julia,** again little more than a foundation. The basilica gets its name from Julius Caesar, who dedicated the first structure in 46 B.C. Like numerous of her sisters in the Forum, the basilica was burned and rebuilt several times, and the last structure dated from those shaky days after the Gothic invasion of 410. Throughout its history, it was used for the hearing of civil court cases, which were conducted in the pandemonium of the crowded Forum, open to anyone who happened to pass by. The building was also reputed to be particularly hot in the summer, and it was under these sweaty and unpromising circumstances that Roman justice, the standard of the world for a millennium, was meted out.

Walking back down the ruined stairs of the Basilica Julia and into the broad area whose far side is bounded by the Curia, we see the **Column of Phocas.** Probably lifted from an early structure in the near vicinity, this was the last monument to be erected in the Roman Forum, and it commemorates the Byzantine emperor Phocas's generous donation of the Pantheon to the pope of Rome, who made it into a church. The emperors of the West had by this time died out, but the Byzantine emperors of New Rome (Constantinople) kept an exarch, or representative, in the West until 731. The exarch at this time was a man with the marvelously Byzantine name of Smaragdus. The exarch usually made his home in Ravenna, possibly because the spectacle of crumbling Rome offended his aesthetic sensibilities. But when he traveled to Rome, this Imperial representative stayed in the dank, rotting palaces on the Palatine Hill. Before the fall of the West, the Palatine had been completely covered with palaces by a succession of emperors; the empty shells, still marvelously rich in decoration, with not too many holes in the ceilings or fallen colonnades, provided temporary quarters to these curious men from the East—that is, when a marauding barbarian general wasn't in residence. We can just imagine Smaragdus traveling to Rome with a gilt statue of his luxuriously evil Eastern monarch, passing his nights in temporarily furnished apartments in some damp and echoing corner of the deserted Palatine. He was probably glad to get the golden statue on the column's top and then be on his way. One wonders how long it stayed there before being snatched.

We now make our way down the middle of the Forum nearly back to the ramp from which we entered. The pile of brick with the semicircular indentation that stands in the middle of things was the **Temple of Julius Caesar,** erected some time after the dictator was deified. Judging from the reconstructions, it was quite an elegant building. As we stand facing the ruins, with the entrance to the Forum on our left, we see on our right three columns belonging originally to the **Temple of the Castors.** This temple perpetuated the legend of Castor and Pollux, who appeared out of thin air in the Roman Forum and were observed watering their horses at the fountain of Juturna (still visible today), just as a major battle against the Etruscans turned in favor of Rome. Castor and Pollux, the heavenly twins—and the symbol of the astrological sign Gemini—seem a favorite of Rome. Their statues grace Michelangelo's Renaissance Campidoglio to this day. The great crumbling brickwork on the Palatine that looms over this portion of the Forum belonged to elaborate palace construction, although it's hard to imagine its elegance from the ruins today.

The next major monument is the circular **Temple of Vesta,** wherein dwelt the sacred flame of Rome, and the **Atrium of the Vestal Virgins.** Everybody's heard of vestal virgins, but what in the world were they? The custom of having young virgins guard an eternal flame probably goes back considerably before the dawn of history to the time when a tribe's menfolk were out at war, and womenfolk were bent double with the task of raising children and preparing food. The young boys were taught the arts of manhood, and what did the young girls do before marriage? They watched after the fires, whose origins were considered holy. It is probably from this ancient custom that the incredible Roman cult of Vesta derives. A vestal virgin was usually a girl of good family who signed a contract for 30 years. During that time, she lived in the ruin we're standing in right now. Of course, back then it was an unimaginably rich marble building with two floors. There were only six vestal virgins during the Imperial period, and even though they had the option of going back out into the world at the end of their 30 years, few did. Those who messed around while the holy vows were in force were buried alive for their trouble (the tombs of several are under Via Goito to this day). The majority, however, remained chaste to the end of their days, and were rewarded with great riches and numerous privileges—they even had their own chariots in a city where vehicular traffic was banned during the day. In return, a vestal had only to watch after the sacred fire, whose continued burning was symbolic of the continuity of Rome. The cult of Vesta came to an end in 394, when a Christian Rome secularized all her pagan temples. A man standing on this site before then would have been put to death immediately.

Stand in the atrium with your back to the Palatine, and look beyond those fragmented statues of former vestals to the **Temple of Antoninus and Faustina.** It's the building with the free-standing colonnade just to the right of the ramp that you first entered the Forum on. Actually, just the colonnade dates from Imperial times. The building behind is a much-later church dedicated to St. Lorenzo. Who were Antoninus and Faustina? He was an emperor, one of the three Antonines (the other two were Marcus Aurelius and Commodus), and he and his wife Faustina ruled Rome for more than 20 years. Upon her death, the empress was deified, and this temple was dedicated to her cult. Not long after (A.D. 161), Antoninus died, and joined his wife in symbolic eternity in this same temple.

Deification was common practice among the imperial families, and after you inspect the beautifully proportioned Antoninus and Faustina temple, head up the Via Sacra away from the entrance ramp in the direction of the Arch of Titus. Pretty soon, on your left, you'll see the twin bronze doors of the **Temple of Romulus.** It's the doors themselves that are really of note here—they're the original Roman doors, and swing on the same hinges they were mounted on in A.D. 306. Romulus is not the legendary co-founder of Rome in this case—he was the son of the emperor Maxentius, who gave him the name in a fit of antiquarian patriotism. Maxentius's last days were far from happy. After the untimely death of his son, which grieved him greatly, he went into battle with a man who further deprived him of his empire, and even his life. That man was Constantine, who, while camped outside Rome, saw the sign of the True Cross in the heavens along with the legend *In Hoc Signo Vinces* (In This Sign Shall You Conquer). He raised the standard of Christianity above his legions and defeated the pagan emperor Maxentius. The emperor of Rome, Constantine the Great, became a Christian.

At the time of his victory (A.D. 306), the great **Basilica of Constantine** (those three gaping arches up ahead on your left) was only half-finished, having been started by the unfortunate Maxentius. However, Constantine finished the job and affixed his name to this, the largest and most impressive building in the Forum. To my taste, the more delicate, Greek-influenced temples are more attractive, but you have to admire the scale, and the engineering skill that erected this monument. The fact that portions of the original coffered ceiling are still intact is amazing.

The basilica once held a statue of Constantine whose little toe is as wide as your waist. You can see a few fragments from this colossal thing—the remnants were found in 1490—in the courtyard of the Conservatory Museum on the Capitoline Hill. As far as Roman emperors went, Christian or otherwise, ego knew no bounds.

From Constantine's basilica, we follow the Roman paving stones of the Via Sacra to the **Arch of Titus,** clearly visible on a rise just ahead. There is, by the way, a little spring to the right of the path, below the arch, whose icy cool waters should be most welcome at this point. Titus was the emperor who sacked the great Jewish temple in Jerusalem, and the bas-relief sculpture inside the arch shows the booty of the Jews being carried in triumph through the streets of Rome, while Titus is crowned by Victory, who comes down from heaven for the occasion. You'll notice in particular the candelabrum, for centuries one of the most famous pieces of the treasure of Rome. In all probability, it now lies at the bottom of the Busento River in the secret tomb of Alaric the Goth. Legend has it that Alaric fell ill—perhaps a curse for having looted the sacred city of Rome (he was the first of many, in August of 410)—while proceeding across Calabria with wagons laden with loot. His last wish was to be buried in a secret spot with the finest of the booty, and accordingly the Busento was diverted, a tomb was dug, and Alaric was laid to rest. The river was set back to its original course and those who dug the tomb were put to death to keep the secret forever.

This is a pleasant spot to pause and observe the vista of the Roman Forum shimmering in the hot sun, perhaps to reflect on all the stories of Rome, or to wonder about all the people who walked down that narrow road you just walked up. This arch has been restored, actually. In medieval times, it was the gate in a wall that stretched about these parts (built by the Frangipani), but was later restored by the man who designed the Piazza del Popolo, Valadier. But while the outer edges date from the 1820s, the friezes inside the arch are original.

When you've gathered your strength, we'll be heading up the Clivus Palatinus, the road to the palaces of the Palatine Hill. With your back to the Arch of Titus, it's the road going up the hill to the left.

THE PALATINE HILL: It was on the Palatine Hill that Rome first became a city. Legend tells us the date was 753 B.C. The new city originally consisted of nothing more than the Palatine, which was soon enclosed by a surprisingly sophisticated wall, remains of which can still be seen on the Circus Maximus side of the hill. As time went on, and Rome grew in power and wealth, the boundaries were extended and later enclosed by the Servian Wall. When the last of the ancient kings was overthrown (509 B.C.), Rome had already extended onto several of the adjoining hills and valleys. As Republican times progressed, the Palatine became a fashionable residential district. So it remained until Tiberius—who, like his predecessor Augustus, was a bit too modest to really call himself "emperor" out loud—began the first of the monumental palaces which were to cover the entire hill.

It's difficult today to make sense out of the Palatine. The first-time viewer might be forgiven for suspecting it to be an entirely artificial structure built on brick arches. Those arches, which are visible on practically every flank of the hill, are actually supports that once held imperial structures. Having run out of building sites, the emperors, in their fever, simply enlarged the hill by building new sides on it.

As I said, the hill was a fashionable residential area through most of the era of the Roman Republic. Among the many distinguished men who called it home were Crassus, the original rich man, and Cicero. All trace of their lavish homes has long since disappeared. The Julio-Claudian emperors completely covered the section of the Palatine known as the Germalus (that part nearest the Capitoline). The middle part of the hill was built up by the Flavian emperor Domitian, a man so (understandably) worried about assassination that he had the walls of his palace covered with mica, so that he could see behind him at all times (they got him anyway). About the last open real estate, at the opposite end of the hill from Tiberius's first palace, was built over by Septimius Severus, at the beginning of the third century. It is the site of his baths, a monumental construction that was, however, outdone by that of his son, Caracalla.

Your entrance ticket to the Forum includes the Palatine, so from the Arch of Titus simply head up the Clivus Palatinus. The road goes only a short way, through a small sort of valley filled with lush, untrimmed greenery. After about five minutes (for slow walkers), you'll see the ruins of a monumental stairway just to the right of the road. The Clivus Palatinus turns sharply to the left here, skirting the monastery of S. Bonaventura, but we'll detour to the right and take a look at the remains of the **Flavian Palace.**

As you walk off the road and into the ruins, you'll be able to discern that there were once three rooms here. But it's really impossible for any but an archeologist to comprehend quite how splendid these rooms were. The entire Flavian palace was decorated in the most lavish of colored marbles, sometimes inlaid with precious silver. The roofs were, in places, even covered with gold. Much of the decoration survived as late as the 18th century, when the greedy Duke of Parma removed most of what was left. The room closest to the Clivus Palatinus was called the Lararium, and held statues of the divinities that protected the imperial family. The middle room was the grandest of the three. It was the Imperial throne room, where sat the ruler of the world, the emperor of Rome. The spot seems still to radiate faint vibrations of the enormous power that once was wielded by a man sitting on a now-vanished throne. The far room was a basilica, and as such was used for miscellaneous court functions, among them audiences with the emperor. This part of the palace was used entirely for ceremonial functions. Adjoining these three rooms are the remains of a spectacularly luxurious peristyle. You'll recognize it by the hexagonal remains of a fountain in the middle. Try, if you can, to imagine this fountain surrounded by marble arcades, planted with mazes, and equipped with mica-covered walls. On the opposite side of the peristyle from the throne rooms are several other great reception and entertainment rooms. The banquet hall was here, and beyond it, looking over the Circus Maximus, are a few ruins of former libraries. Although practically nothing remains except the foundations, every now and again you'll catch sight of a fragment of colored marble floor, in a subtle, sophisticated pattern.

The imperial family lived in the **Domus Augustana,** the remains of which lie in the direction of the Circus Maximus, and slightly to the left of the Flavian Palace. The new building that stands here—it looks old to us but in Rome it qualifies as a new building—is a museum (usually closed). It stands in the absolute center of the Domus Augustana. In the field adjacent to the Stadium well into the present century stood the Villa Mills, a gingerbread Gothic villa of the 19th century. It was quite a famous place, owned by a rich Englishman who came to Rome from the West Indies. The Villa Mills was the scene of many fashionable entertainments in Victorian times, and it's interesting to note, as H. V. Morton pointed out, that the last dinner parties that took place on the Palatine Hill were given by an Englishman.

Heading across the field parallel to the Clivus Palatinus, you come to the north end of the **Hippodrome,** or Stadium of Domitian. The field was apparently occupied by parts of the Domus Augustana, which in turn adjoined the enormous Stadium. The stadium itself is worth examination, although sometimes it's difficult to get down inside it. The perfectly proportioned area was usually used for private games, staged for the amusement of the imperial family. As you look down the stadium from the north end, you can see, on the left side, the semicircular remains of a structure identified as Domitian's private box. I'll note at this point that some archeologists claim the "stadium" was actually an elaborate sunken garden, and perhaps we'll never know exactly what it was. It's quite pleasant to stroll along the grassy, tree-shaded flank that leads past the box, and climb around the remains of royal corridors. Doubtless, some of the famous cats that infest the ruins of ancient Rome will be quietly observing you, waiting for an offer of food. The aqueduct that comes up the wooded hill used to supply water for the **Baths of Septimius Severus,** whose difficult-to-understand ruins lie in monumental piles of arched brick at the far end of the stadium.

Returning to the Flavian Palace, leave the peristyle on the opposite side from the Domus Augustana, and follow the signs for the **House of Livia.** They take you down a dusty path to your left, from which entrance to the house is made. Although legend says this was the house of Augustus's consort, it actually was Augustus's all along. The place is notable for some rather well-preserved murals showing mythological scenes. But more interesting is the aspect of the house itself—it's smallish, there never were any great baths, or impressive marble arcades. Augustus, even though he was the first emperor, lived simply compared to his successors. His wife, Livia, was a fiercely ambitious aristocrat who divorced her own husband to marry the emperor (the ex-husband was made to attend the wedding, incidentally) and according to some historians was the true power behind Roman policy between the death of Julius Caesar and the ascension of Tiberius. She even controlled Tiberius, her son, since she had engineered his rise to power through a long string of intrigues and poisonings.

After you've examined the frescoes in Livia's parlor, head up the steps that lead to the top of the embankment to the north. Once on top, you'll be in the **Farnese Gardens,** which are the

16th-century addition of a Farnese cardinal. They are built on the top of the **Palace of Tiberius,** which, you'll remember, was the first of the great imperial palaces to be put up. It's impossible to see any of it, but the gardens are cool and nicely laid out. You might stroll up to the promontory above the Forum and admire the view of the ancient temples and the Capitoline heights off to the left.

When you've seen this much, you've seen the best of the Forum and the Palatine. To leave the archeological area, you should now continue through the Farnese Gardens, keeping the Forum on your left. Soon you'll come to a stairway that leads to the path from the Arch of Titus. There is an exit just behind the arch, but since it's usually closed, you'll probably have to exit up the ramp you entered by.

THE COLOSSEUM: There's no need to give directions to the Colosseum—you'll be able to see it—but I will wish you luck getting across the howling traffic lanes that surround it. After the great fire of A.D. 64, the emperor Nero snatched up a large amount of land adjacent to the Roman Forum and began construction of his Golden House. The house, whose ruins we'll see later, had such suburban comforts as a fully stocked zoo, swimming pools filled with salt water pumped up from the Mediterranean, and mother-of-pearl floors (here and there). Where the Colosseum stands now was a great reflecting pool for the Golden House. After the death of Nero, and a power struggle that saw four emperors in one year, the stern Vespasian came to power. Vespasian had been raised in the country, where many of the ancient virtues of Rome hadn't yet been corroded by the luxury of the capital. In fact, his humble home was kept exactly as it had been when he was a child, and he would take short back-to-nature vacations there. The decadent luxury of the Golden House embarrassed Vespasian, and perhaps to help along his own popularity too, he began breaking it up and making parts of it available to the public (the palace was unpopular in Rome). In A.D. 72 construction was started on the Colosseum, and a marvel of engineering it is, since the enormous weight is resting in a swamp (Nero's former lake) on artificial supports. The completed stadium, called the Amphitheatrum Flavium, was dedicated by Titus in A.D. 80—"Flavium" refers to the Flavians, an imperial family that included builders Vespasian, Titus, and Domitian.

The Colosseum was covered with marble and could hold 80,000 spectators, who watched games that nearly rendered extinct many species of animals from the Roman empire. In addition to the animal slaughter—a hundred lions might be killed in a morning—untold numbers of men met their death, for the amusement of the mob. The games were quite an event, and everybody went. A third of Rome's population had nothing else to do in any event, except live on the public dole, go to the games, and lounge around the imperial baths. A day at the Colosseum was rather formal—the toga was *de rigueur* dress for men, even though many resented it much the way modern suburbanites hate to put on a tie on Saturday. The seating arrangement was a strictly social matter. The higher you were in society, the lower your seat was—even if you had the money, it was out of the question to "buy" a better seat, if your birth didn't warrant it. Above everybody was a great canopy to shield the spectators from the sun—a canopy so large it roared like thunder in a strong wind.

The sections of the Colosseum that are missing went into the construction of a number of Renaissance palaces, most notable among them the Palazzo Farnese. You can wander around the ruins at any time of the day for no charge. Impressive as it is, it's an evil place, if only because so many men died so violently here. The upper floors are open daily from 9 a.m. to 6 p.m. Admission is 2000 lire ($1.22).

THE ARCH OF CONSTANTINE: A highly photogenic memorial (next to the Colosseum), the Arch of Constantine was erected in honor of Constantine's defeat of the pagan Maxentius (A.D. 306). It is a landmark in every way, physically and historically. Physically, it's beautiful, perhaps marred by the aggravating traffic that zooms around it at all hours, but so intricately carved and well preserved that you almost forget the racket of the cars and buses. Many of the reliefs have nothing whatsoever to do with Constantine or his works, but tell of the victories of earlier Antonine rulers—they were apparently lifted from other, long-forgotten memorials.

Historically, the arch marks a period of great change in the history of Rome, therefore the history of the world. Rome, which had been pagan since the beginning, now had a Christian emperor, Constantine. Converted by a vision on the battlefield, he led his forces to victory, and officially ended the centuries-long persecution of the Christians. By Constantine's time, many a devout follower of the new religion had been put to death (oftentimes horribly) for the sake of his religion, and the new emperor put an end to it. While he did not ban paganism (which survived officially until the closing of the temples more than a half century later), he interceded on an imperial level to stop the persecutions. And by espousing Christianity himself, he began the inevitable development that culminated in the conquest of Rome by the Christian religion. The arch is a tribute to the emperor erected by the Senate in A.D. 315.

TOUR TWO
Via dei Fori Imperiali, The Theater of Marcellus, Piazza Bocca della Verità, The Circus Maximus

THE VIA DEI FORI IMPERIALI: Starting at the Colosseum, the first leg of this tour takes us up to the **Via dei Fori Imperiali,** built in the early 1930s by the Fascist government. This proceeds straight through the middle of the Imperial Forums, built by a succession of emperors to make commerce more comfortable for the merchants of Rome, and to provide new libraries, and more room for assembly, since the original Roman Forum had become too small. (Not only was it too small, it was becoming clogged with marble monuments to fallen Romans, of which there was no lack.) All of the Imperial Forums may be visited daily except Monday from 9 a.m. to 1 p.m. for an admission of 500 lire (31¢).

With your back to the Colosseum, begin walking up the Via dei Fori Imperiali, keeping to the right side of the street. Those ruins across the street are what's left of the colonnade that once surrounded the **Temple of Venus and Roma.** Next to it, you'll recognize the back wall of the Basilica of Constantine. Shortly, you'll come to a large outdoor restaurant, where Via Cavour joins the boulevard we're on. Just beyond the small park across Via Cavour are the remains of the **Forum of Nerva,** built by the emperor whose two-year reign (A.D. 96–98) followed that of the paranoid Domitian.

Nerva's Forum is best observed from the railing that skirts it on the Via dei Fori Imperiali. Again, you'll be struck at just how much the level of the ground has risen in 19 centuries. The only really intelligible remnant is a wall of the Temple of Minerva with two fine Corinthian columns. This forum was once flanked by that of Vespasian, which is, however, completely gone. It's possible to enter Nerva's Forum from the other side, but you can see just as well from the railing.

The next forum up was that of **Augustus,** and was built before the birth of Christ to commemorate the emperor's victory over the assassins Cassius and Brutus in the Battle of Phillippi (42 B.C.). Fittingly, the temple that once dominated the Forum—and whose remains can still be seen—was that of Mars Ultor, or Mars the Avenger. In the temple once stood a mammoth statue of Augustus, which has unfortunately completely vanished. Like the Forum of Nerva, you can enter Augustus's Forum from the other side (cut across the wood footbridge).

Continuing along the railing, you'll next see the vast semicircle of **Trajan's Market,** whose teeming arcades stocked with merchandise from the far corners of the Roman world have long collapsed, leaving only a few ubiquitous cats to watch after things. The shops once covered a multitude of levels, and you can still wander around many of them. In front of the perfectly proportioned semicircular facade—designed by Apollodorus of Damascus at the beginning of the second century—are the remains of a great library, and fragments of delicately colored marble floors still shine in the sunshine between stretches of rubble and tall grass. While the view from the railing is of interest, Trajan's Market is worth the descent below street level. To get there, follow the service road you're on until you come as far as the monumental Trajan's Column on your left, but turn right here and go up the steep flight of stairs that leads to Via Nazionale. At the top of the stairs, about a half block farther on the right, you'll see the entrance to the market. It is open from 9 a.m. to 1:30 p.m. daily except Monday. Admission is 500 lire (31¢). Before you head down through the labyrinthine passageways, you might like to climb the **Tower of the Milizie,** a 12th-century structure that was part of the medieval headquarters of the Knights of Rhodes. The view from the top (if it's open) is well worth the climb.

From the tower, you can wander where you will through the ruins of the market, admiring the sophistication of the layout, and the sad beauty of the bits of decoration that still remain. When you've examined the brick and travertine corridors, head out in front of the semicircle to the site of the former library; from here, scan the retaining wall that supports the modern road and look for the entrance to the tunnel that leads to the **Forum of Trajan.**

Once through the tunnel, you'll emerge in the latest and most beautiful of the Imperial Forums, designed by the same man who laid out the adjoining market. There are many statue fragments, and pedestals bearing still-legible inscriptions, but more interesting is the great **Basilica Ulpia,** whose gray marble columns rise roofless into the sky.

Beyond the basilica is **Trajan's Column,** in magnificent condition—with intricate bas-relief sculpture depicting Trajan's victorious campaign against Dacia at the dawn of the second century. The sculpture depicts in minute detail every event that occurred on the campaign, although from your vantage point you'll only be able to see the earliest stages. At the base of Trajan's Column the emperor's ashes were kept in a golden urn.

If you're fortunate, there will be someone on duty at the stairs next to the column, and you'll be able to get out there. Otherwise, be prepared to walk back the way you came.

Our next stop is the **Forum of Julius Caesar,** the first of the Imperial Forums. It lies on the opposite side of the Via dei Fori Imperiali, the last set of sunken ruins before the Victor Emmanuel Monument. While it's possible to go right down into the ruins, you can see just as well from the railing. This was the site of the Roman stock exchange, as well as the Temple of Venus, a few of whose restored columns stand cinematically in the middle of the excavations. From here, we'll retrace our last steps until we're in front of the white Brescian marble monument around the corner on the Piazza Venezia.

Keeping close to the Victor Emmanuel monument, walk to your left, in the opposite direction from the Via dei Fori Imperiali. You might like to pause at the fountain that flanks one of the monument's great white walls and splash some icy water on your face. There is another fountain just like this on the other side of the monument, and they're both favorite spots for tired visitors. Stay on the same side of the street, and just keep walking around the monument. You'll be on the Via del Teatro Marcello, which takes you past the twin lions guarding the sloping stairs to the Campidoglio (that's on the next tour), and on along the base of Capitoline Hill.

THE THEATER OF MARCELLUS: It stands to the right of the road. You'll recognize the two rows of gaping arches, said to be the models for the Colosseum. It was in a theater much like this (Pompeii's theater in the Campus Martius) that Caesar was murdered in 44 B.C. Julius Caesar is the man credited with starting the construction of this theater, but it was finished many years after his death by Augustus, who then dedicated it to his favorite nephew, Marcellus. The date: 11 B.C. You can stroll around the 2000-year-old arcade, a small corner of which has been restored to what presumably was the original condition. Here, as everywhere, there are numerous cats stalking around the broken marble.

The bowl of the theater and the stage are covered by the Renaissance palace of the Orsini family, now transformed into apartments. You can see the palace walls sitting on top of the ancient arches. Walk around the theater to the right. The other ruins belong to old temples. Soon, you'll walk up a ramp to the street, and to the right is the Porticus of Octavia, dating from the second century before Christ. Note how later cultures used part of the Roman structure without destroying its original character. There's another good example of this on the other side of the theater. There you'll see a church with a wall completely incorporating part of an ancient colonnade.

Returning to the Via del Teatro Marcello, keep walking away from the Piazza Venezia for two more long blocks, until you come to the—

PIAZZA BOCCA DELLA VERITÀ: The first item to notice in this attractive piazza is the perfect rectangular **Temple of Fortuna Virile.** You'll see it on the right, standing a little off the road. Built a century before the birth of Christ, it's still in magnificent condition. Behind it is another temple, dedicated to **Vesta.** Like the one in the Forum, it too is round, symbolic of the prehistoric huts where continuity of the hearthfire was a matter of survival.

THE CIRCUS MAXIMUS: Shades of *Ben Hur.* When you're at Santa Maria in Cosmedin, you're just a block away. The remains of the great arena lie directly behind the block that the church is on. What we see today is only a large field, of awesome proportion, but without a trace of Roman marble. At one time, 250,000 Romans could assemble on the marble seats, while the emperor observed the games from his box high on the Palatine Hill.

The Circus lies in a valley formed by the Palatine Hill on the left, and the Aventine Hill on the right. Next to the Colosseum, it was the most impressive structure in ancient Rome, and was certainly in one of the most exclusive neighborhoods. Emperors lived on the Palatine, while the great palaces of patricians sprawled across the Aventine, which is still a rather nice neighborhood. For centuries, the pomp and ceremony of imperial chariot races filled this valley with the cheers of thousands.

When the dark days of the fifth and sixth centuries fell on the city, the Circus Maximus seemed a symbol of the complete ruination of Rome. The last games were held in 549 on the orders of Totilla the Goth, who had seized Rome in 546 and established himself as emperor. He lived in the still-glittering ruins on the Palatine, and apparently thought that the chariot races in the Circus Maximus would lend credence to his charade of empire. It must have been a pretty miserable show, since the decimated population numbered something on the order of 500 souls when Totilla had recaptured the city three years previous. The Romans of these times were caught between Belisarius, the general from Constantinople, and Totilla the Goth, both of whom fought bloodily for Rome. After the travesty of 549, the Circus was never used again, and the demand for building materials reduced this, like so much of Rome, to a great dusty field.

To return to the other parts of town, head for the bus stop adjacent to the Santa Maria in Cosmedin church. Or walk the length of the Circus Maximus to its far end and pick up the subway to Terminal Station.

TOUR THREE

Piazza Venezia, The Campidoglio, Santa Maria d'Aracoeli, Largo Argentina, The Pantheon, Piazza Navona

PIAZZA VENEZIA: Now you're face to face with **King Victor Emmanuel II**, the man with the luxurious mustaches whose bronze horse stands in the middle of all that white marble. The monument was erected between 1885 and 1911 to celebrate both the king, and the new country he had created. Before Victor Emmanuel, Rome had been the capital of the Papal States, under the direct temporal rule of the pope—a rule that had lasted from 731 to 1870. But with the victory of Garibaldi's forces of united Italy, the pope was driven from the Quirinal Palace to the Vatican, where the papacy remained "imprisoned," as was claimed, until the Lateran Pact of 1929 established Vatican City as a separate state.

The monument in front of you is a curious cross between belle époque, ancient Roman (note the chariots on top with their teams of four horses), and good old Italian overstatement. The effect of all this stone—which, I hear, will never mellow like native Roman travertine—is permanently to blazon the fact of Italian independence on the consciousness.

At the foot of the king's statue is the Tomb of the Unknown Soldier, guarded during the day by two honor guards. The walk to the top looks more forbidding than it really is, and once up there the view is breathtaking. From the right-hand side (as you face the monument) you can see Renaissance Rome with her gleaming domes, and the wooded slopes of the Janiculum Hill across the Tiber. The left-hand side gives one a fine vista of the Imperial Forums, and the Forum Romanum. While the Victor Emmanuel monument is commonly criticized for the insensitivity of both its size and location, it nonetheless has a charm peculiarly its own.

From almost any part of the monument, there's a fine view of the Piazza Venezia below. You'll notice on the left (with your back to the monument) the **Palazzo Venezia,** built in the style of the High Renaissance in the 15th century. There's no baroque busywork on its facade. The small 16th-century loggia (balcony) in the middle of the facade facing the piazza was used by Mussolini to harangue the crowds in the '30s. A long string of kings, popes, cardinals, and ambassadors have lived in the palace. It currently houses a museum founded in 1916. You can visit the rooms and halls containing oil paintings, antiques, porcelain, tapestries, ivories, ceramics, and arms. The museum is open daily except Monday from 9 a.m. to 2 p.m., until 1 p.m. on Sunday. Admission is 2000 lire ($1.22); free on the first and third Saturday and the second and fourth Sunday of each month. For more information, telephone 679-8865.

Now walk toward the Theater of Marcellus, as you did before, on the Via del Teatro Marcello. This time, when you come to the two lions spouting water (on the left), turn and walk up the long shallow stairs which, like the suite of buildings and statues on top of the hill, were designed by Michelangelo in the 16th century.

THE CAMPIDOGLIO: The Campidoglio stands on the summit of the Capitoline Hill, the most sacred of ancient Rome, where the Temples of Jupiter and Juno once stood. This was the spiritual heart of Rome, where triumphant generals made sacrifices to the gods who had given them their victories, and where the earthly homes of the king and queen of heaven stood. The gold-roofed temples of Jupiter and Juno faced the Forum and were approached by the Via Sacra. Later constructions turned their back on the Forum to face the Tiber. On the way up the graceful steps, take a look in the shrubs to the left of the stairway. Deep in the bushes, surrounded by green lawns and flowering plants, is a large cage, and in it are wolves. They perpetuate the memory of the she-wolf who suckled the infants Romulus and Remus.

The top of the stairs is guarded by Castor and Pollux, the same heavenly twins to whom a temple was dedicated in the Forum. But more impressive is the equestrian statue of the emperor **Marcus Aurelius,** which stands in the middle of the piazza. This is the only statue of its type (bronze) to have survived from ancient Rome, and it survived only because it had been tossed into the Tiber by marauding barbarians. For centuries after its discovery, it was thought to be a statue of Constantine the Great, which further protected it, since Papal Rome respected the memory of the first Christian emperor. It's a beautiful statue even though the perspective is rather odd—it was originally designed to sit on top of a column, hence the foreshortened effect. The emperor's stirrups, by the way, are not missing. They were simply unknown in classical times, hence Roman horsemen never used them.

Two of the three buildings that face the piazza are attributed to Michelangelo and his students, and they're a perfect expression of Renaissance balance. The building behind Marcus Aurelius is the **Senatorial Palace,** and while Michelangelo didn't design the facade, the graceful stairway is attributed to him. Note the fountains with their allegorical statuary. The central fountain is presided over by Roma, goddess of the city. The two reclining gentlemen on either side are personifications of two of the empire's greatest rivers, the Nile (look for the pyramids) and the Tiber (look for the infants Romulus and Remus). The palace stands on the site of the Roman Hall of Records, and some of the bronze tablets on which were inscribed the events of the empire still exist.

On the left is the **Capitoline Museum,** with an enormous collection of marble carvings from the ancient world. Many of them are just statues—notable for their age, but that's about it. However, in the first room at the top of the stairs is the eloquently beautiful *Dying Gaul,* actually a copy of a Greek third-century B.C. sculpture. The statue has great dignity and grace, accepting inevitable death with honor and poignant resignation. The connecting rooms house statuary that's nearly as beautiful. Note especially *Cupid and Psyche* (in the same room as the *Dying Gaul*), a jovial red porphyry *Silenus* in the next room, and two delicate fauns, in the large central gallery, that once graced Hadrian's luxurious villa outside Tivoli. The far room holds a collection of busts depicting various of the emperors (you knew that Julius Caesar was bald, but did you know Augustus's ears stuck out? or that Nero had a decidedly decadent fold of flesh under his chin?).

The corridor outside that leads back to the stair is literally a forest of gesticulating marble limbs. The most celebrated torso of them all, however, belongs to the *Capitoline Venus,* an exquisite marble statue complete with nose and fingers. She has an unself-conscious and aristocratic grace. The statue was preserved in a wall for centuries, only to be discovered in perfect condition in the 18th century. Now she lives in her own small room, surrounded by velvet curtains.

Across the piazza is the **Conservatory Palace.** Even if you're weary or in a hurry, you might take just a moment to glance into the courtyard and marvel at the fragments of the enormous statue of Constantine the Great that once stood in his basilica in the Forum. The museum, in my opinion, is more notable for its architectural design and decoration than for the collection it houses. There are several extraordinary pieces here, among them the fifth-century B.C. Etruscan statue of the she-wolf, the ancient symbol of Rome; fragments of the ancient marble map of the Rome of the Caesars (it's in a courtyard in the back), and fragments of the Temple of Jupiter. The nicest thing about the Conservatory Palace is its profusion of splendiferous baroque decoration—murals, gilded furniture, vast ballrooms.

Both the Capitoline Museum and the Conservatory Palace are open daily except Monday from 9 a.m. to 2 p.m.; Tuesday and Thursday in the evening from 5 to 8 p.m.; and Saturday evening from 8:30 to 11 p.m. Admission is 1000 lire (61¢); free on the last Sunday of each month. The same ticket admits you to both museums.

Before you leave the Campidoglio, walk around the right corner (as you face it) of the Senatorial Palace for a look at the Forum. This is a favorite vista of the ruins below, and on a summer's evening you'll find small groups of visitors mixed with Roman couples leaning on the railing surveying the softly lit columns and crumbling temples.

Now, return to the Campidoglio and walk up the stairs that

run between the Senate and Capitoline Museum, keeping close to the wall of the latter. You'll see a ramp leading off to the left and up to the side door of the next stop.

THE CHURCH OF SANTA MARIA D'ARACOELI: This ancient church stands on the site of the Temple of Juno, the pagan queen of heaven. It's a lovely old place, lavishly decorated. Note the intricately carved gold ceiling. Also of interest are the unmatched columns that line the nave. These doubtless come from the Forum below, which, at the time of construction (end of the sixth century), must have been substantially intact. Owing to its considerable age, this church probably bears a strong resemblance to the basilicas of the late Roman Empire. In fact, if you squint your eyes and ignore for a moment all the accoutrements of the Christian present, it's not hard at all to imagine yourself in a hall in ancient Rome. The steps out front were brought from their original site on the Quirinal Hill, where they led to Augustus's Temple of the Sun. They are real calf-breakers, brutally steep in the best Imperial Roman tradition.

At the foot of Augustus's marble stairs, turn right in the direction of the Piazza Venezia. We aren't going to the piazza, however. Instead, cross Via del Teatro Marcello, and walk through the small park on the opposite side of the street. At the far end of the park is the Via San Marco, a heavily trafficked road that connects Piazza Venezia with Largo Argentina, which is where we're headed. (This is the automobile access to Corso Vittorio Emanuele westbound, and that's why there's so much activity.) Largo Argentina, another sunken ruin and a major bus stop, is five blocks from Piazza Venezia.

LARGO ARGENTINA: You'll approach the ruins from the rear. Like other archeological sites in Rome, this one is surrounded by the familiar iron fence, broken here and there by large stone bullets. The temples below the street are quite old, probably dating from Republican times, but no one seems to know much more about them. It is supposedly possible to enter the site and roam about at will, but I've never seen anyone down there, nor even an open gate. The present-day residents are, predictably, cats. Their population seems to be flourishing, although what they do for food is a question. In the evening, you can see old women feeding herds of them from brown bags filled with table scraps. Whether they eat anything else, or whether they ever leave their one-block universe, is hard to say. After you've explored Largo Argentina to your satisfaction, cross Corso Vittorio Emanuele and continue up Via Torre Argentina—the street perpendicular to Corso Emanuele and bordering Largo Argentina on its west side—for three blocks. Looming ahead, you'll see the crumbly brick rear of the Pantheon.

THE PANTHEON: This fabulous ancient monument was built and rebuilt several times. First credit goes to Agrippa, who began it in 27 B.C. The present structure is the result of an early second-century reconstruction by the emperor Hadrian. The Pantheon stands on the Piazza della Rotonda, complete with obelisk and baroque fountain. But during ancient times, the portico opened onto a vast rectangular gallery that formed an impressive courtyard. All that has completely vanished, but the Pantheon itself is in an astonishing state of preservation, considering nearly two millennia of vandalism. Agrippa, whose name still is clearly visible beneath the pediment, dedicated the Pantheon to all the gods of the ancient world. During Imperial times, the roof was covered with gold tiles, the ceiling of the portico was intricately cast bronze, and the interior was decorated with the most precious marbles and gilded bronzes. The centuries have clearly taken their toll. After a series of barbarian pillages, the golden roof was carried off by the Eastern emperor Constans (who was still the nominal ruler of Rome). The Pantheon was later given to the Roman popes for a church by Phocas, emperor in Byzantium. But instead of preserving it, they looted it too. The great bronze ceiling was melted down and cast into cannons by the Barberini pope, Urban VIII. As for the marble, it has long disappeared into a score of buildings, none of which is nearly as magnificent as this. However, the Pantheon still stands in one piece, with the original bronze doors, and an intact roof, which is a single piece of cast concrete! Each column, too, is made from a single piece of granite.

Inside, there's been some attempt at redecoration, but the present appearance comes nowhere near the splendor it had in Hadrian's time. Several famous personages are buried in the Pantheon, among them King Umberto I, Queen Margherita (who, by the way, used to live in what is now the American Embassy's Consular Division), and the painter Raphael. A highly celebrated effect is that of clouds passing over the open dome.

For a moment, it might seem as if the sky is standing still, and you're moving along inside an enormous stone vehicle.

Going through the great bronze doors—said to weigh 20 tons—turn to the left and leave the Piazza della Rotonda on the little street that runs perpendicular to the Pantheon. At the Pantheon, you're only four blocks from the Piazza Navona. It lies due west, and if your sense of direction is good, you'll find it right away. Consult your map carefully, because my giving directions through these nameless little streets might only confuse things further.

PIAZZA NAVONA: Surely one of the most beautifully baroque sites in all of Rome, the Piazza Navona is like an ochre-colored gem, unspoilt by new buildings, or even by traffic. The shape results from the Stadium of Domitian, whose ruins lie underneath the present constructions. Great chariot races were once held here—some of them rather unusual. There was one, for instance, where the head of the winning horse was lopped off as he crossed the finish line and carried by runners to be offered as a sacrifice by vestal virgins on top of the Capitoline Hill. And historians also note that in medieval times the Piazza Navona was flooded by the popes and used to stage mock naval encounters. Today, the most strenuous activities are performed by occasional fire-eaters, who go through their evening paces before an astonished circle of Romans and visitors.

Besides the twin-towered facade of the **Church of Saint Agnes** (17th century), the piazza boasts several other baroque masterpieces. In the center is Bernini's **Fountain of the Four Rivers,** whose four stone personifications symbolize the world's greatest rivers. They are the Ganges, Danube, della Plata, and Nile. It's fun to try and figure out which is which (hint: the figure with the shroud on his head is the Nile, so represented because the river's source was unknown at the time the statue was made). The fountain at the south end, the **Fountain of the Moor,** is also by Bernini and dates from the same period as the church and the Fountain of the Four Rivers. The **Fountain of Neptune,** which balances that of the Moor, is a 19th-century addition. During the summer, there are outdoor art shows in the evening. But a visit during the day is definitely in order. It's the best time to inspect the fragments of the original stadium that remain under a building on the north side of the piazza. If you're interested, walk out at the northern exit, and turn left for half a block. It's astonishing how much the level of the ground has risen since antiquity.

The southern end of the Piazza Navona is only a block and a half from Corso Vittorio Emanuele (merely keep going straight past the Fountain of the Moor). From Corso Emanuele, buses can be taken to any part of town (check the Fermata sign).

TOUR FOUR
Saint Peter's Basilica, The Castel Sant' Angelo

Before we proceed with Tour Number Four, this background information may be in order.

ROME OF THE PAPACY: Rome in the Middle Ages was a quaint, rural town. Narrow lanes with overhanging buildings filled the Campus Martius. Great basilicas were built and embellished with golden-hued mosaics. The forums, stock exchanges, temples, and great theaters of the Imperial era slowly collapsed. The decay of ancient Rome was given an assist by periodic earthquakes, centuries of neglect, and especially the growing need for building materials. For while Rome had receded to provinciality in temporal matters, she was the seat of the Catholic church, a priest state with constant need for new churches and convents.

The story of Rome from the dawn of the Renaissance to the Age of Enlightenment in the 17th and 18th centuries is as varied and fascinating as that of the rise and fall of the empire. The papacy soon became essentially a feudal state, and the pope a medieval (later Renaissance) prince engaged in many of the worldly activities that were to bring criticism upon the church in later centuries. The fall of the Holy Land to the Turks in 1065 catapulted the papacy into the forefront of world politics, primarily due to the Crusades, in which a major part was played by the pope. Until the 14th century medieval power politics took their toll of the Holy Roman Empire. The turbulence and fighting between powerful families, especially in Rome, was climaxed by the removal of the papacy to Avignon, which history books refer to as the "Babylonian Captivity." Until 1377 popes were "protected" in Avignon by the French monarchy from the street battles that raged between opposing Roman families.

The return of the papacy to Rome continued a succession of popes every bit as interesting as that of the Roman emperors.

The great families—Barberini, Medici, Borgia—managed to enhance their status and fortunes impressively when a son was elected pope. The age of siege was not over yet either, and in 1527 the worst sack ever was carried out by Charles V. To the horror of Pope Clement VII (a Medici), the entire city was brutally pillaged by the man who was to be crowned Holy Roman Emperor the next year.

During the years of the Renaissance, the Reformation, and the Counter-Reformation, the city underwent major physical changes. The old centers of culture reverted to pastures and fields, while great churches and palaces were built with the stones of ancient Rome. This building boom, in fact, did far more damage to the temples of the caesars than any barbarian sack. Rare marbles were stripped from the imperial baths and used as altarpieces, or sent to lime kilns. When the Arch of Claudius was found nearly intact in the Corso, it was demolished immediately and the marble put to use elsewhere. So enthusiastic was the papal destruction of Imperial Rome that it's a miracle anything is left.

It was the 19th century that witnessed the final collapse of the Renaissance city-states, of which Rome was one. The Papal States, really a small principality under the temporal jurisdiction of the pope, were eventually absorbed into the new kingdom of Italy (although not without a fight followed by generations of hard feelings). In 1871 Rome became the new capital of a new country. From that year until the Lateran Pact of 1929, the dispossessed popes retired to the Vatican Palace and proclaimed themselves prisoners of the new monarchy. The establishment of Vatican City as a separate state in 1929 normalized relations between Italy and the pope, and so matters stand to this day.

SAINT PETER'S BASILICA: For more than 1000 years St. Peter's was approached through a tangle of medieval streets as confusing as any in the Campus Martius. In the mid-17th century the Vatican "island" was given its superb visual effect with the construction of Bernini's colonnade, and the vast space embraced by the travertine pillars was all the more impressive compared to the tortuously narrow lanes that led to it. It was through these lanes that the last pope who ruled Rome, Pius XI, fled from the advancing armies of Victor Emmanuel in 1870. The pope's retreat to the Vatican palaces in that year was the beginning of an "imprisonment" that was to last for nearly 60 years.

Symbolic of the new church-state rapprochement, and much in the style of Italy in the 1930s, the enormous **Via della Conciliazione** was built. It sliced through the ancient quarters adjoining the Piazza San Pietro and dramatically opened the Vatican. Unfortunately, it did so at the expense of a highly historic district. It also has a sort of world's-fair look to it, a modernity that did not age well. This is the boulevard where your bus will leave you off, and from here, you'll head directly into the wide arms of the colonnade.

The vast piazza can hold 300,000 persons—and, sometimes it seems, all the tour buses they came in—between its twin galleries of nearly 300 travertine Doric columns. This was the site in ancient times of Nero's Circus. Two centuries later it was chosen by Constantine the Great as the site for a church to memorialize the early Christians martyred here, among them Saint Peter. Of Nero's Circus, something actually remains: the magnificent **Egyptian obelisk** (in the center of the piazza, which was ancient when the Romans hauled it back in the first century A.D. A lot of tortured Christian eyes, perhaps those of Peter himself, saw this same obelisk when it decorated the pagan circus. Today, the obelisk, flanked on either side by twin fountains dating from the 18th century, is in perfect harmony with the **17th-century colonnade.** You might like to stroll between the columns, reminiscent of the countless pillared passageways that once stood everywhere in Rome and have now vanished. On the top of the galleries are the statues of major saints, some of whom seem to be waving.

The facade of the basilica is not old by Roman standards (17th century). Its design is owed to Carlo Maderno. The present church took 200 years of off-again, on-again work before it was finally dedicated. Its predecessor, founded by Constantine, was richly impressive, but threatened to collapse. So it was that the pope at the time ordered the construction of a new basilica, one whose design was contributed to by a score of the most famous and creative men of the times—Raphael, della Porta, Michelangelo among them—culminating in the present structure.

Before you enter the basilica, you might glance up to the right at the **Papal Palace,** whose regal apartments have housed the popes for centuries. Recently, however, the holy father has chosen to live in quite simple quarters in the palace.

Once inside the basilica, it's hard to do anything but gasp at the size and magnificence. Take a right turn immediately and walk to a small chapel on the far wall where for centuries Michelangelo's **Pietà** has stood. The *Pietà* is now screened by glass after it was the victim of a senseless attack by a tragically demented man, whose name is best forgotten. The restoration work has been perfect. You'd never know the statue was ever chipped. Michelangelo carved this piece of marble when he was in his early 20s (you'll be able to see his name clearly inscribed on Mary's robe). The story goes that the statue was admired in Michelangelo's presence by several gentlemen who were trying to guess who had sculpted such a beautiful piece. None of them guessed the true artist since Michelangelo was then an unknown. He decided that no one would make this mistake in the future, and at the earliest opportunity, carved his name where we see it today.

After you've gloried in the *Pietà*—most visitors lose track of time standing in front of the sculpture—return to the center of the great nave and look for the red circle of marble on the floor. A historical point: It was on this slab on Christmas day, A.D. 800, that the pope crowned the king of the Franks, Charlemagne, and made him Holy Roman Emperor.

As you walk down the **central nave,** you might examine the marble inlays on the huge columns supporting the roof. The designs are subtle and beautifully executed. Shafts of sunlight illuminate corners of the smaller side naves, each of which is lined with lushly decorated chapels. On one side, you'll see a bronze **statue of St. Peter.** It has been the custom for centuries for the faithful to kiss the saint's right foot, which today has literally been kissed smooth.

The **cupola** was designed by Michelangelo, who is said to have been inspired by the dome on the Pantheon. Below it is the **Baldacchino,** the great bronze canopy over the altar. Bernini was the artist, in the 17th century. The Baldacchino is supposedly made from the bronze ceiling in the portico of the Pantheon, but this is not true. The metal came from Venice. In the sunken area before the altar is the Confession, a standard feature in Rome's great basilicas. This one is unusually extravagant in its decoration. On the altar, note especially the delicate spiral fluting on the columns, and the careful inlays of precious marbles on the column plinths.

In the apse beyond the altar is a gilded bronze sunburst holding a symbolic dove. Below is the **throne of St. Peter,** obviously not meant to be sat on, since it's suspended high above the floor by the combined bronze efforts of Saints Athanasius, Ambrose, Augustine, and John. There are usually seats in this part of the basilica, and it makes a good place to rest and reflect on this mighty temple of Roman Christianity.

You can spend considerably more time admiring the works of art that seem tucked away in each and every corner. For a further view of the church's earthly wealth, head for what was once known as the **Treasury,** the entrance to which is through a door about midway in the left nave. This is a collection of richly decorated ornaments, displayed among equally richly decorated chapels. There you can see jewel-studded chalices, reliquaries, and copes. One robe worn by Pius XII casts a simple note in these halls of elegance. It costs 1000 lire (61¢) to visit the Historical-Artistic Museum, which is open from 9 a.m. to 12:30 p.m. and from 3 to 6 p.m. in summer, to 4:30 p.m. in winter. Later, you can pay an underground visit to the **Vatican Grottoes,** with their tombs—ancient and modern (Pope John XXIII gets the most adulation). They are open from 7 a.m. to 6 p.m. in summer, to 5 p.m. in winter.

The perfect tonic, at this point, is a trip to the top of Michelangelo's cupola for an angel's view of Vatican City, the Tiber, and the domes of Rome in the sunlight beyond. It costs 1500 lire (92¢) to take the elevator to the roof of the basilica, or you can walk up for 1000 lire (61¢). After the elevator trip, there's a considerable distance yet to be walked—up narrow flight after narrow flight, sometimes spiraling, sometimes leaning far to the right just beneath the skin of the dome. You'll finally emerge on a tiny enclosed platform at the top, where you can crane your neck in any direction. The dome is open from 8 a.m. to 6:15 p.m. in summer, to 4:45 p.m. in winter.

To go down to the area around **St. Peter's tomb,** you must apply by letter several days beforehand or at the office of the excavations (tel. 06-69-82). Open from 9 a.m. to noon and from 2 to 5 p.m., it is reached by passing under the arch to the left of the facade of St. Peter's. For 3000 lire ($1.83), you are taken on a guided tour of the tombs that have been excavated 23 feet beneath the floor of the church.

You've now seen the high points of St. Peter's, although admittedly there are so many more noteworthy works of art on the floor of the basilica alone that it would take many books to describe them. I don't advise going to the Vatican Galleries (or the Sistine Chapel) today because, in my experience, that's simply too much to see, let alone absorb in a single day. Please take this advice, and don't try to "do" the galleries after St. Peter's. Go there first thing tomorrow. For now, head down the Via della

Conciliazione right to the banks of the Tiber. A quick turn to the left brings you to—

THE CASTEL SANT' ANGELO: You'll recognize the castle (tel. 655-036) by the medieval turreted wall that surrounds it. The entrance is across from the Ponte Sant' Angelo—the bridge across the Tiber—but before you get too close, look up to the monumental statue of Saint Michael at the highest point of the castle. He looks like he's about to draw his sword, but actually he's sheathing it. The statue commemorates the end of the plague of A.D. 590, which had taken many lives and plunged the city—then no more than a large town, really—into a state of terror. In an effort to enlist divine aid, Pope Gregory I organized a series of processions all over the city. While leading a great assembly of followers, the pope looked across the Tiber and saw, above the crumbling ruins of the imperial tomb of Hadrian, a vision of the archangel Michael covering his shining sword in its scabbard. Gregory took it as a sign that the plague was over, and so it was.

Even before those early times, the castle had occupied an important place in the tapestry of Roman history. It was constructed originally to house the ashes of the emperor Hadrian in fitting splendor. The tomb was round in shape, surmounted by a mound of cultivated earth on which grew decorative plantings. Reconstruction experts suggest that there was probably a chariot-type bronze group in a position the equivalent of St. Michael's. After centuries of decay and depredation, the tomb was pressed into service as a fortification by the popes of the Middle Ages. It underwent successive reconstructions—at one time it even had a moat—the most spectacular of which are the papal apartments of Julius II and the Borgia pope, Alexander VI.

This used to be one of the few monuments in Rome that was not closed during the afternoon. But that, unfortunately, is a thing of the past. Current open hours are 8:30 a.m. to 1 p.m. daily except Monday, and the castle closes an hour early on Sunday. Once through the gate with your 2000-lira ($1.22) ticket, you'll enter a small antechamber with a scale model of the tomb in several of its past incarnations. You then proceed up a ramp that dates from the first Roman construction, past the site of the Renaissance elevator that once cranked the high clergy up and down, and shortly into the funeral chamber of the Roman emperors. While the mausoleum was built for Hadrian—he designed it too, in addition to his opulent villa at Tivoli—several of the succeeding Antonine rulers were buried here as well. Eventually, you emerge into the sunlight in a small court flanked by a weapons museum and a series of frescoed rooms, and filled with stone cannonballs. This court is but one of the many that are hidden all through the castle.

You're at your liberty to poke around as you will, but be certain to see the Cortile of Alexander VI, and the elegant small bath of Clement VII, both beautifully frescoed. The higher realms of the castle contain a series of exquisite Renaissance rooms that comprised the papal apartments. They are divided by twisting stairways and oddly shaped courtyards, and some are gilded and frescoed to the hilt. The castle was not all luxury, however. In fact it has something of a bad name deriving from a good deal of torture that was perpetrated in its many dungeons. Benvenuto Cellini was a prisoner. He was luckier than many, who were twisted, racked, and strangled by Borgias and others in centuries past.

At the top, just below the sword-bearing angel, is a wide terrace with a splendid view of the city. If you walk to the edge, you'll easily be able to identify several landmarks. That glistening, colonnaded pile of white marble off to the left is the Victor Emmanuel monument, and just to its right is the tall, narrow tower of the Senatorial Palace in the Campidoglio. Immediately across the Tiber is the Campus Martius, the site of Renaissance Rome—see if you can pick out the dome of the Pantheon. If you walk over to the right, you'll have a fine view of St. Peter's and the broad Piazza San Pietro. Note, too, the connecting wall that runs between St. Peter's and the castle. This contains the passage used by Clement VII to escape the invasion of 1527, when the pope's policies brought down the wrath of Charles V upon Rome. The sack that followed was worse than any Rome suffered at the hands of barbarians.

TOUR FIVE
The Vatican Museums, The Sistine Chapel

THE VATICAN MUSEUMS: You'll probably be taking bus 64 from Piazza Venezia to the Vatican side of the Tiber: get off and walk to the Piazza San Pietro, which of course is right in front of the basilica (if you're coming from the railway station, take bus 77). The nearest subway station is Ottaviano. The Vatican runs a bus service between St. Peter's Square (to the left, facing the basilica) and the upper entrance of the museums. The way to the museums lies to the right as you face the facade, through the colonnade, past the small newsstand, and under the passageway between St. Peter's and the Castel Sant' Angelo. Once on the street beyond the high arches of the passageway, you'll see a massive wall on your left. Keep following it—a pleasant walk, not overly long—until you come to the main entrance to the museums on Viale Vaticano. The charge for admittance is the highest in Rome—5000 lire ($3.05). General hours are 9 a.m. to 5 p.m. (no admission after 4 p.m.) in July, August, and September. On Saturday, visiting hours are from 9 a.m. to 2 p.m. Except for special closings during religious holidays, hours during all other months are 9 a.m. to 2 p.m.

Too many visitors try to squeeze the Vatican Museums into a day's itinerary that includes half a dozen other sights. This is utter foolishness. There are many museums in the Vatican in addition to Michelangelo's Sistine Chapel, and several papal apartments you'll want to see. It would require much more time than we've got to examine all that's there. Nevertheless, a full day is sufficient for first-timers.

Once inside, up the spiral staircase, and through a few preliminary corridors, you'll come to a small outdoor terrace. To the right is our first stop, the **Pinacoteca,** or picture gallery. To the left is the path through the museums of sculpture, and eventually to the Sistine Chapel. The popes through the ages were great patrons and collectors. The collection of art in the Pinacoteca was started by Pius VI and substantially enlarged by his successors. It's arranged chronologically, starting with gilded polyptychs in the style of Byzantium, and progressing through the Renaissance up to the 20th century. There are some 15 rooms containing the works of such masters as Giotto (a revolutionary against the strict Byzantine confines of Italian art in his day), Beato Angelico, Raphael (there are also some unusual tapestries woven in 16th-century Brussels after some of Raphael's cartoons), da Vinci, Titian, Veronese, Caravaggio (the splendid *Deposition*), Murillo, and Ribera. The gallery rooms are arranged in a circle, so you'll exit through the same door you entered.

We head next for the **Pius Clementine Museum,** whose handsomely decorated rooms contain a vast collection of Greek and Roman sculpture. Of particular note are the porphyry sarcophagi of the mother and daughter of Constantine the Great (fourth century), *Hercules* (a gilded bronze of the first century;

note also the magnificent room it's in), the Hall of the Animals, the *Laocoön* (depicting the punishment of Laocoön by the gods, who were displeased at his warning the Trojans not to bring the Trojan Horse into the city), the *Belvedere Apollo* (a Roman copy of a fourth-century B.C. Greek original), mosaics from the floor of the Villa Hadrian outside Tivoli, and the Belvedere Torso (a fragment of a Greek statue from the first century B.C. that was carefully studied by Michelangelo). There are literally hundreds of other statues lounging in the halls, but I have no space to list them.

The **Chiaramonti Museum,** established by Pius VII, continues the parade of marble. Of the many exquisite pieces from antiquity, look for the bust of Augustus, and a personification of the Nile. Nearby is the Hall of the Chariot, which contains not only the marble chariot that gives it the name, but also the *Discobolus,* a copy of a fifth-century B.C. Greek statue by Myron.

The **Etruscan Museum,** a more recent addition to the Vatican (early 19th century), includes the inevitable mountains of broken crockery, much of it delicately decorated with Etruscan line figures. The Etruscans seem always to have been smiling—a most worthy characteristic. More interesting, perhaps, is the collection of bronze urns (note the imaginative handle designs), and sophisticated gold jewelry. There are also sarcophagi (the museum holds the almost-intact contents of an entire tomb from Cerveteri, a city we'll visit in the one-day trips chapter), some war implements, and a statue of Mars. The Etruscans were dominant in these parts of Italy from roughly the eighth to the sixth centuries B.C.

The **Egyptian Museum,** established by the same pope who began the Etruscan collection, Gregory XVI, houses a fine assortment of statues, mummies, vases, jewelry, pharaohs, all looking suitably and inscrutably Egyptian. There is little in this gallery that does not predate Christ.

The **Vatican Library** represents the literary accumulations of more than 1000 years. Formally organized in the 15th century, the library today holds in excess of a million books, as well as some lovely bronzes, rare manuscripts, a Greek bible from the fourth century, and sketches by Botticelli to illustrate the *Divine Comedy.* The lush decorations of the rooms are as interesting as the glass-enclosed exhibits.

The last stop before the Sistine Chapel is the frescoed apartments of the Borgia pope Alexander VI. The work was completed at the end of the 15th century by Pinturicchio of Umbria and his students, and it reflects the cultivated taste of the pope. In addition to biblical stories, some of the frescoes retell ancient myths, such as that of Isis and Osiris.

Pope Paul VI's **Museum of Modern Art** opened in the Borgia apartments in 1973. It contains both European as well as American art. In fact, out of 65 galleries in the complex, a dozen are devoted to Americans, including such fine pieces as Leonard Baskin's *Isaac*, a five-foot bronze. Other artists represented include Max Weber, José de Creeft, and Abraham Rattner. A quarter of a century ago, the Vatican did not exhibit any works produced after the 18th century. After World War II, Pope Pius XII requested that some salons be opened to display contemporary works of art that had been presented to him. One of his close aides assigned to that task was the late Paul VI. Of course, the Vatican has selected art, both paintings and sculptures, that reflect "spiritual and religious values." However, its representatives have purchased works that refer to other religions as well.

THE SISTINE CHAPEL: Michelangelo devoted 4½ years to painting the beautiful ceiling frescoes of the chapel of Sixtus IV (hence the name "Sixtine" or "Sistine"). Today, throngs of visitors walk around bumping into one another, faces pointed ceiling-ward, admiring the frescoes at the expense of a crick in the neck. One can just imagine the condition of Michelangelo's neck after the job was done—the man's sight was also permanently impaired. The universal story, which I presume is true, is that Michelangelo was almost muscled into the work by Julius II. The artist protested as much as it was possible to protest against so powerful a figure as the pope. In the end, he did not only the ceiling, but also the monumental fresco of the *Last Judgment* on the altar wall.

The familiar figures on the ceiling clearly show the artist's training as a sculptor. They are muscular, mostly nude, and statuesque in every sense of the word. This almost pagan celebration of the naked flesh offended some members of the papal court, among them a man named Biagio. His complaint earned him immortality in a left-handed way, since Michelangelo, on hearing of the complaint, included the man's face—with a pair of ass's ears—among the demons of Hell.

The ceiling follows a progression taken from the Old Testament, and if you know your Bible, you can clearly trace events from the *Separation of Light and Darkness* at the altar end of the chapel, right through to the *Deluge* at the other end of the room. Intermediate events, such as the *Creation of Adam* and the *Expulsion from the Garden of Eden,* lie in between and are easily identified.

The paintings that line both side walls of the chapel go almost unnoticed under such an impressive ceiling. Again the topics are biblical, and the artists are famous in their own right—Botticelli, Cosimo Rosselli, Pinturicchio, and Luca Signorelli, among them. Some of the more recognizable of the topics include *Moses Crossing the Red Sea,* the *Sermon on the Mount,* and the *Last Supper.* There are 12 frescoes altogether.

The Sistine Chapel is actually the pope's private chapel, and in this room are held the secret conclaves in which the pope is elected.

After leaving the Sistine Chapel, you may want to attend at least two more recently opened museums. One is the **Ethnological Museum,** which promises 3000 objects and 3000 years of history on a walk of 2100 yards. This museum contains works of art and objects from the world's major countries. The section devoted to China is of particular interest. It's most surprising to see Buddhist art displayed within the citadels of the Vatican. The other museum is the Museo Storico or **History Museum,** founded by Paul VI. It contains the carriages of popes and cardinals, as well as uniforms and equipment.

When you've absorbed the glories of the Vatican, it's a long, opulently decorated walk through corridor after corridor back to the main entrance on Viale Vaticano. The Vatican museums run a bus service to and from St. Peter's Square, and there is an excellent service of city buses from the nearby Piazza Risorgimento.

THE VATICAN GARDENS: Separating the Vatican on the north and west from the outside world are 58 acres of lush, carefully tended gardens, filled with winding paths, brilliantly colored flowers, groves of massive oaks, ancient fountains and pools. In the midst of this shadowy setting is a small summer house, the Casina Pio IV, built for Pope Pius IV in 1560 by Pirro Ligorio. With the exception of Wednesday and Sunday, tours of the Vatican Gardens leave daily from the Information Office for Pilgrims and Tourists, near the Arco delle Campane, in St. Peter's Square. Visits are exclusively organized by the Information Office.

PAPAL AUDIENCES: Private audiences with the pope are very difficult to obtain. Public audiences with the pope are held regularly, usually on Wednesday morning. Depending on the season, the actual hour of this audience is likely to vary. In summer, audiences take place in St. Peter's Square. However, in the off-season they are held at 11 a.m. in the large Paul IV Hall, close to the south side of St. Peter's. Anyone is welcome.

To attend a general audience, you can obtain a free ticket from the office of the Prefecture of the Pontifical Household, which lies at the far reach of the northern colonnade of St. Peter's Square. Hours are from 9 a.m. to 1 p.m. on Tuesday and from 9 a.m. until just before the papal appearance on Wednesday.

Americans can apply to the **Bishops' Office for United States Visitors to the Vatican,** 30 Via dell'Umità (tel. 678-9184). Requests for invitations should be sent as far in advance as you know your schedule (always specify if any person in your party is handicapped). It's often good to have some kind of testimonial from a church authority in your hometown, although that is not absolutely necessary. The Vatican has relaxed its dress code in recent years, although women, of course, are asked not to wear revealing clothing.

In summer the pope appears at his summer residence at Castel Gandolfo. He says a few words at noon, prays, and bestows his blessing upon the throng gathered there.

Two Supplementary Tours

I'm including two additional itineraries for you to insert in your schedule as you will. Neither is long. Rather, they are strolls through parts of the city I thought you might like to see and know about.

TOUR SIX

Piazza Barberini, Via Veneto, Porta Pinciana, The Borghese Gardens, The Pincio, Piazza del Popolo

PIAZZA BARBERINI: The Piazza Barberini lies at the foot of several important Roman streets: Via Barberini, Via Sistina, and Via Veneto among them. It would be a far more pleasant spot were it not for the considerable amount of traffic swarming around its principal feature, Bernini's *Fountain of the Triton.* Day and night for more than three centuries, the strange figure sitting in a vast open clam has been blowing water from his triton. Off to one side of the piazza is the Piccadilly Restaurant and above it, the clean aristocratic side facade of the Palazzo Barberini. Rome has always been a city of powerful families. The Renaissance Barberini reached their peak when a son was elected Pope Urban VIII. And it was this Barberini pope who encouraged Bernini and gave him so much patronage.

As we start up the Via Veneto, look for the small fountain on the right-hand corner of the Piazza Barberini. There you'll see another of Bernini's many works, the small *Fountain of the Bees.* At first they look more like flies, but they are the bees of the Barberini, the crest of that powerful family complete with the crossed keys of St. Peter above them. The crossed keys were added to a family crest when a son was elected pope.

VIA VENETO: The posh, tree-lined Via Veneto still looks as elegant as it did in the 1950s when it reached its peak. Those *dolce vita* days, when Middle East businessmen in fez and sunglasses sat surrounded by bevies of blonde beauties in the sidewalk cafés, when movie stars promenaded with rich old men in monocles, are gone, although admittedly you can still see scenes of the above sort on rare occasions.

> You might, as you survey these attractions, stop at the **Church of the Capuchins,** where the bones of 4000 monks have been artistically arranged in various geometric and representational patterns. There is, appropriately, a design that shows the "grim reaper" amid a sea of skulls and thighbones. You'll find it just below the church.

Via Veneto makes a large S-curve, and just where it straightens out for the last time, you'll see the swank U.S. Embassy, whose Consular Division is in a rose-colored palace where the queen of Italy once lived. From the embassy on up to the Aurelian Wall are the most chic of the cafés, which still carry on a thriving business despite the depletion of the celebrity roster. These cafés, with their brightly colored umbrellas and awnings, are perfectly designed for people-watching. They straddle the sidewalk, and there's no way to stroll up Via Veneto without going through the middle of half a dozen of them.

The end of the Via Veneto comes with a final burst of plush hotels and Harry's Bar. Right in front of us is the hulking brickwork of the Aurelian Wall, begun in A.D. 271. The gate, however, is a bit newer.

THE PORTA PINCIANA: This gate derives its name from the Pincian Hill. It was built in A.D. 546 by the Byzantine general Belisarius, who was, at the time, seeking to assert the rule of Eastern Rome over the fallen capital of Western Rome. The city was in a shambles after more than a century of barbarian assaults, which had looted it of nearly all its ancient treasure. The last emperor of the West had long fallen (A.D. 476), and the pope was the real power in Rome. Even the pope was gone, however, the city being depopulated as a result of the constant upheaval. The Goth in question was Totilla, and he defeated Belisarius. Belisarius won in the end, and laid the dead Goth at the feet of his emperor in Constantinople.

THE BORGHESE GARDENS (VILLA BORGHESE): While Belisarius was building the Pincian Gate, the land just outside was the sometime campground of Totilla. All trace of the Goth has long been smoothed away, and today we see a perfectly exquisite (albeit well-used) 17th-century country estate, with the addition of modern roads. The land was developed by Cardinal Scipio Borghese, a high churchman belonging to another of Rome's mighty families. In later years a Borghese prince was to marry Napoleon's sister Pauline. The most striking feature of the Borghese Gardens (aside from the palace, whose museum is described in Chapter V), are its trees—stark and eerie looking, their trunks rising some 50 or more feet into the air without a single branch, only to burst forth in an evergreen canopy high above. Few activities are quite as pleasant as a slow stroll through the Villa Borghese on a sunny afternoon, pausing to admire carefully planned 17th-century vistas, ornamental fountains, and the magnificent trees.

From the Pincian Gate, cross the street and bear right down the path through the trees. Soon you'll see the equestrian statue of King Umberto I. That statue faces the Piazza di Siena, through a bit of intermediate territory. The piazza is a perfect oval ring, lined with elegant pines—a fine place for a picnic if you have time. Beyond the road at the far end of the piazza lies another section of the park whose iron fence you'll have to follow (to the left) for a while. Turn right at the gate and walk straight in. Soon you'll come to a delightful small lake, complete with Greek temple and rental rowboats.

Retrace your steps to the road and turn right. A walk the equivalent of several blocks brings you to another tract of gardening, this one dating from the 19th century.

THE PINCIO: Standing on the summit of the Pincian Hill on the ancient site of the gardens of Lucullus is the Pincio, a formal garden laid out by Napoleon's architect, Valadier. There are almost as many busts here as there are trees—almost all with new noses, since it seems a favorite sport to chip off the old marble ones. The main attraction of the Pincio is a wide terrace that overlooks the city from a vantage point high above the Piazza del Popolo. From the ornate balustrade, there's a fine view across the Tiber that includes the wooded slopes of Monte Mario and the Janiculum with the white dome of St. Peter's in between. It's a most romantic view, especially at sunset. And for an evening stroll, take the stairs to the right that lead down the hill, past several fountains lit with golden orange lights at night, until finally you arrive at the piazza below.

THE PIAZZA DEL POPOLO: Aside from the Pincio, this exquisitely balanced piazza is the only Roman reminder of the once-considerable influence of Napoleon. Valadier placed the central fountain, the flanking semicircular retaining walls, and the hillside of fountains. The matching baroque churches on either side of the Corso date from the 17th century. Like every part of Rome, this piazza has a long history. It was also a part of Lucullus's estate—a lavish one—and later was the burial site of several emperors, Nero among them. The area was supposedly haunted by that imperial ghost until a medieval pope tore down the tomb and consecrated the site. The obelisk is thousands of years old. It originally was Roman booty from Heliopolis and once stood in the Circus Maximus. It's surrounded today by four marble lions, carved with the initials of 19th-century tourists. At night, the thin sheets of water from the lions' mouths are illuminated by spotlights hidden in the marble basins below. A fashionable meeting place these days, the Piazza del Popolo boasts two sidewalk cafés—Canova, and the much better known Rosati—which are ideal for watching expensive Italian cars full of expensive Italians doing expensive things.

There are buses from the Piazza del Popolo straight down the Corso to Piazza Venezia and other points in town.

TOUR SEVEN

The Spanish Steps, The Mausoleum of Augustus, Ara Pacis (The Altar of Peace), The Fontana di Trevi, The Quirinal Hill

THE SPANISH STEPS: The Scalinata di Spagna and the adjoining Piazza di Spagna both take their name from the Spanish Embassy, which was in a palace here during the 19th century. The Spanish, however, had nothing to do with the construction of the Steps. They were built by the French, and lead to the French church in Rome, Trinità dei Monti. The twin-towered church behind the obelisk at the top of the Steps is early 16th century. The Steps themselves are early 18th century. The French are in the church to this day, and the adjoining Villa Medici is now a French school.

The Spanish Steps are at their best in spring, when the many flights are filled with flowers. You'll see a wide variety of types, mostly young people, sitting around here any time of the year. In the fall and winter, the population is much more sparse, with only an occasional Roman soaking up a few of the sun's warming rays. It is a rare visitor who hasn't sat for a while on one of the landings—there's one every 12 steps—perhaps to read a letter from home, or observe the other sitters. It's interesting to note that in the early 19th century the Steps were famous for the sleek young men and women who lined the travertine steps flexing muscles and exposing ankles in hopes of attracting an artist and being hired as a model. The fountain at the foot was designed by Bernini's father at the end of the 16th century, and it's reputed to have the sweetest water in Rome. Almost any time of year, you'll see thirsty travelers suspending young children in the air just far enough to allow their small mouths to close on the thick jets of pure mountain water. The fountain is called the **Barcaccia.**

There are two nearly identical houses at the foot of the Steps on either side. One is the home of Babington's Tea Rooms (see Chapter III); the other was the house where the English romantic poet John Keats lived . . . and died. Today, the **Keats-Shelley Memorial,** at 26 Piazza di Spagna, has been bought by English and American contributors and turned into a museum. The rooms where Keats lived are chock full of mementos of the poet, musty leather books, original drafts of poems, and some interesting correspondence and reminders of Shelley, Byron, and other friends and contemporaries. From the windows, there's a view of Rome that's hardly changed since the poet was alive. Keats was much depressed at the time of his death, and it was perhaps a small comfort to him, being able to observe the architectural beauty outside his window. The house is open from 9 a.m. to 1 p.m. and from 3:30 to 6 p.m. daily in summer, from 9 a.m. to 1 p.m. and from 2:30 to 5 p.m. in winter, daily except Saturday and Sunday. Admission is 2000-lira ($1.22).

In the past this area was a favorite of English lords, who rented palaces hereabouts and parked their coaches where the Fiats rest today. Americans predominate in the 20th century, especially since the main office of American Express is right on Piazza di Spagna and dispenses all those letters (and money) from home.

There's a street called Via della Croce which intersects the northern end of Piazza di Spagna perpendicularly from the left. We'll follow this street for four blocks, passing women selling fruit between parked cars and small workrooms filled with dust, where old men are repairing 16th-century gilt frames, until we come to Via del Corso. We continue straight across the Corso, where the street takes a sharp turn to the left. At the first intersection, we turn right, and across the piazza is our next stop.

THE MAUSOLEUM OF AUGUSTUS: This seemingly indestructible pile of bricks has been here for 2000 years, and will probably remain for another 2000. Like the larger tomb of Hadrian across the river, this was once a circular, marble-covered affair with tall cypress trees on the earth-covered dome. Many of the emperors of the first century had their ashes deposited in golden urns inside this building, and it was probably due to the resultant crowding that Hadrian decided to construct an entirely new tomb for himself. The imperial remains stayed intact until the fifth century, when invading barbarians smashed the bronze gates and stole the golden urns, probably emptying the ashes on the ground outside. The tomb was restored in the '30s. You cannot enter, but you can walk around looking inside.

THE ARA PACIS (THE ALTAR OF PEACE): Across Via Ripetta, the main street on the far side of the tomb, is an airy glass-and-concrete building right on the banks of the Tiber at Ponte Cavour. Within it is one of the treasures of antiquity, the Altar of Peace, built by the Senate during the reign of Augustus as a tribute to that emperor and the peace he had brought to the Roman world. On the marble walls can be seen portraits of the imperial family—Augustus, Livia (his wife), Tiberius (Livia's son and the successor to the empire), even Julia (the unfortunate daughter of Augustus, exiled by her father for her sexual excesses). The altar was reconstructed from literally hundreds of fragments scattered in museums for centuries. A major portion came from the foundations of a Renaissance palace on the Corso. The reconstruction—quite an archeological adventure story in itself—was executed by the Fascists during the '30s. The Ara Pacis is open from April 1 until the end of September from 9 a.m. to 2 p.m. and from October 1 until the end of March from 8 a.m. to 2 p.m. (from 4 to 7 p.m. on Tuesday, Thursday, and Saturday). Admission is 300 lire (18¢). Closed Monday.

THE FONTANA DI TREVI (TREVI FOUNTAIN): As you elbow your way through the summertime crowds around the Trevi Fountain, it's hard to believe that this little piazza was nearly always deserted before *Three Coins in the Fountain* brought the tour buses. Today, it's a must on everybody's itinerary. The fountain is an 18th-century extravaganza of baroque stonework ruled over by a large statue of Neptune. While some of the statuary is the work of other artists, the man who gets the credit for the entire project is Nicolo Salvi. The tradition of throwing coins into the fountain is an evolution of earlier customs. At one time visitors drank water from the fountain; later they combined that with an offering to the spirits of the place. In our inflationary world, we don't even get the drink of water, but just make the offering. To do it properly, hold your lire in the right hand, turn your back to the fountain, and toss the coin over your shoulder, being careful not to bean anyone behind you. Once done, the presiding spirit of the fountain will see to it that you will one day return to Rome.

On one corner of the piazza, you'll see an ancient church with a strange claim to fame. In it are contained the hearts and viscera of several centuries of popes. This was the parish church of the popes when they resided at the Quirinal Palace on the hill above, and for many years each pontiff willed those parts of his body to the church. To reach the Quirinal, take the Via Lucchesi from the church for two blocks, where it intersects with Via Doloria. Turn left and you'll see the steps to the Quirinal straight ahead.

THE QUIRINAL: At the top of the stairs, you'll be in a wide pink piazza with the palace of the president of Italy on your left. Until the end of the Second World War the palace was the home of the king of Italy, and before that it was the residence of the pope. In antiquity this was the site of Augustus's Temple of the Sun. The steep marble steps that lead to Santa Maria in Aracoeli on the Capitoline Hill once led to that temple. The great baths of Constantine also stood nearby, and that's the origin of some of the fountain statuary.

From here, your closest public transportation is on Via Nazionale, reached by taking Via della Consulta between the Palazzo della Consulta and the little park.

Café on Via Veneto

Chapter V

ADDITIONAL ATTRACTIONS

FOR VISITORS with more time, I offer this brief compendium of secondary sights, arranged in no particular order.

In Central Rome

MUSEO DELLE TERME: On the Piazza della Repubblica (entrance faces Piazza dei Cinquecento). Admission is 1500 lire (92¢). It's free on the first and third Saturday and the second and fourth Sunday of each month. Hours: 9 a.m. to 2 p.m., on Sunday and holidays to 1 p.m.; closed Monday.

The museum takes its name from the Baths ("Thermae") of Diocletian, whose late-third-century structure it shares with the Church of Santa Maria degli Angeli. You might take a peek at the church (the door opens directly onto the Piazza della Repubblica), converted in the 16th century by Michelangelo from its original function as "tepidarium," or chamber with lukewarm baths. The later baroque renovation consists largely of trompe-l'oeil marble columns and slabs. Still, it gives a good idea of the scale of a late Imperial Roman bath—in addition to the tepidarium, there was a "frigidarium" with cold-water baths, and a "calidarium" with hot-water baths.

The entrance to the museum is outside the church, past the Piazza della Repubblica (which follows the outline of the exedra of Diocletian's Baths), and around the corner to the left. The first few rooms are cavernous, windowless chambers full of sooty statuary, some fabulous old mosaics and sarcophagi, and a marble fragment of the frigidarium or cold-water pool.

Whether you're a fan of ancient sculpture or not, the galleries here are guaranteed to make you one. Among the masterpieces assembled in the various rooms, be sure to see the *Venus* from Cyrene, the green masterpiece *Birth of Venus*, the *Apollo of the Tiber*, and two marble copies of Myron's fifth-century B.C. *Discus Thrower*, the well-muscled bronze *Pugilist* (Boxer) from the first century B.C., and a Greek bronze called *The Hellenistic Ruler*. Especially interesting are the salvaged frescoes that once decorated one of Livia's villas. Her eyes, and probably those of her husband Augustus, once rested on these walls, which represent a darkly lush garden. Outside the museum halls, on the opposite side from the garden, there's a lovely 16th-century cloister, filled with bits of marble and mosaic from the past.

THE GALLERIA BORGHESE: The museum (tel. 858-577) lies in the Borghese Gardens, an easy walk from Via Veneto and the Pincian Gate. There is a 4000-lira ($2.44) entrance charge. Year-round hours: 9 a.m. to 2 p.m., on Sunday to 1 p.m., and it is open every day except Monday.

The museum is housed in an early 17th-century casino or summer palace, built by Cardinal Scipio Borghese for entertainments and at the same time as a home for his art treasures.

Most visitors go here to see Canova's statue of Pauline Bonaparte Borghese, the sister of Napoleon. Actually, there are numerous other works of art—both painting and sculpture—as well as the opulently decorated palace itself.

There are several other marble sculptures, notably by Bernini —see especially his *David*, and the better known *Apollo and Daphne*. Also on the ground floor of the palace are interesting 17th-century busts of Roman emperors, and a few pieces of Roman statuary from antiquity. Upstairs is a treasure house of painting including works of Raphael (*Young Woman with a Unicorn* and a *Deposition from the Cross*), Pinturicchio, Botticelli, Caravaggio (a fine *Young Bacchus* is here, as well as *St. Jerome*), Correggio, Titian, Veronese, Bellini, and even some non-Italians, such as Cranach and Rubens.

PALAZZO DORIA PAMPHILI AND GALLERY: On the Piazza del Collegio Romano, off Via del Corso, this private residence is open from 10 a.m. to 1 p.m. on Tuesday, Friday, Saturday, and Sunday only. Admission is 2000 lire ($1.22) for the gallery, and another 2000 lire for the private apartments.

What an absolutely delightful palace this is! And it gives us so much insight into Roman life. The public entrance is actually on the far side, off the Piazza del Collegio Romano. You mount a few flights of steps and emerge in an anteroom adjacent to the gallery, where you buy your tickets.

The Palazzo Doria is still privately owned, the occupant being an elegant princess who can be recognized around town, shopping in the open-air market at Campo dei Fiori just like the rest of us. Her family palace is typical of that of a great Roman family of the 18th century. There are not just palatial rooms here—much of the building (which is tremendous) is tenanted by shops, offices, even apartments for tenant families. And this is not the result of shrinking fortunes. Roman palaces have always housed ground-floor shops (probably a carryover from Imperial times) and a population comprised of family members on down to common tenants who occupy the less-desirable quarters on the higher floors. Sandwiched between are the regal apartments of the most important family members. And in the case of Palazzo Doria, they are regal indeed.

The picture gallery, which houses a private collection, skirts a central court and is opulently decorated with trompe-l'oeil frescoes, statuary, and paintings. The most notable of the latter is Velázquez's portrait of Pope Innocent X, who belonged to the Pamphili family. There's also an airy, high-ceilinged sculpture gallery filled with porphyry satyrs and stern marble emperors, most of which, I'm told, were dug up on the Doria-Pamphili's extensive country estates.

Surrounding the gallery is the most interesting part of the palace, the private apartments. These consist of a beautifully maintained series of public rooms, many in high 18th-century style—a ballroom, a family chapel, yellow, green, and red rooms, studies, and dining rooms, all furnished and (when the tourists are away) still in use. The palace provides the best opportunity I know of for a close-up view of aristocratic life as it is and as it was. The crystal chandeliers, silk wall coverings, gilded furniture, brooding oil portraits, Renaissance tapestries are all here, and they're gorgeous.

ETRUSCAN MUSEUM OF VILLA GIULIA: At 9 Piazza di Villa Giulia (tel. 360-1951), this museum is open all year from 9 a.m. to 2 p.m.; closed Monday. Admission is 2000 lire ($1.22).

Like the Palazzo Borghese, the Villa Giulia was built as a country house, and it too has been engulfed by the spreading city. Its slightly out-of-the-way location in the northwestern corner of the Borghese Gardens makes it strangely difficult to find. A 67 or 67b bus from Via Due Macelli (near Piazza Barberini) will take you past the Spanish Steps, past the Piazza del Popolo and through the gate, down Via Flaminia to Via di Villa Giulia, which is but one long block from the museum. Alternatively, you can take a no. 30 tram, if you're ever near its route, which circumnavigates the city.

The Etruscans are a celebrated mystery. They seem to have sailed to Italy in large groups around 800 B.C., presumably from Asia Minor. Although just why they arrived in force in Italy, we don't know. The only possible record of them comes from the 13th-century B.C. Egyptian inscriptions that describe raids on the Nile delta by a people called the "Turuscha." Within two centuries they had brought much of central Italy under their control, forcing the native Italians to support them. The Roman monarchy, whose demise by revolution signaled the start of the Roman Republic, was probably an Etruscan aristocracy. Their subsequent fall from power was swift, and eventually even their language was forgotten. Today we have some 8000 Etruscan inscriptions left from tombs and the like—we simply cannot make any sense out of the language, and the inscriptions remain untranslated to this day. The Villa Giulia, built by Pope Julius III (hence the name), houses another few tons of pottery shards, as well as more interesting bronze and gold remains.

Outside the museum, the rear courts and gardens of the palace are well worth exploration, especially the intricate "nympheum," a multilevel architectural courtyard so named for the statues of nymphs among the fountains on various levels.

GALLERIA NAZIONALE: The Palazzo Barberini is one of the most magnificent baroque palaces in Rome. Entered at 13 Via Quattro Fontane, right off the Piazza Barberini, it was begun by Carlo Maderno in 1627 and completed in 1633 by Bernini, whose lavishly decorated rococo apartments are on view. The palace houses the Galleria Nazionale (tel. 475-4591), which is open from 9 a.m. to 2 p.m.; closed Monday. It charges 2000 lire ($1.22) for admission.

On the first floor of the palace, a splendid array of printings includes works that date back to the 13th and 14th centuries, most notably a *Mother and Child* by Simone Martini. Also praiseworthy are paintings by Florentine artists from the 15th century, including art by Beato Angelico and Filippo Lippi.

Some of the salons display 15th- and 16th-century paintings by such artists as Andrea Solario and Francesco Francia. Il Sodoma has some brilliant pictures on display at the gallery, including *The Rape of the Sabines* and *The Marriage of St. Catherine.* One of the best known paintings is Raphael's beloved *La Fornarina,* the baker's daughter who was his mistress, posing for his madonna portraits. Titian is represented by a stern portrait of Philip II. Other artists exhibited include Tintoretto, El Greco, and Holbein the Younger. Many visitors come here just to see two magnificent Caravaggios: *St. John the Baptist* and *Narcissus.*

BASILICA OF ST. JOHN IN LATERAN: In the Piazza San Giovanni in Laterano, the basilica is open daily with no admission charge.

This predecessor of the Vatican lies hard by the city wall in the southern part of town. Bus 85 goes directly there from the Piazza S. Silvestro, with an intermediate stop at the Colosseum, and bus 88 leaves from the Piazza Cavour.

The Lateran family was one of ancient Rome's wealthiest, and their lands and palace were situated where today's basilica stands. Their fortunes took an abrupt turn for the worse in the first century A.D., when Plautius Lateranus, a notorious playboy and bon vivant, was involved in a plot to murder the emperor Nero. Being the nephew of one of the emperor's favorite generals didn't save him in this case. He was executed and his family lands and palace were confiscated. The property was later restored to the family, and after several years it came into the hands of Constantine's wife, Fausta. After his defeat of Maxentius and his conversion to Christianity, the young emperor went another step and donated the lavish palace of the Laterans to a surely astonished pope, who was more used to the persecutions of Diocletian.

All through the Middle Ages, until the riots of medieval Rome combined with politics to force the pope to Avignon, the papacy resided at the Lateran. The present basilica is the fifth or sixth on the site, the others having succumbed to earthquakes, fires, and papal remodelings. The facade was designed in 1735 by Galilei, but other portions of the buildings predate it by as much as 500 years. Inside, under a huge golden ceiling, is much sculpture and painting. The doors to the central nave once stood on the Senate House in the Roman Forum.

Other points of interest include the Baptistery built by the emperor Constantine, and the **Scala Santa,** or Holy Stair, across the piazza. The custom is to mount the steps on one's knees.

BASILICA OF ST. PAUL OUTSIDE THE WALLS: On the Via Ostiense, a short distance outside the ancient Roman city walls (but too far to walk), the basilica is open daily with no admission charge.

Built over what is believed to be the tomb of St. Paul, the great basilica on the Via Ostiense is the fourth of the great patriarchal churches of Rome belonging to the Vatican even though it lies outside the Papal City. Rebuilt in the 19th century after a tragic fire, the church dates from the reign of the emperor Constantine. The subdued lighting effect on the interior is created by the alabaster windows, through which light pours as if through stained glass. The aisles of the ornate church are lined with massive columns and studded with mosaic medallions of the popes of the Church of Rome. The cloisters adjoining the church were designed in the 13th century by Vassalletto, who also created the basilica's greatest work of art, an elaborate candelabrum. Every day the Benedictine fathers officiate at holy services at St. Paul's. Adjoining the cloister a shop offers a number of souvenirs for sale, including rosaries and bottles of Benedictine liqueur. The shop is open weekdays.

THE DOMUS AUREA (GOLDEN HOUSE OF NERO): On Via Labicana, facing the Colosseum, the Domus Aurea's year-round hours are 9 a.m. to two hours before sunset; closed Monday. Admission is 1000 lire (61¢).

This bit of conspicuous consumption so embarrassed Vespasian that he spent the better part of his reign disassembling it. After the great fire of A.D. 64, Nero confiscated a square mile of the newly cleared land adjacent to the Forum and erected a palace of such sumptuous proportions and decor that it became a symbol of popular disaffection. After the year of chaos that followed Nero's death (there were four emperors in the year 69), Vespasian took control of the empire, control that was to stay in the Flavian family for 30 years. Vespasian had been reared in the country, far from the excesses of overindulgent Rome. He was probably genuinely disgusted with the extravagance of the Domus Aurea—there were once woods with wild game here as well as mother-of-pearl floors, golden fixtures, and all sorts of mechanical gimmicks including a planetarium. Although the

120-foot statue of Nero remained on the property for another century, Vespasian eliminated most other artifacts, and his son, Titus, finished the job. The ornamental lake was donated as the site for the Colosseum, parts of the palace were pulled down for new public baths, and the interiors were stripped of much decoration.

As the Middle Ages advanced on Rome, and the level of the land rose, the Domus Aurea literally dropped out of sight, only to be discovered in the Renaissance by men like the painter Raphael, who had to get in by chopping holes in the ceilings, holes that are still visible. The frescoes they found inside were the perfect thing for decorating the palaces and churches of Renaissance Rome, and the little "grotesques" (the name comes from "grotto" since the palace seemed to be built underground) of garlands, cornucopiae, and cupids spread all over Rome. The decorations on Adam mantelpieces are inspired by the walls of the palace of Nero.

To be truthful, the ruins are rather hard to imagine in palatial condition, and the floorplan seems confused at best. The almost 2000-year-old frescoes are fascinating, however.

A Few Sights Farther Out

THE APPIAN WAY: The Via Appia Antica straddles a ridge of countrified land to the south of Rome just beyond the Gate of Saint Sebastian. These days, there's a Via Appia Nuova (New Appian Way), but it's an uninteresting, modern boulevard through land marked by modern construction. The old (Antica) Via Appia is the ancestress of all the roads of Europe, and much of its original Roman paving still remains beneath the asphalt. It was originally built 300 years before the birth of Christ to connect Rome with her growing possessions to the south, and later it became lined with the marble monuments of dead patricians. During the infant stages of Christianity, some important catacombs were here.

Most travelers visit the Appian Way on a tour—itinerary number four of almost any tour company makes the trip—but there is a public bus (118) that does the same. You can board bus 118 from in front of the Colosseum, right near the Arch of Constantine, and it will take you past the Baths of Caracalla, down a narrow road lined with private villas hidden behind high walls, and eventually out through the battlemented towers of the Gate of St. Sebastian.

The first stretch of the Via Appia Antica is paved smoothly. There are several important monuments along this stretch, the first being the **Church of Domine Quo Vadis?**, where legend has it that St. Peter saw a vision of Christ. Peter asked Jesus, "Lord, where are you going?" which is what *Domine, quo vadis?* means. Jesus replied that He was going to Rome to be crucified. The comment was especially meaningful, since St. Peter's reason for being in this part of the countryside was that he was fleeing Rome and possible execution. The vision had the sobering effect of convincing the saint to abandon his hopes of escape, and return to Rome and martyrdom. There is a slab in the church that shows the footprints of Jesus, but it is reputed to be a copy, the original being in the Church of St. Sebastian down the road.

The **Catacombs of Saint Callixtus** were named after a pope of the early third century. There are numerous other catacombs in and around Rome, but these are the most visited. The catacombs are at 110 Via Appia Antica (tel. 513-6725). From the Colosseum, a visitor should catch bus 118, asking the driver to let you off at the catacombs. A staff of multilingual friars conducts bands of foreigners into the musty vaults all day every day except Wednesday. Down below, you'll see the Christian city of the dead whose accidental discovery so amazed 16th-century Rome. Of course, we know now that the early Christians never lived here, but it was the resting place of many an early pope and saint as well as thousands of their followers.

Among the many eerie corridors, lined with the crypts of persons who died almost 2000 years ago, look especially for the statue of Saint Cecilia. This lady was a Roman patrician, put to death in her father's palace for her faith (it was on the site of today's Trastevere). She was subsequently elevated to sainthood, and was later the object of a ninth-century body hunt. When the corpse was found in these catacombs, tradition has it that it looked like that of a sleeping maiden, not the least decayed. Known as the catacombs par excellence, this was the first official cemetery of Christian Rome. It was more than 11 miles long on five levels, with thousands of tombs and hundreds of crypts, some of them decorated with original frescoes now known all over the world. The last scientific discovery (1852) was made by John B. de Rossi, great archeologist of the 19th century. Visiting hours in summer are from 8:30 a.m. till noon and from 2:30 to 6 p.m. (to 5 p.m. in winter). Admission is 1000 lire (61¢).

The nearby **Tomb of St. Sebastian,** called the Catacombe di San Sebastiano, lies at 136 Via Appia Antica (tel. 788-7035). The tomb of the martyr is in the basilica (church). His original tomb, however, was in the catacomb that is under the basilica. From the reign of the emperor Valerian until the emperor Constantine converted to Christianity, the bodies of Saint Peter and Saint Paul were hidden in this catacomb. The big church here was built in the fourth century, and this is the only Christian catacomb in Rome that is always open. None of the catacombs, incidentally, is a grotto; all are dug from tufo, a soft volcanic rock.

The tunnels here, if stretched out, would reach a length of seven miles. In the tunnels and mausoleums are mosaics and graffiti, along with many other pagan and Christian objects, even from centuries before Constantine. Visiting hours are from 8:30 a.m. to noon and from 2:30 to 5 p.m. (summer schedules are a bit longer). The catacombs are closed every Thursday, but otherwise charge an admission of 1000 lire (61¢).

The circular, turreted tower ahead on the left is the **Tomb of Cecilia Metella,** a lady of Republican times who is remembered today primarily because of her tomb's refusal to collapse. The circular structure is faced with the original travertine marble, and some of the ornamental frieze, as well as Cecilia's name, is clearly visible. The turrets on top date from the Middle Ages, when the tomb was incorporated into the defenses of the Caetani family.

Soon after the tomb is the end of the 118 bus run, and the beginning of the truly ancient zone of the Appian Way. Not even tour buses go beyond this point, however, so you'll either have to explore it on foot or by rental car. Much more of the basalt paving-stone surface is visible here, and pillars, statues, and arches lie at either side of the road. Best time to come is during the week, when the picnic traffic is light and you can examine the ruins in 19th-century leisure. Across the desolation of the campagna, you can see the lower reaches of the Alban Hills, and the gaunt arches of the Claudian Aqueduct. The tombs between the stone pines are those of the Roman upper class, and the feeling out here is much as it must have been millennia ago.

EUR: The initials (pronounced "a-oor") stand for **Esposizione Universale di Roma** and Mussolini meant it to be the most impressive world's fair Europe had ever seen. Construction began in the late '30s, and a complex of palaces, stadiums and ornamental lakes began to take shape in anticipation of the opening date of 1942. The war slowed construction, eventually stopping it altogether, and leaving vast marble areas with no purpose. The postwar government inherited the site and decided to make it into an administrative center free from the congestion of central Rome. Today it has grown into that plus a complex of expensive villas and apartment houses.

Bus 93 leaves from Terminal Station and, once past the city wall, picks up a sweeping superhighway called Via Cristoforo Colombo. After average-looking outskirts—open land until a few years ago—you'll suddenly descend into a wide valley whose far ridge is lined with the cool glass towers of EUR, reflected in wide lakes at the valley's bottom. The sweeping, Washington, D.C.–type vistas of EUR have a certain 1930s elegance. The entire place lacks the human spontaneity of Rome's twisted avenues, but substitutes an almost 21st-century look instead. Much of the architecture from Il Duce's time looks like Egyptian tombs, but the parks are nice, and the views impressive. In the wooded areas behind the circular glass Palazzo dello Sport are posh homes, the 20th-century equivalents of the palaces that once stood on the Aventine Hill. There are a number of porticoed buildings shining starkly in the sun and a nearby basilica (St. Peter and St. Paul) that also has a left-handed splendor to it.

Your real destination in EUR, aside from the parks and views, is the **Museum of Roman Civilization**, which stands on the Piazza G. Agnelli, charging an entrance fee of 1000 lire (61¢), free on Sunday. It is open daily from 9 a.m. to 2 p.m., to 1 p.m. on Sunday. Closed Monday, the museum is also open on Tuesday and Thursday until 5 p.m. Inside you'll find a fascinating scale model of Rome at the beginning of the fourth century. If you've studied maps of the city and have learned your way around, the model's a great help in unraveling the mystery of what Rome looked like 17 centuries ago. Also in the museum are bronze tablets from the Capitoline Hill, still engraved with the laws and events of the empire, plus exhibits on the agriculture, science, medicine, clothing, astrology, leisure activities, and home life of the men and women who lived in Imperial Rome. The museum is a bit hard to find—it's at the end of Via della Civiltà Romana, only two blocks diagonally from the rear of the Palazzo di Congresso. EUR can also be reached by subway from Terminal Station; the stop is Esposizione.

THE JANICULUM HILL (GIANICOLO): On these placid wooded slopes, the forces of Pope Pius IX and those of Garibaldi met in a historic battle in 1870. The outcome was virtually a foregone conclusion. Today, Romans come up here to admire the splendid view of Rome across the Tiber. Of the great battle, only a few statues remain to remind us of those days when Rome was the provincial capital of the Papal States.

The view is especially breathtaking at dawn when the city is blessedly silent and bathed with that Roman hue of pale pink. Getting here at dawn, however, is a logistical problem unless you have a car, or *dolce vita* friends. Seeing the park during the day doesn't present as many problems. Bus 41 meanders the length of the greensward, and you can catch it quite close to the Ponte Sant' Angelo, on the side opposite Hadrian's tomb. Remember that Corso Vittorio Emanuele crosses the Tiber just a few blocks from Sant' Angelo.

THE ENGLISH CEMETERY: It might sound morbid to suggest that you visit a graveyard on your trip to Rome, but this one is well worth the trip. It's easily accessible by subway—get off at the Piramide stop—and bus 95 from Piazza del Popolo and Piazza Venezia also stops within a block.

The cemetery adjoins the pyramid of Caius Cestius, a first-century B.C. Roman tribune, and his pyramid in turn adjoins the city wall and the Gate of St. Paul, erected by Belisarius during his struggles with Totilla the Goth. Inside the graveyard is a romantic 19th-century world of prone marble angels, elegant cypress trees standing in quiet rows, and sad misty inscriptions. "Here lies one whose name was writ in water," reads the bitter epitaph of John Keats. Buried beside him is Joseph Severn, his best friend and deathbed companion. The carefully tended paths contain the graves of much of the foreign community of the 19th century—Charles Mills, the man whose villa was on the Palatine Hill, is here, as well as Goethe's son, and Percy Shelley. Look too for the grave of Rosa Bathurst and the extravagantly grief-stricken inscription on the tomb—in English on one side, in Italian on the other. The young woman was killed when her horse slipped into the Tiber from a high embankment in 1824, 15 years after her father had mysteriously disappeared while on a mission between Vienna and Berlin.

Toward the Tiber, beyond the atmospheric precincts of the English Cemetery, rises a small hill with a cross on top. This is

Monte Testaccio (Potsherd), created wholly from broken pots that were thrown on this spot throughout the period of the Roman Empire. This was the site on the Tiber where barges carrying goods from the port at Ostia Antica were unloaded; every time a pot broke, it was tossed here and this small mountain is the result.

THE FLEA MARKET: Buses 91 and 92 travel the distance between Piazza Venezia and the Porta Portese, on the south side of Trastevere. Every Sunday morning, and into the afternoon, this is the site of a sprawling flea market, noteworthy less for its bargains than for its perspectives into everyday Italian life. From the wide, paved Piazzale Portuense, the market extends for block after block, looking more like an outlet store than a bazaar. Wooden stalls are crammed with transistor radios, clothing, bolts of brightly colored fabric, imitation antique globes, all sorts of gilded gimcrackery, and cooking appliances. Men demonstrate how to broil a chicken over a tin of Sterno; an old circus performer draws a large crowd that watches him being wrapped in chains only to make a miraculous escape (50 lire, please); strolling musicians play songs that everyone knows the words to. Farther down from the Portese Gate, there are stalls with 16th-century books in leather binders that have long lost their coloring, and a smattering of antiques—some good, some not.

THE FORO ITALICO: This is another of the works of Mussolini—a large obelisk with his name blazoned vertically proclaims the fact from its position on the Tiber in front of the Forum. Bus 67 from Piazza della Repubblica or Piazza Barberini makes the long trip past Piazza del Popolo into the northern reaches of the city, and eventually crosses the Tiber right at the Foro Italico. Alternatively, you can get bus 32 from Piazza Risorgimento, which is quite close to the entrance of the Vatican Museums.

The Foro Italico is high 1930s, and as such has curiosity value for everybody, whether they lived during the era or not. It is a complex of sports arenas—the pools were used during the Olympics held in Rome several years back. But the modern facilities aren't what's interesting here. The raw spirit of fascism is everywhere and that's what the place is all about. Look at the mosaics, using the word "DUCE" as a design repeated thousands of times in black and white tiles over the acres of open area. Also in the pavements are designs of young men giving the Nazi salute, or riding around in trucks building the militaristic world of Italy in the '30s. It's hard to resist a sort of fascination with all this misdirected energy, the place is such a strong statement of the times in which it was built. Beyond the mosaics and uninspired statuary is a great arena, built to befit a latter-day emperor of the sort Mussolini obviously fancied himself. It's called the Stadium, and it's surrounded completely with marble musclemen of impressive proportions.

Rather an anachronism, tucked off in this unvisited corner of Rome, the Foro Italico is nonetheless a fascinating insight into the times that preceded World War II.

THE JEWISH MUSEUM: The **Museo di Arte Ebraica della Communità Israelitica di Roma,** at Lungotevere Cenci (Tempio), is the permanent exhibition of the Jewish community of Rome. It contains Jewish ritual objects and scrolls from the 17th to the 19th centuries, as well as copies of tombstones, paintings, prints, and documents illustrating 2000 years of Jewish history in Rome. The collection of silver ceremonial objects is important, as is a selection of ancient ceremonial textiles. Of exceptional interest are documents of Nazi domination. Visitors are admitted free on Monday, Tuesday, Thursday, and Friday from 10 a.m. to 2 p.m., on Wednesday to 1 p.m. and from 2:30 to 5:30 p.m., and on Sunday from 10 a.m. to 1 p.m. Call 65-64-648 for more information.

Michelangelo's "Pietà"

Chapter VI

A SHOPPING TRIP

I WON'T pretend that Rome is Italy's finest shopping center (Florence and Venice are), nor that its shops are unusually inexpensive—many of them aren't. But even on the most elegant of Rome's thoroughfares, there are values mixed in with the costly boutiques, and I've therefore arranged this chapter to discuss the city's top shopping streets. The method, obviously, is to stroll these streets, ferreting out the best values they offer, comparison-shopping on those stretches that hold no particular appeal to the budget-minded tourist.

I don't know who numbered Rome's streets—doubtless it was done centuries ago—but many times you'll find the numbers start on one side of the street, run all the way down that side in sequence to the far end of the street, then change sides and run all the way back. Therefore, 500 is sometimes across the street from 1. So, duly warned, you're ready to stroll what I consider the city's major shopping thoroughfares.

Via Frattina

Via Frattina runs off Piazza di Spagna and is probably the busiest shopping street in town. You'll frequently find it closed to traffic, converted into a pedestrian mall thronged with shoppers moving from boutique to boutique.

Starting at Piazza di Spagna, as you walk down the street, in between antique shops and beauty parlors, you'll see one boutique after another.

There's the toy store, **Girotondo,** 25 Via Frattina (tel. 679-3576). It's stocked to overflowing with all manner of dolls, games, and delightful diversions for children.

Anatriello Bottega del Regalo, 123 Via Frattina (tel. 678-9601), is chock full of high-quality gifts such as silver candelabra, elegant table lighters, and tea sets.

Some of these storefronts are fabulous looking all by themselves. Many of them are little masterpieces of Italian contemporary design.

Vanilla, 37 Via Frattina (tel. 679-0638), a boutique for women, offers an unusual collection of sometimes offbeat items, including handmade, elaborately decorated sweaters and imaginative accessories.

On the other hand, **VIP,** 43 Via Frattina (tel. 679-0951), is an outfitter for prosperous-looking Italian businessmen, who like well-cut—not too flashy—clothes.

Castelli, 54 Via Frattina (tel. 679-0339), is a perfume-cosmetic-jewelry boutique, with another branch at 61 Via Condotti. The Via Frattina branch comes complete with a full-service beauty salon and fashion section. Here you can luxuriate in every kind of beauty treatment, including sauna baths and body massage.

Finally, **Fornari,** 71–72 Via Frattina (tel. 672-524), has been providing fine silver to an international clientele for more than half a century. The Via Frattina showroom consists of two floors, on which are displayed the precision-crafted items that have earned this establishment the reputation of being the finest silversmith in Rome. Elegant silver trays and boxes, complete tea services, small gift items, handsome silver table settings, and many fine antique pieces, as well as modern gift items, are on display and can be shipped anywhere in the world. It's great fun to browse around inside, inspecting the "objets" in elegantly curved brass and glass cases. In addition, the store has added a whole section of elegant dishes and glassware, everything related to wedding listings for brides.

Via Francesco Crispi

This is a short street that crosses Via Sistina a block from the top of the Spanish Steps. Within a block of the intersection in either direction are several excellent shops for small, not overly expensive gifts.

Stampe d'Arte F.lli Panatta, 117 Via Francesco Crispi (tel. 679-5948), is up the hill toward the Borghese Gardens. Here you'll find excellent prints in color and black and white, covering a variety of subjects from 18th-century Roman street scenes to astrological charts. Also, there is a good selection of antique reproductions of medieval and Renaissance art—extremely attractive and reasonably priced as well.

Pappagallo, 115 Via Francesco Crispi (tel. 678-3011), is a suede and leather factory. The staff at this "parrot" makes their own goods here, including bags, wallets, suede coats—all manner of leather goods. The quality is fine too, and the prices are most reasonable.

At the corner of Via Sistina is **A. Grispigni,** 59 Via Francesco Crispi (tel. 679-0290), with a large assortment of leather-covered boxes, women's purses, compacts, desk sets, and cigarette cases. Many items are inlaid with gold, including Venetian wallets and Florentine boxes.

More leather is down the street at **A. Antinori,** 47 Via Francesco Crispi (tel. 679-0713). This well-established shop is a place for distinctive high-quality gifts, including billfolds, all kinds of attractive Venetian and Florentine boxes, desk sets, cigarette cases, bags, frames, albums, purses, and luggage items.

Via Sistina

This street, after Via Frattina, is good for browsing, and women tourists will occasionally find exciting items on sale.

The boutiques begin at Piazza Trinità dei Monti, at the top of the Spanish Steps. On that little piazza, facing the elegant Hassler Hotel, are these deluxe establishments.

La Mendola, 15 Piazza Trinità dei Monti (tel. 678-9025), is known around the world for its original prints (which the shop designs itself) stamped on uncrushable silk jersey, silk chiffon, wool jersey, and washable matt jersey. The models in Rome cost less than what they sell for in chic department stores and boutiques in the U.S. The store stocks out-of-season dresses in sizes 6 to 16, many of which are personally designed by Michael la Mendola, the voluble owner. With an attractive and articulate staff, in an unusual showroom dotted with antiques and Oriental rugs, he offers good advice on what looks best on his many loyal clients from around the world. His beautiful assistant is named Alessandra.

Anna Manieri, 16 Piazza Trinità dei Monti (tel. 679-4288), is a well-dressed American from Philadelphia who, years ago, decided to move to Rome. Today she designs, and with the help of six or seven persons, creates couture and semi-couture dresses for day and evening wear. You'll go down a curving marble staircase past a statue of Aphrodite before being greeted enthusiastically at the door of Mrs. Manieri's high-ceilinged showroom by Chérie, her poodle.

Moving down the Via Sistina toward Piazza Barberini, you'll discover one small shop after another. Among them:

Leather boots and bags are sold at **Elena,** 81–82 Via Sistina (tel. 678-1500).

Tomassini di Luisa Romagnoli, 119 Via Sistina (tel. 461-909), offers delicately beautiful lingerie and negligees, all the original designs of Luisa Romagnoli. Her creations of frothy nylon, shimmery Italian silk, and fluffy cotton come both ready to wear and custom-made.

Alex Shey, 42 Via Sistina (tel. 679-3181), cuts clothes for women who prefer a tailored, big-city look which is high fashion, although ready-made.

Pancani, 117 Via Sistina (tel. 461-434), has a wispier, boutique look in muted pastels. Inventory at this small shop (whose ceiling contains a fanciful fresco by well-known Roman artist, Novella Parigini) includes well-cut clothes, sometimes in cashmere, for younger, semi-trendy women.

Via Condotti

This is the poshest shopping street in Rome, although many of the larger stores have a few small and moderately priced items. Wise shoppers are advised to take a look at the goods displayed on the Spanish Steps before a tour of Via Condotti. Here, artisans good and bad lay out their wares on old velvet cloths—usually paintings, beads, silver and turquoise jewelry, some of it quite good—and bargain for the best offer. If nothing here interests you, then head down Via Condotti. New Yorkers will regard many of the stores on Condotti as direct transplants from Fifth Avenue (although it was usually the other way around).

Krizia, 77 Piazza di Spagna (tel. 679-3419), near the corner of the famous street but still on the piazza, is the only outlet in Rome for some of Italy's most lighthearted and best received women's designers.

Then, starting from the top of the street, near the Spanish Steps, you'll find an array of shops that, as many visitors to Rome sometimes ruefully admit, send them into an absolute orgy of spending. Some highlights include—

Fabrizio Runci, 93 Via Condotti (tel. 679-5819), is a deluxe haberdashery, with excellent ties, shirts, suits, leather goods, and women's garments.

Gucci, 8 Via Condotti (tel. 678-3232), is a legend, of course, an established firm since 1900. Its merchandise consists of high-class leather goods, such as suitcases, handbags, wallets, shoes, and desk accessories. It also has departments complete with elegant men's and women's wear. Sold there are beautiful shirts, blouses, and dresses, as well as ties and neck scarves of numerous designs. Among these are many accessories, including Gucci's own perfume.

And **Bulgari,** 10 Via Condotti (tel. 679-3876), has the diamonds to wear with anything.

Behind all the chrome and mirrors at 13 Via Condotti is **Valentino** (tel. 678-3656), a swank emporium for men's clothing. Here you can become the most fashionable man in town, but only if you can afford those high prices. Valentino's women's clothes are sold around the corner, in an even bigger showroom at 15 Via Bocca di Leone (tel. 679-5862).

Federico Buccellati, 31 Via Condotti (tel. 679-0329), is one of the best known silversmiths in Italy, selling neo-Renaissance creations that will change your thinking about the way silver is designed. They sell jewelry as well.

Salvatore Ferragamo, 66 Via Condotti (tel. 678-1130), sells elegant men's clothes in an ambience reeking of Italian style. A few stores away, at nos. 73–74 (tel. 678-8402), the same designer sells clothes, purses, and accessories for women. Across the street, **Fornari,** 80 Via Condotti tel. 679-4285), specializes in sumptuous small jewelry and gift items for both sexes. The collection includes gold jewelry for both men and women, striking rings of traditional and modern design, unusual bracelets, key rings, chains, and necklaces, plus an array of charms.

Other good spots for (at least) window shopping include—

Cucci, 67 Via Condotti (tel. 679-1882)—not to be confused with Gucci. This has been a leading name in custom tailoring and shirt-making since 1912. Here you'll find beautifully made knitwear, sports shirts, and cashmere sweaters for both women and men. Many original designs are always available. Cucci's also features handsome ties and scarves, along with an exclusive line of handmade moccasins.

Sergio Valente Beauty Center, 11 Via Condotti (tel. 679-4515), offers every cosmetic indulgence—fashion hair styling, coloring, scalp treatments, facials, manicure, massage, and sauna —in bright, luxurious surroundings. English is spoken.

Note: Via Condotti is actually at the heart of quite a stylish shopping area, which extends into the side streets in both directions. You might enjoy browsing on some of these other streets, particularly amid the aforementioned boutiques (for men and women) on Via Frattina, and Via della Vite.

Via Borgognona

Sandwiched between the already-recommended Vias Condotti and Frattina is yet another one of Rome's exclusive shopping streets, the Via Borgognona, beginning near the Piazza di Spagna. This street has some of the most elegant clothing in Rome—but at high prices. In fact, observers of the Rome fashion scene are beginning to think that stores on this fashionable street are quickly approaching the desirability of the addresses on the adjacent Via Condotti.

Carlo Palazzi, 7c Via Borgognona (tel. 678-9143), will make you a suit to order in the latest of styles, using the most carefully chosen and refined of materials. In addition, this men's store will also make custom shirts. To go with your suit and shirt, you'll find a tasteful selection of belts, ties, and shoes. And of course you can always find high-fashion ready-to-wear suits, shirts, and accessories.

Givenchy, 21 Via Borgognona (tel. 678-4058), is a Rome outlet for this world-famous Paris fashion house, one of the great couturiers.

Gucci Boutique, 25 Via Borgognona (tel. 678-3232), holds the Italian colors in this exclusive boutique devoted to the finest in leather handbags (soft, superb finish), as well as a stunning collection of belts and other Gucci fashion items such as scarves, ties, luggage, women's shoes, and wallets.

Fendi, 36a–39 Via Borgognona (tel. 679-7641), is fun, amusing, and witty, selling trendy purses and leather goods for women.

Scotch House, 36 Via Borgognona (tel. 678-2660), is an attractively cramped women's boutique with friendly saleswomen and a floor-to-ceiling collection of fashions by eight European designers, including Sonia Rykiel, Pancaldi, and Angelo Tarlazzi.

Gianni Versace Uomo, 29 Via Borgognona (tel. 679-5292), is the biggest Roman outlet for the famous designer's menswear line. The tastefully upbeat clothes are displayed in a long format of stone floors and white-lacquered wall.

La Bohème, 5 Via Borgognona (tel. 679-2908), sells fun, fanciful, and sexy clothes for women under 25.

Gianni Versace Boutique Accesori, 41 Via Borgognona (tel. 678-1732), offers a full line of glamorous leather goods and accessories for women.

Missoni, 38b Via Borgognona (tel. 679-7971), is the main outlet in Rome for this imaginative designer.

Gianfranco Ferre, 6 Via Borgognona (tel: 679-7445), is the outlet for his men's line. His women's line is sold at no. 42b on this same street (tel. 678-0256).

Via Veneto–Via Barberini

There's quite a bit of shopping here, especially along the Via Veneto (although at truly high tabs). Shoe and glove stores and the like are interspersed with hotels and chic cafés.

Ribot, 98a Via Veneto (tel. 483-485), offers exclusive ties, Peter Scott and Ribot exclusive cashmeres, all Burberry lines including suits, jackets, and sportswear, and the beautiful knitwear from Avon-Celli. It is in front of the Excelsior Hotel.

The elegant new store of **Raphael Salato,** 104 Via Veneto (tel. 484-677), near the Excelsior Hotel, is where the style-conscious woman goes for the latest in shoe fashions. The selection of unusual and well-crafted shoes is wide. In addition, Raphael Salato stocks an exclusive line of children's shoes. Other stores in Rome include 149 Via Veneto (tel. 493-507), where men's and women's shoes are sold.

Bruno Magli, 70a Via Vento (tel. 464-355) and 94 Via Barberini (tel. 486-850), offers dressy footwear for both sexes. Magli also has shops at 1 Via del Gambero (tel. 679-3802) and 237 Via Cola di Rienzo (tel. 351-972).

Also in the area are several other stores of note:

Anqelo, 36 Via Bissolati (tel. 464-092), a custom tailor for discerning men. Angelo Vittucci has been featured in such publications as *Esquire* and *Gentlemen's Quarterly.* He employs the best craftspeople and cutters, and his taste in style and design is impeccable. Custom shirts, suits, dinner jackets, even casual wear, can be made on short notice. A suit, for instance, takes about three days. If you haven't time to wait, Angelo Vittucci will ship anywhere in the world.

Nickol, 30 Via Barberini (tel. 474-0869), is a modern shoe emporium, featuring shoes for the whole family. Women's footwear is particularly stylish, and there's a wide sampling in many colors and fabrics. For men, soft leather shoes are available. Most children's sizes are kept in stock as well, and the staff speaks English.

Limentani Franco, 78 Via Barberini (tel. 475-1122), is a specialty leather shop, with a good assortment of handbags, women's shoes, and gloves. It has good-quality items sold at moderate prices.

La Barbera, 74 Via Barberini (tel. 483-628), has been in business since 1837, building a substantial reputation in the field of optical equipment. The store also carries a full spectrum of related wares: cameras, films, binoculars, opera glasses, and microscopes. You can have prescription glasses reproduced in 48 hours. For those fashionable hangouts on the Via Veneto and the Piazza del Popolo, take a look at Barbera's collection of sunglass frames—more than 5000 varieties.

Via del Corso

Now that traffic has been curtailed on this main thoroughfare of Rome, a variety of unusual shops has sprung up, particularly on the section near the Piazza del Popolo.

Sav, 129–130 Via del Corso (tel. 679-5655), sells belts, a wide variety of luggage, and women's purses of all degrees of conservatism. Near the landmark Hotel Plaza, it has a modern design and is not as expensive as some of the shops a few blocks away.

Elsy, 106 Via del Corso (tel. 679-2275), features women's clothing on two levels of ultramodern, warmly accented floor space.

Grillis, 166 Via del Corso (tel. 679-3650), has an elegant assortment of shoes, suitcases, purses, and leather goods. Clients indicate the item they like from the long expanses of display window fronting on the street. Sales clerks then bring the item into the oval-shaped ground-floor showroom for closer inspection.

Strada, 443 Via del Corso (tel. 679-0608), is a disco and beachwear-conscious boutique for men and women where everything that has become trendy within the past ten minutes in Rome is displayed in a hi-tech, low-camp format of Polynesian palms and glistening chrome. Near the corner of the Via del Carozze the store, depending on your salesperson, can be a lot of fun.

Doiminici, 14 Via del Corso (tel. 361-0591). The store is so trendy that it's difficult even to see the sign in front. The understated facade, a few steps from the Piazza del Popolo, shelters an amusing and lighthearted collection of men's and women's shoes in a pleasing variety of vivid colors. The style is aggressively young-at-heart, and the children's shoes are adorable.

Via Nazionale

One of the city's busiest shopping thoroughfares, Via Nazionale runs from Piazza della Repubblica (with its great Fountain of the Naiads in front of the Baths of Diocletian) down almost to Piazza Venezia. There is an abundance of leather stores—more reasonable than in many other parts of Rome—as well as a welcome element of stylish boutiques.

Our first stopover is right near the beginning of the Via Nazionale. **Cesare Diomedi Leather Goods,** 96–97 Via Vittorio Emanuele Orlando (tel. 464-822), offers one of the most outstanding collections of leather goods in Rome. And leather isn't all you'll find in this small, two-story shop, with its attractive winding staircase. There are many other distinctive gift items—small gold cigarette cases, jeweled umbrellas—that make this a good stopping-off point for that last important item. Upstairs is a wide assortment of elegant leather luggage and accessories.

Down Via Nazionale, at the corner of Via Torino, is **Arte dell' Arredamento,** 6 Via Nazionale (tel. 461-1034), offering an outstanding collection of fabrics and Oriental rugs.

Pitti, 11 Via Nazionale (tel. 461-567), presents a wide selection of gloves, luggage, and smaller pieces inlaid with gold designs.

At **Marte's,** 14–16 Via Nazionale (tel. 461-048), you'll find inexpensive boots and casual shoes for both sexes.

Marie Louise, 23–24 Via Nazionale (tel. 475-0878), attracts with its exceptional collection of silk foulards and stoles and women's knitwear—mostly in strong prints and bright colors.

Marisa, 234A Via Nazionale (tel. 461-669), has boutique items and trendy fashions for the style-conscious playgirl.

Winton, 209–210 Via Nazionale (tel. 475-5918), features restrained but chic fine leather and suede clothing for men and women. You'll also find a good assortment of men's shirts, trousers, and ties, plus sweaters for both sexes.

Louis, 198 Via Nazionale (tel. 464-614), is a moderately priced shoe emporium for both men and women.

Alexia, 76 Via Nazionale (tel. 464-890), offers good buys in purses for women and for businessmen, as well as a stylish selection of leather coats and furs.

Opposite the travertine marble palace of the Banca d'Italia is **Socrate,** 89b Via Nazionale (tel. 484-530), dispensing low-key, excellently cut, and high-quality men's clothing, much of it wool and suede.

Borsalino, 157B Via IV Novembre (tel. 679-4192), is chock-full of rakish hats reminiscent of the 1930s. The most famous hatmaker in all of Italy, the world even, offers all sorts of other styles too, for both women and men. The store also sells ultra-well-made trousers and suits as well.

Fiorucci, 236 Via Nazionale (tel. 463-175), was at one time inimitable, but now copies have sprung up. Still, Fiorucci is fun and hyper-trendy, with a logo (two smiling cherubs with dilated pupils and sunglasses) that still inspires a smile.

BOX 233, 233 Via Nazionale (tel. 475-4518), sells avant-garde, chicly up-to-date, and relaxedly casual clothes for men.

Via dei Coronari

Like Via Condotti, this street should be seen whether or not you buy. Buried in a colorful section of the Campus Martius (Renaissance Rome), Via dei Coronari is an antiquer's dream, literally lined with magnificent vases, urns, chandeliers, breakfronts, chaises, refectory tables, candelabra—you name it. You'll find the entrance to the street just north of the Piazza Navona. Turn left outside the piazza, past the excavated ruins of Domitian's Stadium, and the street will be just ahead of you. There are more than 40 antique stores within the next four blocks, and on my last trip I saw in the windows brocade dining chairs, inlaid secretaries, marble pedestals, claw and ball tables, gilded consoles, and enamel clocks, among countless other treasures. Keep in mind that stores are frequently closed between 1 and 4 in the afternoon.

Miscellaneous

At **E. Fiore,** 31 Via Ludovisi (tel. 475-9296), near the Via Veneto, you can choose a jewel and have it set according to your specifications. Or make your selection from a rich assortment of charms, bracelets, necklaces, rings, brooches, corals, pearls, and cameos. Also featured are elegant watches, silverware, and goldware. Fiore's also does expert repair work on your own jewelry and watches.

Basile, 5 Via Belsiana (tel. 678-9244), is slightly isolated from the other chic shops of Rome but within walking distance of some of the most important of them. This is the only store in the city that sells women's clothes from the Milanese factories of the famous Italian clothier. The store positively reeks of Italian taste and style, the service is friendly and gracious, and the apparel is well made and sophisticated.

Emporio Armani, 28 Via del Babuino (tel. 678-4325). In a format of black lacquer accents and neutral-colored carpeting, this store sells the famous line of men's clothes at slightly less expensive prices than its twin at Giorgio Armani, 102 Via del Babuino (tel. 679-3777).

Murano Veneto, 13 Via Marche (behind the Hotel Excelsior) (tel. 474-1995), offers a magnificent collection of Venetian blown glass, including chandeliers, art objects, fine mirrors, sculptures, and giftware, in a variety of colors and styles. Shipments are guaranteed.

Galleria d'Arte Schneider, 10 Rampa Mignanelli (tel. 678-4019), an art gallery run by an American professor of art, Robert E. Schneider, is worth a visit. It's near the Spanish Steps.

Lombo, 25a Via XX Settembre (tel. 463-759), is an excellent place to find gifts—crystal and china pieces, glassware, sterling, and the like.

Roman Forum

Chapter VII

ROME AFTER DARK

WHEN THE SUN goes down, lights across the city bathe palaces, ruins, fountains, and monuments in a theatrical white light. There are actually few evening occupations quite as pleasurable as a stroll past the solemn pillars of old temples, or the cascading torrents of Renaissance fountains glowing under the blue-black sky. Of the fountains, that of the **Naiads** (Piazza della Repubblica), of the **Tortoises** (Piazza Mattei), and, of course, the **Trevi** are particularly beautiful. The **Capitoline Hill** is magnificently lit at night, its measured Renaissance facades glowing like jewel boxes surrounding the statue of Marcus Aurelius. Behind the Senatorial Palace is a fine view of the **Roman Forum.** If you're staying across the Tiber, **Piazza San Pietro** (in front of St. Peter's Basilica) is particularly impressive at night without the tour buses and crowds. And a combination of illuminated architecture, Renaissance fountains, and, frequently, sidewalk stage shows and art expositions, is at the **Piazza Navona.** If you're ambitious and have a good sense of direction, try exploring the streets to the west of Piazza Navona, which look like a stage set when they're lit at night.

Café Life

The most famous of the cafés of Rome are on the Via Veneto. While they line the streets from Piazza Barberini all the way to the Pincian Gate, the best are near the latter landmark. They include Doney, Harry's Bar, and the Caffé de Paris. These three are the best known on the Via Veneto.

This area, once exclusive and expensive—now only expensive—is still a sophisticated part of town. Stores sell jewels and airline tickets.

Cadillacs with Connecticut license plates and Rolls-Royces bearing medallions reading "GB" line the streets.

Those old enough to remember the 1950s may recall Marcello

Mastroianni fighting off the paparazzi (Rome's aggressive band of freelance photographers) in *La Dolce Vita.* Well, they're still here, except the clientele isn't as exotic as it was in the '50s. However, you'll probably want to spend at least one night on the Via Veneto. Few dare to return home having missed it.

The **Caffè de Paris,** 90 Via Veneto (tel. 465-284), a landmark, is a good place to get the night started. Tables spill out onto the sidewalk in summer, and the passing crowd walks right through the maze. In winter, "see-through" booths are enclosed. Here you can have drinks from 10,000 lire ($6.10) and sandwiches from 9000 lire ($5.49).

Doney, 145 Via Veneto (tel. 493-405), is the other most frequented café. It has endured while others have come and gone. Doney is now considered more fashionable than the Caffè de Paris. You might not find an Italian here, but you'll meet plenty of your fellow countrymen, along with other Europeans. Go here for drinks from 10,000 lire ($6.10) and sandwiches from 9000 ($5.49), prices that match those of the Caffè de Paris.

Harry's Bar, 148 Via Veneto (tel. 474-5832), is the choicest watering spa along this gilded street, as of this writing. It has no connections with the world-famous Harry's Bars at such cities as Florence, Venice, and Paris. In many respects, the Roma Harry's is the most elegant of them all, with its tapestry walls, elaborate wood paneling, curvy pilastering, and sconces. If you're lonely, you might meet some companions here.

You can have pretty good, but outrageously priced, food here as well, taking your meal in summer (if you prefer) at one of the sidewalk tables. Two drinks will cost from 18,000 lire ($10.98). If it's crowded, your reception is likely to be hysterical from the waiters. Closed Sunday.

The fashion-conscious denizens of Rome, known as the *bella gente,* or beautiful people, are seldom seen on the Via Veneto any more. Instead they make a point to be seen (especially after midnight) on the **Piazza del Popolo.** There is on this square an element of excitement in the air, the feeling that something interesting is just about to happen. The little outdoor tables of the two leading sidewalk cafés sprawl far and wide. They're surrounded by expensive Italian sports cars, elegant women with German accents, and men in leather pants.

The chicest place to go for a drink is **Rosati,** 4–5 Piazza del Popolo (tel. 360-5859). This place has been in business since 1923. Originally it was more or less an ice-cream parlor. Light food items are available, but most people order either a drink, a beer, or a dish of ice cream, sitting out front at one of the clothed tables spreading out into the piazza like a housing development.

Low, growling Maseratis cruise slowly by while young Italian men in silk shirts hang from the car windows, eyeing sleek blonde girls. There is a constant stream of expensive automobiles cruising by Rosati at night.

Drinks are more expensive, of course, if you select a table. But who wants to stand at the bar? Coffee at a table begins at 2800 lire ($1.71), with pastries costing from 5000 lire ($3.05).

Canova Café, Piazza del Popolo (tel. 361-2231). Although the management has cluttered up the interior with boutiques selling expensive gift items, which include luggage and cigarette lighters, many Romans still consider this to be the place to be on the Piazza del Popolo. The Canova has a sidewalk terrace for pedestrian-watching, a chrome-accented bar in an anteroom, and an inner seating area with velvet-covered walls, parquet floors, and comfortable banquettes. In summer, you'll have access to a quiet courtyard whose walls are covered with ivy and where colorful flowers grow in terracotta planters. Expect to spend around 9000 lire ($5.49) for two Campari sodas. Closed Monday.

Just as the Piazza del Popolo lured the chic and sophisticated from the Via Veneto, several other cafés in the colorful district of Trastevere, across the Tiber, are threatening to do the same for Popolo. Fans who saw Fellini's *Roma* know what the **Piazza Santa Maria,** deep in the heart of Trastevere, looks like. The square—filled with milling throngs in summer—is graced with an octagonal fountain and a church dating from the 12th century. On the piazza, despite a certain amount of traffic, children run and play, and occasional spontaneous guitar fests are heard when the weather's good. For drinks, try either the Di Marzio or the Galeassi.

Café-Bar di Marzio, 14B Piazza di Santa Maria in Trastevere (tel. 581-6095), is a warmly inviting place, strictly a café (not a restaurant), with both indoor and outdoor tables at the edge of the colorful square with a view of its famous fountain. Coffee here costs around 2000 lire ($1.22) and beer ranges from 3500 lire ($2.14).

Galeassi Café, 3 Piazza di Santa Maria in Trastevere (tel. 580-3775), right on the square, offers an outdoor terrace as well as an inner room with paneled walls and dozens of bottles of wine arranged on a shelf above the heads of the many clients. If after a drink you should stick around to partake of the Roman specialties, count on spending from 30,000 lire ($18.30) to 45,000 lire ($27.45). Closed Monday.

Alternatively, you could try **Antico Caffè Greco,** 86 Via Condotti (tel. 678-2554). This spot is considerably older than the other cafés mentioned. In fact, it has been serving drinks in its front-room bar since 1760. Over the years it has attracted such habitués as Goethe, Stendhal, and D'Annunzio. Lying half a block from the foot of the Spanish Steps, it still retains a 19th-century atmosphere. The waiters wear morning coats—most effective looking—and seat you at small marble tables. Beyond the abovementioned carved wooden bar are four or five small, elegant rooms, whose walls are covered with silk and hung with oil paintings in gilded frames. Most people drop by for an apéritif at 4200 lire ($2.56), a coffee for 2300 lire ($1.40). You can also order light sandwiches at 2000 lire ($1.22), little more than hors d'oeuvres, really. Prices, incidentally, are slightly lower at the bar.

Sant'Eustachio, 82 Piazza Sant'Eustachio (tel. 656-1309). Strongly brewed coffee might be considered one of the elixirs of Italy, and many Romans will walk many blocks for what they consider a superior brew. One of the most celebrated espresso shops is on a small square near the Pantheon, where the city water supply comes from a source outside Rome which the emperor Augustus funneled into the city with an aqueduct in 19 B.C. Rome's most experienced judges of espresso claim that the water plays an important part in the coffee's flavor, although steam forced through ground Brazilian coffee roasted on the premises has an important effect as well. Stand-up coffee at this well-known place costs around 1000 lire (61¢). Purchase a ticket from the cashier for as many cups as you want, and leave a small tip (about 100 lire—6¢) for the counterman when you give him your receipt. It's open from 8 a.m. till 1 a.m. every day except Monday.

Café Alemagna, 181 Via del Corso (tel. 679-2887), is a monumental café usually filled with busy shoppers. On the premises are just about every kind of dining facility a hurried resident of Rome could want, including a stand-up sandwich bar with dozens of selections from behind a glass case, a cafeteria, and a sit-down area with waiter service. The decor includes high coffered ceilings, baroque-style wall stencils, glove lights, crystal chandeliers, and black stone floors. Pizza slices range from 1200 lire (73¢), sandwiches and pastries from 2500 lire ($1.53). It is open daily except Sunday from 7:30 a.m. to 9 p.m.

Another favorite p.m. activity is to visit a chic ice-cream parlor. Fanciers of "gelato" for gelato's sake head for the Piazza Navona and the outdoor tables of **Tre Scalini,** 28–32 Piazza Navona (tel. 654-1996), opposite side of the piazza from Il Domiziano. The specialty of the house, called a "tartufo," is a frozen chocolate concoction topped with whipped cream. It's really good and exceptionally filling. At a sidewalk table, you can order one for 3500 lire ($2.14). Tre Scalini is especially pleasant as it's on a forever-interesting piazza. Closed Wednesday.

If you simply like ice cream, without going too far, just stop at **Giolitti.** This justifiably famous ice-cream emporium is at 40 Via Uffici del Vicario (tel. 679-4206), which is around the corner from the Hotel Nazionale, just after Piazza Montecitorio, where there is the House of Commons, adjacent to Piazza Colonna. Giolitti is on a narrow street, and its single string of outdoor tables, as well as its wide internal hall, is a favorite meeting place. The whipped-cream-topped coppa Giolitti goes for 4000 lire ($2.44) at a table. The coppa Olympica and coppa Primavera cost 6000 lire ($2.66) at a table. During the day, good-tasting snacks are served also. Many take ice cream out to eat on the streets; others enjoy it in the post-Empire splendor of the salon inside. You can have your "coppa" until 2 a.m. every day except Monday, when the place is closed.

Culture

The **Teatro Goldoni,** just north of the Piazza Navona and tucked away on the little Vicolo dei Soldati, presents a medley of theatricals in English. You might call 656-1156 to see what's playing when you're in town. Not only are plays in English presented, but so are concerts, both classical and pop. Incidentally, there's a well-stocked bar in the handsome 18th-century foyer, serving snacks, local specialties, and afternoon teas.

Opera is a major tourist attraction in Rome, appealing especially to persons who probably wouldn't dream of going at home. The reason for this attraction is the unabashed splendor of the staging. When, after all, was the last time you saw charging horses, camels, and elephants on a stage? The stage is not in the opera house; rather it's in the awesome ruins of the Baths of Caracalla. The summer-season productions there include *Rigoletto, Aïda,* and ballet. Everyone goes to see *Aïda.* The sets, costumes, and especially the wildlife (horses and camels for sure) of the Verdi classic never fail to provoke enthusiastic applause from an appreciative audience. Tickets can be purchased at the Opera House box office, a block south of the Via Nazionale at 64 Via Firenze. The Opera House (tel. 461-755) sells tickets from 9:30 a.m. to 1 p.m. and from 5 to 6:30 p.m. daily. On the day of the performance only, you can also purchase tickets at the Baths of Caracalla. However, the box office there doesn't open until 8 p.m. Bus 93 from in front of the Terminal Station will take you to the Baths of Caracalla. For the return, special buses bring you back to the center of town. Performances are held practically every day (or every other day) throughout the summer. Check at the Opera House for times. Bring a jacket or sweater, as it occasionally gets chilly even in summer.

You may also want to attend the Rome Opera House itself, **Teatro dell'Opera,** 1 Piazza Beniamino Gigli (tel. 461-755), off the Via Nazionale, should you be in the Italian capital for its season, usually from the end of December till June. Tickets for the finest seats in this historic theater cost as much as 40,000 lire ($24.40), while other seats begin at a modest 10,000 lire ($6.10). Good gallery seats are available in the 6000-lire ($3.66) to 15,000-lire ($9.15) range.

Concerts, given by the orchestra of the Academy of St. Cecilia, take place in the ruins of the Basilica of Constantine (referred to as the Basilica of Maxentius by the St. Cecilia people). Details, such as prices and schedules, are available by phoning the academy at 673-617.

Perhaps to make up for inconvenient hours at other times, several of Rome's museums are happily open a few evenings each week. Visiting a museum in the evening is a delight, since there's rarely anyone else there with you. The **Conservatory Palace,** on your right as you arrive at the top of the Capitoline Hill via Michelangelo's stairs, is open every Saturday evening from 9 to 11. In addition to the baronial halls, the museum houses the she-wolf of Rome, an Etruscan sculpture of the fifth century B.C. that has been the symbol of the city for more than 3000 years.

The city's attic, the **Museum of Rome** on the Piazza San Pantaleo, is also open Tuesday and Thursday evenings from 5 to 7:30, and is enjoyable to combine with a visit to Tre Scalini (see above).

Movies

The **Pasquino** is a small theater showing English-language films of rather recent vintage. The average charge is 5000

($3.05). Phone the theater at 580-3622 if you want to know what is playing. It's on a little street called Vicolo del Piede, just a block from the aforementioned Piazza Santa Maria in Trastevere. In fact, it makes quite a pleasant evening to catch a show at Pasquino, then have a drink or cappuccino afterward at one of the cafés on the square, where you can admire the village atmosphere and fine architecture, even observing (or participating in) the scene around the fountain.

Nightclubs and Discos

There are no inexpensive nightclubs in Rome, so be duly warned. Another important warning: During the peak of the summer visiting days, usually in August, all nightclub proprietors seem to fold their doors and head for the seashore. Many of them operate alternative clubs at coastal resorts. Some of them close at different times each year, so it's hard to keep up to date with them. Always have your hotel check to see if a club is operating before you make the trek there. Drink prices range from 10,000 lire ($6.10) to 20,000 lire ($12.20) at the clubs recommended below, unless otherwise stated.

Bella Blu, 21 Via Luigi Luciana (tel. 360-8840). This is currently the most elegant nightspot in Rome. You may have trouble getting in if the doorman doesn't think you are chic and/or rich. Visiting film stars gravitate here, as do Roman aristocrats. In the Parioli district, this is technically a disco (which begins at 11 p.m.), although you can go early and dine at 9:30 p.m. if you want to. It's necessary to reserve a table. The piano bar is quite popular from 9 p.m. till midnight. Closed Monday.

Gil's, 11a Via Romagnosi (tel. 361-1348), rivals Bella Blu as the most chic rendezvous point in Rome. There are those who claim that Gil's pedigree is even bluer blooded than Bella Blu's. The designer wanted to give you the impression that you are entering a mammoth tent of some sheik in the Sahara. Sand-filled aquariums line the walls. This is definitely an '80s kind of club, unlike some Roman nightspots where the nostalgic aura of the '50s lingers.

Gil, incidentally, one of the leading makeup artists in Rome, is said to be one of the owners. Doors open at 10:30 nightly, but no one shows up until much later. Evening clothes are the appropriate garb.

La Pergola Bar, Cavalieri Hilton, 101 Via Cadlolo (tel. 31-51), adjoins the world-famous restaurant of the same name. On the top floor of the Hilton International, the panoramic bar has a view that encompasses most of Rome, while its guest list includes drop-ins from the restaurant (see the dining chapter), guests from the hotel (see the hotel chapter), and a wide range of the chic, the trendy, the glittering, and the unattached who drive or taxi up from the city below. The decor is black with brass accents and includes a dramatic bar area, a medium-size dance floor, and a labyrinthine arrangement of warmly tinted velvet banquettes clustered into intimate niches and groupings. Disco music plays from 10 p.m. until 2 a.m. The first drink costs 14,000 lire ($8.54) during the week, around 18,500 lire ($11.29) on weekends. The second drink costs slightly less, around 10,000 lire ($6.10). Residents of the Hilton are allowed a reduction in the price of the first drink. There is a large terrasse area where dancers can promenade and cool off between sessions.

For elegant drinking only, try **La Cabala,** the bar above the Hosteria dell' Orso ("Inn of the Bear"), at 25 Via Dei Soldati (tel. 656-4250). it is close to the Tiber in the northern part of the Campus Martius. It's a legend in Rome, and has been for years. Today it is most chic, drawing heavy patronage from Americans, who dress to the teeth. It would be worth a visit if only for the pure ostentation of the decor.

I like the Inn of the Bear less and less as a restaurant, but **La Cabala** is still a fine place to go for a drink. The building housing the Hostaria and bar has a rich history. It was once a simple inn, constructed in 1300. Reportedly, St. Francis of Assisi once stayed here, as did Dante during the Jubilee Year. Later, as a hotel, it was to attract such guests as Rabelais, Montaigne, and Goethe.

Club 84, 84 Via Emilia (tel. 475-1538), has for a long time been a leading choice on the elegant after-dark circuit of Rome. Well-known combos perform here until 3 a.m. The disco dance floor is small and very intimate. Mostly couples patronize the club.

Paradise, 97 Via Mario de' Fiori (tel. 678-4838), is noted both for its adventurous combination of nightclub, disco, and restaurant, and for the glamorous acts it books. In the past they have included Diana Ross and splashy, Paris-type revues, often with young women from England and the United States. The artistic direction assures first-class shows, a well-run restaurant, an attractive bar, and recently released disco music played between the live musical acts. A drink is included in the price of a meal (although wine is not) at around 55,000 lire ($33.55) and up. A drink without dinner costs around 25,000 lire ($15.25), while the second drink goes for 18,000 lire ($10.98). Open seven days a week, the establishment presents shows at 10:30 p.m. and 12:30 a.m.

Capriccio, 38 Via Liguria (tel. 489-961), off the Via Veneto, is underneath a popular restaurant featuring top-notch service, food, and wines in a beautiful roof garden. A meal costs 50,000 lire ($30.50) and up. Downstairs, music for dancing is provided for those who prefer a nonfrenetic atmosphere. Two orchestras play nightly. The nightclub is closed in July and August, although the restaurant remains open all year.

Much More, 52 Via Luigi Luciani (tel. 870-504), is the *grande discoteca* of Rome. Every night, except Monday, it pulsates with life, and it also stages tea dances on Saturday and Sunday afternoons. It lies on the same street as the most sophisticated nightclub in Rome, the Bella Blu, out in the Parioli district, but each establishment attracts an entirely different clientele. Back in the 1970s this place was a movie palace, but most of today's crowd is far too young to remember the previous decade. Hours are from 11 p.m. to 3 a.m. Occasional live rock concerts are presented.

Jackie O', 11 Via Boncompagni (tel. 461-401), is still around, but it's not as chic as it was in its heyday. Nowadays the doorman is far less strict about who he will let into these glittering precincts. There is a restaurant serving very expensive food inside, as well as a piano bar. You go to the Jackie O' section for dancing and to Graticola for dining. This was—and still is to some extent—a haven for what used to be called "the beautiful people." Beautiful they may be, but they are a fickle lot when it comes to nightclubs.

Easy Going, 9 Via della Purificazione (tel. 474-5578). Rome has never been able to match the variety of gay nightclubs of New York or San Francisco, but this amusingly decorated two-level club near the Piazza Barberini is by far the best known gay disco in the Italian capital. Set behind speakeasy-style, white lacquered doors with a peephole, the club charges around 15,000 lire ($9.15) entrance fee per person, which gives the guest the right to one drink. This can be consumed at the upstairs bar, whose walls and cubbyholes are decorated with pseudo-baroque frescoes of cherubs fornicating, or at the downstairs level, which is the more popular and where the illustrations are far more risqué. The art includes a silver-colored statue of the Americans planting the flag on Iwo Jima "au naturel," a slickly contemporary bar area, and a very small dance floor where would-be lookalikes from *Gentlemen's Quarterly* stand in poses of studied indifference. It opens at 11 p.m., but if you want to wait till it gets interesting, go even later.

Scarabocchio, 8 Piazza dei Ponziana (tel. 580-0495), is both a nightclub and a disco with a disc jockey. It's an ivy-covered building on a charming little square. A glass floor inside is illuminated for dancing to both recorded and live music. It attracts a fashionable, dressy crowd that arrives late.

Mississippi Jazz Club, 16 Borgo Angelico (tel. 654-0348), is the best place in Rome to hear jazz. Every night, a jazz concert with Dixieland is presented. In air-conditioned comfort, you can enjoy this laid-back atmosphere of American music with Italian style. You get good drinks at the bar, and if you're hungry the waiter will serve you a pizza. On Saturday and Sunday afternoons, you can attend jazz tea dances.

La Cage aux Folles, 9 Via Gregoriana (tel. 679-0490). Although the name might imply otherwise, this is a disco for young heterosexuals—usually under 25—who pack into its neon-lit cellar every evening except Monday from 9:30 till closing (usually around 4 a.m.). Dress codes range from 1950s retro to understated punk. The entrance fee of 10,000 lire ($6.10) includes the first drink. It's especially crowded on a day many Romans consider boring (Sunday), when it opens for an additional session from 4 to 7:30 p.m.

Folkloric Evenings

Fantasie di Trastevere, 6 Via di Santa Dorotea (tel. 589-2986), provides a lusty, theatricalized evening where you'll be instantly immersed in the bravura and gaiety of uninhibited Roman nightlife. The setting is the former Teatro Tiberino, a so-called people's theater where the celebrated actor, Petrolini, made his debut. It was a small printing operation when Constante Brugnoli took it over, transforming it into the present "fantasy." You dine on hearty regional cuisine while you're entertained by folk singers and musicians performing in provincial attire. Some of their songs are old Roman and Neapolitan favorites; others are esoteric. The show lasts two hours—so try for a table no later than 9:30 p.m. Expect to pay from 75,000 lire ($45.75) for a full-course meal, although the cost of your wine from the Roman hill towns is extra. Closed Sunday.

L'Arciliuto, 5 Piazza Monte Vecchio (tel. 659-419), will revive the romantic in you. It was the former studio of Raphael. In fact, in its restoration a rare fresco by the great master was discovered. In this atmosphere of sienna-colored walls and vaulted ceilings, you can quietly sip drinks and listen to one of Italy's best known musicians, Enzo Samaritani, who opened the club after winning wide audiences for his recordings. He performs these personalized, warm, and graceful concerts in a subdued candlelight setting, with many guests sitting on sofas, as in a living room. The club lies only a short walk from the Piazza Navona. But it's easy to get lost.

Da Meo Patacca, 30 Piazza dei Mercanti (tel. 581-6198), is a theatrical fantasy for dining in Trastevere. Meals are served in a vaulted cellar, while you're entertained by strolling musicians and singers who come around to serenade. The decor is rustic, in the country-tavern style, with farming paraphernalia on the stone walls, including ox yokes and Sicilian carts. All this extravaganza was created in 1959 when Remington Olmsted visited the Eternal City while he was playing Judd in *Oklahoma!* He has since sold the restaurant. The antipasto is big enough to finish you off for the evening. The menu is likely to feature everything from quail on the spit to wild boar to corn on the cob. You also get thick-cut sirloins and chicken on a spit. A pasta specialty is wide noodles with hare sauce, or you might begin with onion soup. Another good dish is the Roman mixed grill. Ice cream follows. Expect to pay from 45,000 lire ($27.45) and up for a meal. In summer, alfresco tables are placed on the piazza itself.

The success of Da Meo Patacca prompted Mr. Olmsted to open **Da Ciceraucchio,** on the same square, although he has now sold it too. It was once a sunken jail, its vine-covered walls dating back to the heyday of the Roman Empire. The address is 1 Via del Porto (tel. 580-6046). Featured here are steaks and chops, charcoal-broiled right out in the open. Plenty of local wine is on tap. Bean soup is a specialty, although you may prefer to begin with grilled mushrooms or spaghetti with clams. Beefsteak is one of the most popular items, and you can get it charcoal-grilled. Complete dinners are served here nightly, except Monday, costing from 40,000 lire ($24.40).

On the same square is **Ar Fieramosca,** 3 Piazza dei Mercanti (tel. 589-0289), which is named after a medieval knight. It is decorated in the rustico style, and is known for its charcoal-grilled meats, its huge buffet, and its pizzas. Expect to pay at least 40,000 lire ($24.40) for a complete meal. The restaurant is closed on Wednesday.

Some Elegant Bars

Fontana Hotel, 96 Piazza di Trevi (tel. 678-6113), has very quickly become one of the most unusual and chicest little bars in Rome. While there is soft piano music played from 6 p.m. till 2 a.m., it is the situation that counts. The bar is on the top floor of a converted 13th-century monastery that has been turned into a tasteful and charming little hotel. The Piano Bar, in contrast, is in stark black and white. Picture windows have been inserted between the beamed walls, allowing for a spectacular view of the illuminated Trevi Fountain at night. Drinks begin at 10,000 lire ($6.10), or whatever the waiter thinks you'll pay. An elevator will take you to the top.

Baretto, 55 Via Condotti (tel. 678-4566), as its name implies, is a postage-stamp-size bar that has become the darling of many glamorous Romans who are amused by the chicly discreet black decor and the fact that there is no sign over the entrance. A small canopy marks the entrance on one of Rome's most exclusive shopping streets. Inside its cramped quarters you'll have trouble finding a seat, but the ambience may be worth the visit. It is open from 11:30 a.m. in time to catch the Gucci shoppers, closing at 9:30 p.m. It is also closed on Sunday.

The Arch of Titus and the Colosseum

Chapter VIII

ONE-DAY TRIPS FROM ROME

ROME IS FORTUNATE to be surrounded by a countryside that has delighted Romans and foreigners for thousands of years. The attractions are varied—beaches, ancient temples, Renaissance palaces—and all are within easy trip distance. While I have outlined means of public transportation, here's where a rental car really comes in handy.

Tivoli

An ancient town, Tivoli has origins that probably predate those of Rome itself. At the height of the empire "Tibur," as it was called, was a favorite retreat for the rich. Horace, Catullus, Sallust, Maecenas, and a few emperors (notably Hadrian) maintained lavish villas here near the woods and waterfalls. It was popular enough to warrant a Roman road, the Via Tiburtina, whose modern descendant funnels trucks and tour buses into today's Tivoli. During the Middle Ages, Tivoli achieved a form of independence, which was to last through her rise in fortunes during the Renaissance. This latter period saw real-estate investment by several of the wealthier princes of the church, especially Cardinal Ippolito d'Este. By the late 19th century, Tivoli had been incorporated into the new kingdom of Italy, and her former privileges of independence passed into history.

Below the foothills on which Tivoli is built lies a gently sloping plain, the site of the **Villa of Hadrian** (A.D. 135). Today the ruins cover slope after slope of the rolling terrain, fully 180 acres of villa. Hadrian was a widely traveled and highly cultured man. He was also something of an amateur architect, and much of the villa was designed by him. It was built as a heaven on earth in which to spend a long and luxurious retirement, a retirement surrounded by a court that numbered in the hundreds. Having traveled extensively as a general, Hadrian had seen much of the world, and he sought to recreate in his villa at Tibur those sights that most pleased him. Hadrian did not wish to build replicas of just rooms, or even palaces he had seen: he reconstructed entire valleys complete with the temples that had made them famous (the Canopus on the estate is one example). Much of the ruin is readily recognizable, and it's easy to wander around the hot baths and the cold baths and experience a real sense of the villa as it once was. In addition to the Poekile, the Lyceum, the valley of Tempe (named after a vale in Thessaly), the Academy, and the beautiful Canopus (a replica of a sacred canal linking the Nile to the Temple of Serapis), there was even an Inferno. (This last attraction is in an olive grove lying in a portion of the villa that hasn't yet been excavated, so it's hard to visit.)

Hadrian didn't live long enough to enjoy the full pleasure he expected from the villa; he died of a painful and undiagnosed illness three years after its completion. Legend has it that he was able to perform miracles on his deathbed—restoring sight to the blind and that sort of thing.

The villa is open from 9 a.m. to 7:30 p.m. (till 5 p.m. in winter), charging 3000 lire ($1.83) for admission. It's free on Sunday.

The Villa Adriana, as the signs call it, lies just off Via Tiburtina to the right before Tivoli. Buses connect it directly with Rome (leaving from the Piazza della Repubblica).

FOOD AND LODGING: It's possible to spend the night in Tivoli, or perhaps you'd prefer a weekend, exploring the hill towns at leisure, without having to make the difficult trip in and out of Rome.

The **Residence Torre S. Angelo,** Via Quintilio Varo (tel. 23292), is an adapted 15th-century Roman castle, where you can live in serenity. On the ledge of a hill, it was built of natural cut stone, with a five-story square tower, a tiled roof, and a magnificent view from most rooms. Bedrooms are consistently rustic, with terracotta tile floors and 17th-century country-style furnishings. Singles with private bath rent for 45,000 lire ($27.45), increasing to 110,000 lire ($67.10) in a double with private bath. The dining room is lofty and baronial, with huge beams, tall windows, and tiled floors. The guest lounges as well have fashionable colors and rustic furnishings intermixed with more sophisticated pieces, such as 16th-century oil paintings and one-of-a-kind antiques. You can alternate days of sightseeing with periods of relaxation around the swimming pool.

An attractive idea for an overnight stay in Tivoli or for a

At Tivoli the clutter and clamor of 20th-century Italy is forgotten in two perfect gems from the Renaissance, the Villa d'Este and the Villa Gregoriana. The more important by far is the **Villa d'Este,** so named after the 16th-century cardinal who transformed it from a government palace (it had been built in the 13th century as a Benedictine convent) into a princely residence that remained in the cardinal's family until 1918.

The 16th-century frescoes and decorations of the place are attractive, but unexceptional. The garden on the sloping hill beneath is another story—a perfect fairytale of the Renaissance, using water as a medium of sculpture, much the way the ancients used marble. There are fountains in every imaginable size and shape. Pathways are lined with 100 fountains, and stairs are flanked with cascades on either side. There are fountains you can walk under, fountains you can walk over, and long reflecting pools with surreal trees in between. The fountains have names—*Owl and Bird,* the *Oval Fountain, Fountain of Glass*—and in centuries past, might possibly have concealed practical jokes. The Renaissance aristocracy were immensely amused by a shot of water in someone else's eye.

The villa is open from 9 a.m. to two hours before sunset, charging 4000 lire ($2.44) for admission. Sunday is free. The fountains are floodlit every evening, except Monday, from 9 p.m. till midnight. Entrance then is 5000 lire ($3.05), which may go even higher.

Whereas the Villa d'Este dazzles with man-made glamor, the **Villa Gregoriana** relies more on nature. At one point on the circuitous walk carved along a slope, visitors stand and look out onto the most spectacular waterfall (Aniene) at Tivoli. The trek to the bottom on the banks of the Annio is studded with grottoes, plus balconies opening onto the chasm. The only problem is, if you do make the full journey, you may need to have a helicopter summoned to lift you back up again (the climb is fierce). From one of the belvederes is an exciting view of the Temple of Vesta on the hill. The gardens were built by Pope Gregory XVI in the 19th century. The villa is open from 9 a.m. to one hour before sunset daily and costs 900 lire (55¢) to enter.

Tivoli is 20 miles from Rome on the Via Tiburtina, about an hour's drive with traffic. Alternatively, you can take a bus from Via Gaeta downtown. Buses leave about every 15 minutes.

well-prepared meal might be the **Eden Sirene,** which lies behind an ochered neoclassical facade at the end of an alley at 4 Piazza Massimo (tel. 21352). The restaurant is on a long terrace, which you'll reach from a flight of marble steps that begins near the hotel entrance. The Ceruleo family runs this idyllic place, where summertime diners can choose between two terraces, each of which is built above a steep ravine with views of the gardens of the Villa Gregoriana and the Temple of Vesta, and a splashing waterfall where, on sunny days, the local housewives still do their laundry. Of course, on cold nights, you can dine inside in one of the two spacious rooms, with pink napery and lots of rustic artifacts.

Typical Italian meals range from 30,000 lire ($18.30) up, and could include cannelloni Sirene or chicken from Valdarno. It is closed Monday and for a few days every year between Christmas and New Year's. If you're planning on spending the night, the establishment maintains some 14 rooms. Bathless singles cost around 15,000 lire ($9.15), while bathless doubles go for 25,000 lire ($15.25). Doubles with bath cost 35,000 lire ($21.35).

Restaurant Sibilla, 50 Via della Sibilla (tel. 20281), is a landmark restaurant with a second-century B.C. temple in its private garden. In fair weather, you can choose one of a collection of tables running right up to the foundation of what the friendly owners, Enzo and Maria Fritella, claim is the oldest remaining temple in Italy. Called the Temple of Vesta (also known as Sibilla), it is occasionally visited by art historians who travel many miles just to see it. You, however, can combine your cultural visit with well-prepared regional cooking, scents from the overhead wisteria, and the views across the precipice to a crashing waterfall. An elegant interior room has terracotta walls, old lace in gilt frames, and a mosaic tile floor. Specialties are cannelloni, trout freshly caught in the Annio, and a mouthwatering soufflé. If you decide to dine here, you'll be interested to know that you have been preceded by French author and statesman Vicomte Chateaubriand in 1803 and by Princess Margaret of Britain in 1965. The price of a complete meal, depending on what you order, will range from 25,000 lire ($15.25) up.

Albergo Ristorante Adriano, Villa Adriana (tel. 529-174), might be the perfect stopover point either before or after you visit Hadrian's Villa. At the bottom of the villa's hill, in an ochered building a few steps from the ticket office, it offers terrace dining under verdant plane trees in summer or indoor dining in a high-ceilinged room with terracotta walls, neoclassical moldings, and

Corinthian pilasters painted white. Menus include roast lamb, saltimbocca, a variety of veal dishes, deviled chicken, a selection of salads and cheeses, and simple desserts. Expect to spend about 18,000 lire ($10.98) to 27,000 lire ($16.47) per person.

Palestrina

For those of you who rent a car, the Temple of Fortuna Primigenia at Palestrina is an ideal sight to combine with the Villa Adriana. The drive from Rome is on Via Prenestina, a much more untrafficked roadway than Via Tiburtina. Like Tibur, ancient Preneste (as Palestrina was called) was a superb holiday spot, the favorite of Horace and Pliny, and even Hadrian, who maintained a villa here.

The town was really known for the great temple, which covered most of the hill where Palestrina stands today. In its inner sanctum was an oracle, to which thousands journeyed regularly from Rome over the ancient stone road. As it was the fashion for emperors to enlarge and beautify temples and public facilities, the Temple of Fortuna grew to fabulous proportions. But its magnificence fell into rapid decay at the end of the fourth century, when pagan temples were ordered closed by the Christian Imperial government of Theodosius. During the Middle Ages it was a stronghold for a string of families—the physical situation on top of Mount Ginestro was perfect—the last of which, the Barberini, erected a palace at the summit of the temple. The great sanctuary was almost forgotten until World War II, when Allied bombers made runs on Palestrina and uncovered the ruins with exploding bombs.

Today Palestrina consists of a modern town at the foot of Mount Ginestro, the excavated levels of the temple on the slopes above, the Barberini palace at the highest point of the temple (with a fascinating museum), and a fantastic tangle of medieval streets on the crown of the mountain. In the Barberini museum is a collection of Etruscan odds and ends, a mosaic of the Nile at flood from the Fortuna sanctuary (a beautiful piece on the top floor of the museum), and a view of the surrounding countryside that certainly makes you feel like a Renaissance prince.

From November to February hours are 9 a.m. to 4 p.m. in March and October to 5 p.m., in September to 5:30 p.m., in May to 6:30 p.m., and June through August to 7:30 p.m. Admission is 1500 lire (92¢).

Palestrina is 23 miles from Rome, and you can either take the twisting Via Prenestina, or the Autostrada (A2), getting off at Valmontane; the latter routing requires much less time. Buses leave Rome from Via Castro Pretorio.

The Castelli Romani

The name means "Roman Castles," which they're not. The castelli are really a series of little hill towns, grouped on mountain slopes around two lakes. Some are extremely ancient, and all have been popular as holiday retreats at least since the days of the empire. The best way to visit the castelli is with a car, especially since many of the towns don't have enough to keep you occupied for more than an hour or so. Without a car, you will have to take one of the many buses serving the castelli.

Marino is the closest to Rome (only 15 miles); it's about 4½ miles off the Via Appia Nuova quite near Ciampino Airport. Much of Marino's original charm has fallen victim to modern builders, but the town is still the place to go each October, during the grape harvest. At that time, the town's fountains are switched from water to wine, and everyone can drink for free.

Rocca di Papa is the most attractive of the hill towns, and it lies only some six miles from Marino. The best road if you're driving is over 217 to the junction with 218, where a left turn is made. Before the intersection, you'll be high on a ridge above Lake Albano—the views of the lake, the far woods, and the papal palace of Castel Gandolfo on the opposite mountain are superb. Just before Rocca di Papa is the entrance to the toll road to Monte Cavo. Once a temple to Jove stood on top of this mountain, and before that, the tribes of the area met with King Tarquin (the Proud) before Rome was a republic. Atop the mountain is a restaurant with reasonable prices and a perfectly incredible view of the surrounding Alban Hills and hill towns. Down below, Rocca di Papa has nothing but a number of charming streets and churches. A legend of dubious origin claims that Hannibal once camped just below the town in a wooded hollow.

From Rocca di Papa, it's only a short drive to **Nemi**, a tiny town clinging to a woody precipice above the lake of the same name. The ancient Romans knew these parts well. A temple to Diana once stood in the valley and the lake was called her "looking glass." Today there's not much to see, however. If October is the time for Marino, May is the ideal time for Nemi, when a festival is held in honor of the local strawberries.

Looking from any of the balconies in Nemi, you'll see what

looks like an airplane hangar in the valley right by the lake's shore. This unprepossessing building has the important-sounding name of "Museo delle Navi Romane," and until the last war, it held remains of two luxurious barges that floated in the lake during the reign of Caligula (assassinated A.D. 41). The boats, which were fitted out lavishly with bronze and marble, were sunk during the reign of Claudius (he succeeded the insane Caligula), and were entirely forgotten until Mussolini drained the lake in the '30s. The barges were found, set up in a lakeside museum, and remained as a wonder of ancient Rome until the Nazis burned them (out of spite) during their retreat from Rome and environs in World War II.

Castel Gandolfo is our next stop, and the road leads us through a few charming towns on the way. **Genzano,** on the other side of Lake Nemi, has beautiful views of the countryside, and a 17th-century palace that belonged to the Sforza-Cesarini.

Ariccia is an ancient town that sent representatives to meet with Tarquin the Proud on top of Monte Cavo 2500 years ago. After many centuries of changing hands, especially between medieval and Renaissance families, it has taken on a suburban look. The palace in the middle of town is still private, belonging to the Chigi family.

Albano practically adjoins Castel Gandolfo. It has a fabulous history—this is the reputed site of Alba Longa, the mother city of Rome—but it's quite built up today.

Now we come to **Castel Gandolfo,** the summer residence of the pope. The papal palace, a 17th-century edifice designed by Carlo Maderno, stands practically on the foundations of another equally sumptuous summer residence, the villa of the emperor Domitian. Unfortunately, the palace, the gardens, and the adjoining Villa Barberini can't be visited. You'll have to content yourself with the pretty piazza out front with its church and fountain by Bernini.

Finally, **Frascati** is the best known hill town of them all, lying only 13 miles from Rome out the Via Tuscolana. Some 1073 feet above sea level, Frascati is celebrated for its white wines. Golden vineyards cover the surrounding northern slopes of the outer crater ring of the Alban hills. From its lofty perch, a panoramic view of the campagna and the other castelli can be seen.

At one time Frascati was the chicest mountain resort for Roman society, the wealthy patricians erecting villas there, with elaborate gardens and spectacular fountains. Later the town belonged mainly to the papacy. From that period dates the most important villa, the **Villa Aldobrandini,** which owes part of its look to Maderno, the designer of the facade of St. Peter's. To visit the gardens, which are open only in the morning, go to Azienda di Soggiorno e Turismo, 1 Piazza Marconi (tel. 940-331). They are closed on Sunday. The villa was built for a wealthy cardinal.

About three miles past the villa, motorists can reach **Tuscolo,** a spot known to the ancients with an amphitheater dating from the first century B.C. From here, one of the most spectacular views in all the castelli is possible.

Finally, the **Villa Torlonia,** bombed in the Second World War, has been converted into a public park, celebrated for its Theater of the Fountains, with a spectacular "sound, light, and water" display in summer.

To sample some of that golden white wine yourself, in Frascati head for **Cantina Comandini,** 1 Via E. Filiberto, right off the Piazza Roma. Comandini Antonio welcomes you to his wine cellar, a "rustico" tavern in which he sells Frascati wine from his own vineyards. You can stop off here and drink the vino on the spot at only 2200 lire ($1.34) per liter. Mr. Antonio, if he has the time, might also take you on a tour of his grottoes where his select vintage bottles are carefully placed. The tavern is closed on Sunday.

Lido di Ostia

The history of this congested beachfront goes back only to 1926 when the first highway linking Rome to the coast was built. Prior to that, it was a malaria-ridden waste, unvisited and unwanted. Lido di Ostia is also served by the subway system, so it's easy to reach. That fact is, however, a mixed blessing, since the beach crowds can get quite heavy on weekends.

If you're spending a day at the beach, the best place for a meal is **Vecchia Pineta,** Piazzale dell'Aquilone (tel. 562-9277), near the end of the Metro stop. Seafood, naturally, is the specialty. For an opener, I'd suggest zuppa di cozze, a savory kettle of mussels from Gaeta Bay, served in a piquant marinade sauce. Other specialties include risotto con scampi, raviolini alla crème, and fritto di calamari, gamberi, e moscardini. For a complete seafood dinner, expect to pay from 30,000 lire ($18.30).

Ostia Antica

Ostia was the port of Rome and a city in its own right. The currents and uneven bottom of the Tiber prevented Mediterranean shipping from going farther upstream. Merchandise was transferred to barges for the remainder of the trip. Ostia's fate was tied closely to that of the empire. At the peak of Rome's power the city had 100,000 inhabitants—hard to imagine looking at today's ruins. Ostia was important enough to have a theater (still standing in reconstructed form), numerous temples and baths, great patrician houses, and a large business complex. Successive emperors enlarged and improved the facilities, notably Claudius and Trajan, but by the time of Constantine (fourth century) the tide was turning. The barbarian sieges of Rome in the fifth century spelled the end of Ostia. Without the empire to trade with and Rome to sell to, she quickly withered, reverting within a few centuries to a malarial swamp without a trace of Roman civilization. The excavations, still only partial, were started by the papacy in the 19th century, but the really substantial work took place between 1938 and 1942 under the Fascist government.

Ostia Antica is one of the nicest afternoons you can spend near Rome. It's relatively secluded, and the ruins are fascinating. There are perfect picnic spots beside fallen columns or near old temple walls, and it's even easy to reach. The subway lets you off across the highway that connects Rome with the coast. It's just a short walk to the excavations. While you're there, be sure to see the museum with its fine collection of statuary found in the ruins. Entrance to the grounds is 3000 lire ($1.83), and hours are from 9 a.m. till one hour before sunset. Closed Monday.

Fregene

On the coastline north of the Tiber lies Fregene, a town under the jurisdiction of Rome. Fregene is known for its magnificent pine trees, which have a fine story behind them. They were planted in an age when rich men did large things. The land in the late 1600s belonged to the Rospigliosi, one of Rome's powerful families. Clement IX, a Rospigliosi son who became pope, planted a forest 2½ miles long and 2624 feet deep, and 300 years later we have the pines of Fregene. The forest was planted to protect the inland areas from the sea winds, which damaged crops, but today they form a scenic background for a collection of posh villas and a golden-sand beach. Although most of the beach has been divided by concessionaires (with more attractive results than at Lido di Ostia), there are various slivers of free beach within walking distance of the bus stop. In addition to the beach, large areas of the pine forest have been preserved as a park, making for some really good walks.

If you're driving, the best way to Fregene is on Via Aurelia, which you can pick up behind St. Peter's and the Vatican. Once past the outskirts, the road is excellent and toll free.

La Conchiglia ("The Shellfish"), 4 Piazzale a Mare (tel. 64-60-229), in Fregene, is a beachfront hotel and restaurant. Built in pine woods with excellent sea views, La Conchiglia has an all-white circular lounge, with curving wall banquettes facing a cylindrical raised fireplace hearth. Cubical upholstered chairs sit in loggias, and large green plants add a resort note. In the cocktail lounge, a circular bar faces the terrace and is padded with foot-wide plastic rolls, somebody's idea of chic. In high season, full board ranges in price from 85,000 lire ($51.85) to 100,000 lire ($61) per person, including service and taxes. If you're stopping by only for a meal, you can dine in the circular, bamboo-covered garden restaurant. There, the best beginning is a home-made gnocchi, followed by scampi al curry or one of the many good-tasting meat dishes.

Anzio–Nettuno

Anzio has the dubious distinction of being the birthplace of both Caligula and Nero, two of history's greater misrulers. From its position in the ancient world as a fashionable seaside resort and major port (thanks to Nero), Anzio followed the familiar pattern after the collapse of Rome, and reverted to swamp. The city was rescued from periodic Saracen raids by the papacy, which eventually rebuilt the port in the late 17th century. Anzio and adjoining Nettuno are resorts again in the 20th century, but it's really too far from Rome for just a day at the beach.

Many Americans remember Anzio from January 22, 1944, the date of the Allied landing that led to the liberation of Rome. The vast U.S. cemetery at Nettuno is a grim souvenir of those terrible years. It is still the goal of many pilgrims visiting graves of those who died during that week some 40 years ago. Likewise, the British cemetery at Anzio is still visited.

Anzio is nearly 44 miles from Rome—much of the road has heavy traffic—and a car is the fastest and most convenient way to get there. There is public transportation from Via Carlo Felice in Rome.

The Etruscan Mystery

As Livy's Trojans landed in ancient Italy, so did the Etruscans. Who were they? We still don't know, and the many inscriptions they left behind—mostly on graves—are no help since the Etruscans' language has never since been deciphered. We deduce the date of their arrival on the west coast of Umbria as several centuries before Rome was built, probably around 800 B.C. Their religious rites and architecture show an obvious contact with Mesopotamia. That they came from the general area is further likely due to some 13th-century B.C. Egyptian monuments whose inscriptions describe raids on the Nile delta by a warlike people called the "Turuscha." But why did they come to Italy? Perhaps they were forced from their home, literally pushed into the sea with no choice but to find a new homeland. We know that they arrived in Italy in large numbers and within two centuries had subjugated Tuscany and Campania and the Villanova tribes who lived there. The Etruscans appeared disinterested in having land of their own to till. Rather they forced the Latin tribes to work the land for them and support them as an aristocratic class of princes.

While the Etruscans built temples at Tarquinia and Caere (present-day Cerveteri), the few nervous Latin tribes who remained outside their sway consolidated power at Rome. They remained free of the Etruscans until about 600 B.C. thanks mainly to the presence of Greek colonies on the Italian coast, which tended to hold back Carthaginians on one side and Etruscans on the other. But the Etruscan advance was as inexorable as that of the later Roman Empire, and by 600 B.C. there was an Etruscan stronghold in the hills above Rome. The frightened tribes concentrated their forces at Rome for a last stand, but were swept away by the sophisticated Mesopotamian conqueror. And when the new overlords took over, they not only introduced gold tableware and jewelry, bronze urns and terracotta statuary, and the best of Greek and Mesopotamian art and culture, but they made Rome the government seat of all of Latium.

Roma is an Etruscan name, and the kings of Roma had Etruscan names too—Numa, Ancus, Tarquinius, even Romulus. Under the combined influences of the Greek and Mesopotamian east, Roma grew enormously. A new port was opened at Ostia.

The artists from Greece carved statues of Roman gods who looked like Greek divinities. The "Servian" army was established, and since soldiers had to provide their own horses and armor, the result was that the richest citizens carried the heaviest burden of protection. We can see now how this classification by wealth, which also affected voting and law-making, stemmed from a democratic concept of the army, but led to an undemocratic concept of society.

Two former strongholds of the Etruscans can be visited today, Cerveteri and Tarquinia.

The best way to reach Cerveteri is on the Via Aurelia through the rolling hills of the Roman campagna. You'll eventually see the city's medieval walls up in the hills on your right; on the left are the modern towers of Ladispoli, a rapidly growing seaside town.

Cerveteri is older than Rome. It stands on the site of a major Etruscan stronghold called Caere. It's the Etruscan heritage that brings visitors to Cerveteri today, for while the Caere of the living has long vanished, the Caere of the dead still exists in an amazing state of preservation. Next to their city, the Etruscans built an important necropolis, a city of tombs. Most of the circular, dome-shaped graves date from the seventh century B.C., and several have been found completely intact, untouched since their doors were sealed 2600 years ago. The necropolis lies on the other side of a small valley from the medieval battlements, and it's still surrounded by grape fields. There is no sound here (songbirds are eaten in Italy) except the rather ghostly moans of wind in the pine trees. Only a portion of the necropolis is excavated, but it's quite extensive. You can climb in and out of the tombs, decorated inside as Etruscan homes were. Note the absence of the arch, an architectural innovation of the later Romans. Many of the treasures in the Villa Giulia in Rome came from Caere, and many other priceless pieces of that distant culture are on display in the Orsini Castle in the medieval part of Cerveteri. The necropolis, 1¼ miles north of Cerveteri, is open May 1 to September 30 from 9 a.m. to 7 p.m. (otherwise, 9 a.m. to 4 p.m.). Closed Monday. Admission is 2000 lire ($1.22).

The castle has been converted into a delightful museum—interesting without being defeatingly large. It contains a rare collection of Etruscan pottery, among other exhibits.

When you're through visiting the necropolis and the museum, it's pleasant to stroll around the twisting lanes of the town, pausing perhaps at the battlements to survey the vastness of the

ITALY
AUSTRIA
SWITZERLAND
FRANCE
Dolomites
LAKE MAGGIORE
LAKE OF COMO
LAKE GARDA
MILAN
VENICE
YUGOSLAVIA
PAVIA
GENOA
Italian Riviera
RAVENNA
ADRIATIC SEA
FLORENCE
SIENA
PERUGIA
ASSISI
ROME
Sardinia
NAPLES
ISCHIA
CAPRI
TYRRHENIAN SEA
PALERMO
Sicily
TAORMINA
SYRACUSE
MEDITERRANEAN SEA

countryside. The Tyrrhenian Sea glitters in the sunshine, and Ladispoli rises like a dream city on the shore.

An even more striking museum is at **Tarquinia,** 13 miles above the port of Civitavecchia, which was the port of Rome in the days of Trajan. The situation of Tarquinia is commanding, with a view of the sea. It is remarkably medieval in appearance, with its fortifications and nearly two dozen towers. The **Tarquinia National Museum,** Piazza Cavour (tel. 856-036), is housed in the Gothic Renaissance Palazzo Vitelleschi, dating from 1439. It displays a large number of sarcophagi and Etruscan exhibits removed from the nearby necropolis. But the reason people drive up here all the way from Rome is to see a pair of winged horses, removed from the fronton of a temple. This work by some unknown artist numbers among the great masterpieces ever discovered of Etruscan art. The museum is open daily except Monday from 9 a.m. to 2 p.m., to 1 p.m. on Sunday. Admission is 2000 lire ($1.22).

The tombs are about four miles southeast of the town itself. Inquire at the museum about a guided tour. The most important tombs here are chambers hewn out of rock, containing well-preserved paintings. Actually, the necropolis covers more than 2½ miles of windswept ground, containing hundreds upon hundreds of tombs—not all of which have been visited by the "tombaroli" or grave-robbers. A guide shows you the most important tombs. The paintings give an intimate glimpse of the daily life of the Etruscans, including their customs, beliefs, and religion. One of the most important dates from the fifth century B.C. Paintings there depict guests at a banquet, lying on beds, waited on by naked ephebes. Colors include red and pale pink from iron oxide, blue from the dust of lapis lazuli, and black from charcoal. To visit the necropolis, you leave from the museum from 10 a.m. to 1 p.m. in winter and also during the afternoon in summer.

Chapter IX

FLORENCE

ON THE BANKS of the Arno, Florence had been a Roman stronghold since the first century B.C., but it was not until after A.D. 1200 that it began to come into its own as a commercial and cultural center. During the 13th century the merchants and tradesmen organized the guilds that were to control the economy and government of Florence for nearly 150 years. These guilds supervised the construction of several important buildings of the city, and with their newfound wealth, commissioned works of art that were to adorn the churches and palaces.

This revival of interest in art and architecture brought about the Italian Renaissance, an amazing outburst of activity between the 14th and 16th centuries that completely changed the face of the Tuscan town. During its heyday under the benevolent eye (and purse) of the Medicis, the city was lavishly decorated with churches, palaces, galleries, and monuments, making it the world's greatest repository of art treasures. The list of geniuses who lived or worked here reads like a "who's who" in the world of art and literature: Dante (he "invented" the Italian language here), Boccaccio, Fra Angelico, Brunelleschi, Donatello, da Vinci, Raphael, Cellini, Michelangelo, Ghiberti, Giotto, and Pisano.

Efforts to preserve Florence as the "jewel of the Renaissance" have been successful, in spite of the calamities it has suffered during the past 400 years. Wars and floods have damaged some of its treasures. All the medieval bridges that once spanned the Arno are gone, destroyed by Nazi mortar attacks in World War II—except for the Ponte Vecchio ("Old Bridge"), where pedestrians still browse through the tiny jewelry and goldsmith shops that line the bridge. The flood of 1966 temporarily took the glow off the "jewel" also, but today Florence shines again almost as brightly as it did in the days of Michelangelo.

The best overall view of the city is from the **Piazzale Michelangelo** (take bus 13 from the Central Station), an elevated plaza on the south side of the river. If you can ignore the milling crowds and souvenir peddlers who flood the square, you can enjoy a spectacular view of old Florence, circled by the hazy hills of Tuscany. If you look up into the hills, you can also see the ancient town of Fiesole, with its Roman ruins and splendid cathedral.

The Major Sights

But the rich sightseeing attractions of Florence cannot be fully appreciated from afar. Many of its treasures cry out for a closer inspection, beginning with—

THE CATHEDRAL OF SANTA MARIA DEL FIORE: The cathedral of Florence, called simply the **Duomo,** is a splendid pile of green-and-white marble in geometric patterns, the climax of the Florentine-Gothic style of architecture. Begun in 1296 by Arnolfo di Cambio, it became a subject of such architectural controversy that it was not consecrated until nearly 150 years later. The controversy revolved around the monumental task of constructing the cathedral's dome: how could anyone build a dome to span 138½ feet? Some pretty wild suggestions were made, including filling the Duomo with a mountain of earth and building the dome on top of it. Finally, in 1417 the authorities accepted the design of Brunelleschi, who began building in 1420, tying in concentric layers as he went, using a herringbone system to absorb the strain of the inward curve. The overall effect of the dome atop its octagonal drum is one of the most striking sights of the city—and its most famous landmark.

The inside of the cathedral is almost plain in contrast to its grand exterior, but it does contain several important works of art, including the dome fresco of the *Last Judgment* by Vasari and Zuccari, a bronze urn by Ghiberti, and several terracottas by della Robbia. Some of the stained-glass windows were designed by Donatello and Ghiberti. You can climb to the top of the dome and more closely inspect the engineering feat of Brunelleschi and at the same time enjoy a delightful panorama of the city. It is open daily except Sunday from 8:30 a.m. to 12:30 p.m., and from 2:30 to 5:30 p.m. Admission is 3500 lire ($2.14). For another 2000 lire ($1.22) you can visit the basement of the cathedral, where recent excavations have revealed the ruins of the Cathedral of St. Reparata, dating from the fifth century.

Many of the treasures of the Duomo have been removed for

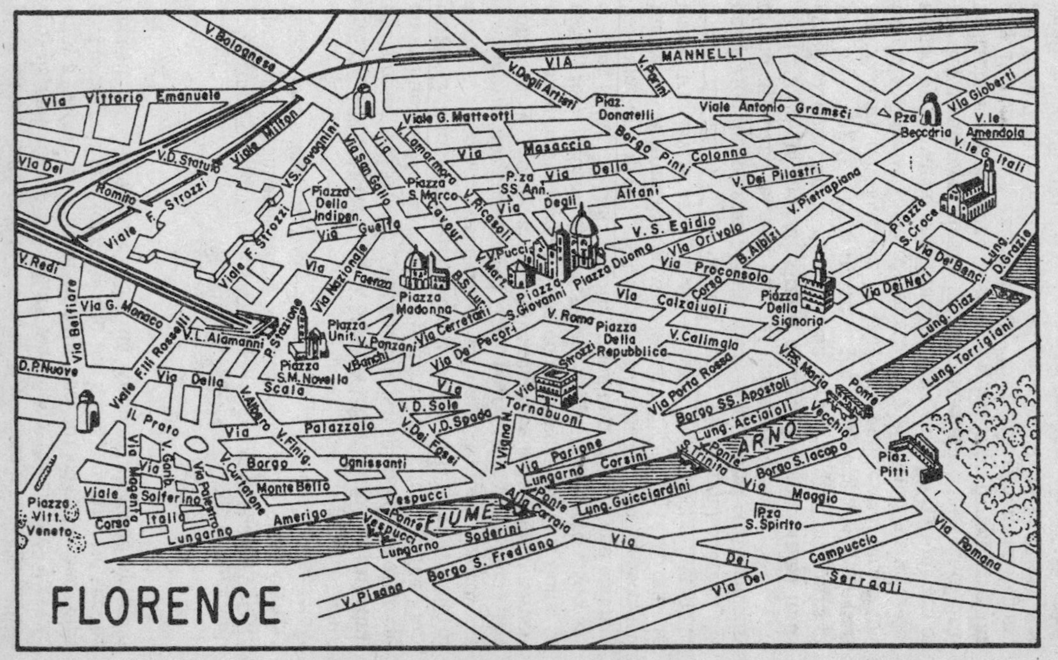
FLORENCE
V. Bolognese
VIA MANNELLI
Via Vittorio Emanuele
V. Degli Artisti
V. Parini
Viale G. Matteotti
Piaz. Donatelli
Viale Antonio Gramsci
Pza Beccaria
Via Gioberti
V. le Amendola
V. le G. Itali
Via Dei
V.D. Statuto
Viale Milton
V.S. Lavagnini
Via San Gallo
V. Lamarmora
Via Masaccio
Borgo Pinti
Colonna
Romito
Viale F. Strozzi
Piazza Della Indipen.
Piazza S. Marco
P.za SS. Ann.
Via Della
V. Dei Pilastri
V. Pietrapiana
Cavour
V. Ricasoli
Via Degli Alfani
Via Guelfa
V. S. Egidio
Piazza S. Croce
Via Dei Benci
Lung. D. Grazie
V. Redi
Via Nazionale
Faenza
Piazza Madonna
V. Pucci
Via Orivolo
B. Albizi
Via Proconsolo
Via Dei Neri
Via Belfiore
Via G. Monaco
Viale F.lli Rosselli
V.L. Alamanni
P. Stazione
Piazza Unit.
V. Panzani
Via Cerretani
B.S. Lor.
V. Mart.
Piazza S. Giovanni
Piazza Duomo
Corso
Via Calzaiuoli
Piazza Della Signoria
Lung. Diaz
D.P. Nuove
Piazza S.M. Novella
V. Banchi
Via De' Pecori
V. Roma
Piazza Della Repubblica
V. Calimala
Lung. Torrigiani
Via Della Scala
V. Alloro
V. Strozzi
Via Porta Rossa
V.P.S. Maria
Ponte Vecchio
IL Prato
V.D. Sole
V.D. Spada
Via Tornabuoni
Borgo SS. Apostoli
Lung. Acciaioli
ARNO
Via Palazzolo
V. Finig.
V. Dei Fossi
V. Vigna N.
Via Parione
Lungarno Corsini
S. Trinita
Ponte
Borgo S. Iacopo
Piaz. Pitti
Via V. Garib.
Via Magenta
Via Palestro
V. Curtatone
Borgo Ognissanti
Monte Bello
Viale
Solferino
Piazza Vitt. Veneto
Corso Italia
Lungarno Amerigo Vespucci
Ponte Vespucci
FIUME
Ponte Alla Carraia
Lung. Guicciardini
Via Maggio
Pza S. Spirito
Lungarno Soderini
Borgo S. Frediano
Via Dei Serragli
Campuccio
Via Romana
V. Pisana

safekeeping to the **Museo dell'Opera del Duomo,** 9 Piazza del Duomo, facing the apse of the cathedral. The star attraction of this museum is now the unfinished *Pietà* by Michelangelo, which is in the middle of the stairs. It was carved between 1548 and 1555 when the artist was in his 70s. In this vintage work, a figure representing Nicodemus (but said to have Michelangelo's face) is holding Christ. The great Florentine intended it for his own tomb, but he is believed to have grown disenchanted with it and to have attempted to destroy it. Also here you'll find designs and models of the Duomo, along with marble choir galleries (cantorie) by Luca della Robbia and Donatello that once hung over the sacristy doors. Other sculptures by Donatello include *Jeremiah* and *Habakkuk*. The museum is open weekdays from 9:30 a.m. to 1 p.m., and from 2:30 to 5:30 p.m. (Sunday until 1 p.m.), and charges 3500 lire ($2.14) for admission.

GIOTTO'S BELL TOWER: Although better known for his great skill in fresco painting (his creation of pictorial depth helped bring about the Renaissance in painting), Giotto was also a noted architect, appointed to preside over the construction of the Duomo after the death of Arnolfo di Cambio. It was in this capacity that he began his own monument in 1334, just three years before his death. Adjoining the right nave of the cathedral, the 274-foot campanile was only partially completed when it became Giotto's own tombstone. The upper stories, pierced with Gothic windows and covered with marble inlay, were added by Pisano, who, along with Luca della Robbia, decorated the lower portion with a series of bas reliefs. For 3500 lire ($2.14) you can enter the tower and climb the seemingly endless stairs. At the top is a memorable view—the sienna buildings of Florence at your feet, and the blue-green Tuscan hills in the distance. The tower is open daily from 8:30 a.m. to 12:30 p.m. and from 2:30 to 5:30 p.m.

THE BAPTISTERY OF SAN GIOVANNI: Facing the Duomo, the octagonal Baptistery is a splendid example of Romanesque architecture as only the Florentines could interpret it. Dating from the fifth century, it was virtually rebuilt in the 11th and 12th centuries with particularly Florentine innovations. The facade is covered with green-and-white marble, and set into three sides are magnificent bronze doors decorated with gilded bas reliefs. The south doors are the oldest, completed in 1336 by Andrea Pisano, and depicting scenes from the life of John the Baptist, the patron saint of the Baptistery.

The greatest treasures, however, are the East and West Doors, artistically created by Ghiberti under a commission awarded him by the cloth guild of Florence. The enterprise, one of the curtain raisers on the Renaissance, cost the guild 22,000 florins (a 15th-century Florentine could live in luxury on only 200 florins a year), and took Ghiberti a total of 52 years. After the second door was unveiled in 1452, Michelangelo adjudged it so beautiful that he dubbed it "The Gateway to Paradise." Ghiberti used biblical themes in his panels, including "The Meeting of Solomon and Sheba," thought to symbolize the union of the Eastern and Western churches, an event that was proclaimed from the steps of the nearby Duomo in 1439.

The Baptistery is open daily (no admission is charged). On the inside, you can admire the 13th-century mosaics that line the dome.

THE UFFIZI GALLERY: Outside the Prado and the Louvre, no art museum in the world can compare with the Uffizi. The 16th-century building stretches from the Palazzo Vecchio to the Arno, and was begun by Giorgio Vasari in 1560 for Cosimo di Medici, who wished to create a massive structure to house all the civic offices "for the greater ease of the public." When the Palazzo Vecchio was vacated by the Medicis later in the century for the more comfortable Pitti Palace, the administrative offices were moved to the "Old Palace," leaving the Uffizi free to be used for the art collections of the Medicis. When the Medici dynasty came to an end in 1737, the gallery became a public institution that today attracts nearly a million visitors each year.

In spite of its size and multitudinous works of art (about 2500 paintings alone, plus miniatures, statues, and more than 100,000 drawings and prints), the museum is easily navigated, since the galleries are grouped by periods and schools. But don't expect to see everything in one day. Laid out progressively, the galleries begin with Room 1 (classical sculptures) and extend through Room 5 (Italian and French paintings of the 18th century). The largest concentration of paintings is on Italian works of the 15th and 16th centuries (more than 400 of these alone). Room 2 is probably the most popular in the entire gallery. Here you'll find the works of Botticelli, including his *Birth of Venus* and *Primavera,* two of the world's most celebrated paintings.

Room 18, the octagonal "Tribune," is the most splendid in the museum, even when it contains no exhibits. The floor is inlaid with marble in geometric designs, and the domed ceiling is studded with pearl shells. The room's most prominent spot is occupied by the *Medici Venus,* a magnificent Greek sculpture, along with later copies of fourth-century Greek sculptures of *The Wrestler* and *Apollo.*

Although the bulk of the paintings in the Uffizi are works by Italian artists, from Giotto through the 18th-century painter Crespi—and including such masters as Raphael, Michelangelo, Fra Angelico, Filippo Lippi, Mantegna, Bellini, Titian, and Tintoretto—other countries are represented as well. Albrecht Dürer's *Madonna and Child,* Jan Brueghel's *The Great Calvary,* two self-portraits by Rubens, and three by Rembrandt are just a few of the works by northern painters.

The Uffizi is open daily, except Monday, from 9 a.m. to 7 p.m. (Sunday to 1 p.m.). Admission is 5000 lire ($3.05).

THE ACADEMY GALLERY: The museum at 60 Via Ricasoli (tel. 214-375) is visited mainly for one exhibit: Michelangelo's awesome statue of *David.* For years the 17-foot statue weathered the elements on the Piazza della Signoria, but was finally moved to the protection of the gallery in the 1870s. It stands alone in a great circular room, surrounded by hushed groups of admirers. Elsewhere in the gallery are half a dozen other masterpieces by Michelangelo, including the "Slave" series. The gallery of paintings includes works by Botticelli, Orcagna, Monaco, Lippi, Fra Bartolomeo, and Lorenzo di Credi. The Academy is open daily, except Monday, from 9 a.m. to 2 p.m. (on Sunday to 1 p.m.), and charges 2000 lire ($1.22) for admission. Free on Sunday.

THE MEDICI CHAPELS: Michelangelo left his mark on Florence in many places, but nowhere can you feel so completely surrounded by his works as in the Medici Chapels, adjoining the Basilica of San Lorenzo. Commissioned in 1520 by Cardinal Giulio di Medici (later Pope Clement VII), the chapels were designed as mausoleums for the "Signori" of Florence. Entering from the Piazza Madonna degli Aldobrandini, you'll find yourself wandering through a great maze of rooms, some of mammoth proportions, and all decorated with a lavishness of detail and integrity of materials that seems unbelievable today. The most impressive of these is the "New Sacristy," containing the tombs of two of the lesser Medicis, but some of Michelangelo's best works. Unfortunately, the only two members of the Medici family to be immortalized in marble in the tombs were the delicate Giuliano and the viciously ambitious Lorenzo II. Their statues preside over the sarcophagi, which are adorned with Michelangelo's allegorical masterpieces of *Dawn, Dusk, Night,* and *Day.* Lorenzo the Magnificent, the artist's mentor, is entombed in the same chapel, near an unfinished *Madonna and Child.* The chapels are open every day from 9 a.m. to 7 p.m. (to 4 p.m. in winter) on weekdays, and from 9 a.m. to 12:30 p.m. on Sunday. Closed Monday. Admission is 4000 lire ($2.44).

In a sepulchral chamber, beneath the chapel, a recent discovery brought to life 50 drawings by Michelangelo. It was called his "doodling sheet." The drawings are reached by going through a trapdoor, then down a winding staircase. The public is admitted in groups of about ten people at half-hour intervals. Michelangelo depicted such figures as the Laocoön, the great Hellenistic figure group, as well as Jesus risen, and the legs of Duke Giuliano. The drawings were done in charcoal on the rough plaster walls. Some, however, may be by students.

PIAZZA DELLA SIGNORIA: As the "front yard" of Florence's city hall, the Palazzo Vecchio, the Piazza della Signoria was the center of the city's political life from around A.D. 1300. In its heyday it was the scene of hangings (including the execution of the zealous monk, Savonarola, an event marked by a medallion in the square), book burnings, assassination plots, as well as some everyday lobbying. Today the square is a favorite tourist attraction, not only because of its historical significance, but for its wealth of artistic sights as well.

On the piazza is the **Fountain of Neptune,** a massively detailed work by Ammannati. Created in the 16th century, it portrays the sea god surrounded by his following of water creatures and woodland nymphs. Also on the plaza is a copy of Michelangelo's *David,* substituted for the original after it was removed to the safety of the Academy Gallery in 1873. Opening onto the square is the **Loggia dei Lanzi,** a spacious open hallway dating from the 14th century. It is lined with several important sculptures, all of them outshone by Cellini's brilliant masterpiece *Perseus Holding the Head of Medusa.*

On the adjoining side of the plaza is the great stone mass of the **Palazzo Vecchio** (tel. 27681), whose 308-foot tower by

Arnolfo di Cambio soars upward from the ramparts. Begun at the end of the 13th century, about the same time as the Duomo, the "Old Palace" was the seat of the Florentine government in the time of the tradesmen's guilds, and later became the palace of the Medici. Its rather stark facade is offset by a row of important statues, including Donatello's portrayal of *Judith Slaying Holofernes.* Placed at the palace after the expulsion of the Medici, it was a symbolic warning to tyrants. Although the interior of the palace today contains offices of city employees, several important salons and halls are open to the public. The most popular of these is the dei Cinquecento, the "Hall of the 500," with frescoes and sculptures by Vasari and his 20 assistants. Near the entrance is a sculpture by Michelangelo, his allegorical interpretation of *Victory.* You can also visit several small, but richly decorated salons with works by Vasari, Bronzino, and Verocchio. It is open every day except Saturday from 9 a.m. to 7 p.m. (Sunday and holidays, 8 a.m. to 1 p.m.). The palazzo charges 3500 lire ($2.14) for admission.

THE PITTI PALACE: Begun in the mid-15th century to a design by Brunelleschi, the Renaissance palace on the left bank of the Arno, just five minutes from the Ponte Vecchio, was once the "other" residence for the Medici clan. It was later the royal palace of Victor Emmanuel II, king of Italy, but today it is a museum, consisting of the **Silver Museum** (Museo degli Argenti), the **Royal Apartments,** the **Gallery of Modern Art,** and, most important, the **Palatine Gallery.** Devoted mainly to Renaissance works, the Palatine is especially rich in Raphaels, including his famous *Madonna of the Chair,* and the portrait of his mistress under the title *La Fornarina* ("the bakery girl"). Other works by Titian, Botticelli, Fra Bartolomeo, Filippo Lippi, Tintoretto, and Andrea del Sarto round out the Italian group, but such northern masters as Rubens and Van Dyck are also represented, as is Spain in the works of Velázquez and Murillo.

The Silver Museum, on the ground floor of the palace, is noted for several works, including the Medici Vase, by Buontalenti, delicately carved in lapis lazuli with a gold enameled mount. All the museums, except the Gallery of Modern Art, may be visited for the one entrance fee of 4000 lire ($2.44), and are open daily, except Monday, from 9 a.m. to 2 p.m. (to 1 p.m. on Sunday).

Behind the palace are the extensive **Boboli Gardens,** designed and executed by Tribolo, a landscape artist (on canvas and in real life), in the 16th century. Studded with fountains and statues, it provides an ideal setting for a relaxing break between museum visits. The gardens are also the setting for Fort Belvedere, an imposing structure that dominates the hillside and offers a spectacular view of Florence. The gardens are open daily in summer until 6:30 p.m. (till 4:30 in winter).

THE NATIONAL MUSEUM (BARGELLO): Begun in 1254, the medieval palace at 4 Via del Proconsolo was once a powerful military fortress. Today, as a museum, it exhibits the arms and armor used during the more violent periods of its history, along with a fine collection of decorative art. But the real attraction at the Bargello is the splendid array of medieval and Renaissance sculpture. There's another *David* by Michelangelo here, although not nearly as virile as the one in the Academy Gallery. Nor does it stand up to the most famous *David* here—Donatello's free-standing bronze creation, nude (except for boots and bonnet) atop the severed head of Goliath. Also by Donatello is his heroic and extremely lifelike interpretation of *St. George.* Michelangelo is represented in several works, including his *Bacchus,* a bust of Brutus, and a bas relief of a *Madonna and Child with John the Baptist.*

Benvenuto Cellini was one of the last of the great Renaissance sculptors, a protégé of Cosimo di Medici, whose idealized bronze bust is displayed. Included are an *Apollo* and *Narcissus,* as well as early versions of the magnificent *Perseus* which stands in the Loggia dei Lanzi. Other rooms contain a number of terracottas, some by Luca della Robbia. Also look for the bronze relief by Ghiberti depicting *The Sacrifice of Isaac.* The magnificent panel, enclosed within a quatrefoil shape, won the award for the artist in the competition for the doors of the Baptistery of San Giovanni near the Duomo. The museum is open every day except Monday, from 9 a.m. to 2 p.m. (to 1 p.m. on Sunday and holidays). Admission is 3000 lire ($1.83).

MUSEUM OF SAN MARCO: In 1437 Michelozzo began the renovations on a broken-down convent on what is today the Piazza San Marco, turning it into a monastery for the Dominicans. The pious Cosimo di Medici had a special affection for the San Marco monastery, and often stayed in the guest room reserved for such distinguished visitors as the pope. Fra Angelico, one of the resident friars, made his unique contribution to Florentine art by decorating the previously bleak cells with magnificent frescoes that are still colorful today, even though they were created more than 500 years ago.

One of his most famous works is *The Last Judgment,* a panel contrasting the beautiful angels and saints on the left with the demons and tortured sinners of hell on the right. Among his other works are a masterful *Annunciation,* and a magnificently colorful *Virgin and Child.* In all, the museum contains the largest collection of Angelico's panels and paintings. Other artists worked on the rooms as well: Ghirlandaio's *Last Supper* is extremely realistic; Fra Bartolomeo's portraits of Savonarola (the zealot was arrested in a cell here) and his *Madonna and Child with Saints.* Open daily except Monday from 9 a.m. to 2 p.m. (to 1 p.m. on Sunday), the San Marco Museum charges 3000 lire ($1.83) for admission; free on the first and third Saturday and the second and last Sunday of each month.

THE CHURCHES OF FLORENCE: Since art and religion went hand in hand in the years preceding and during the Renaissance, you'll find some of the greatest treasures in the city in its numerous churches. The great Franciscan **Church of Santa Croce** is an imposing Gothic monument, designed by Arnolfo di Cambio with frescoes by Giotto. The adjoining Pazzi Chapel was designed by Brunelleschi and contains terracottas by della Robbia. The church is the site of the tombs of such Italians as Michelangelo, Machiavelli, Galileo, Rossini, Ghiberti, and Alfieri.

Additionally, inside the monastery of this church, the Franciscan fathers established the **Leather School** at the end of World War II. The purpose of the school was to prepare young boys technically to specialize in Florentine leatherwork. The school has flourished and has produced many fine artisans, who continue their careers here. Stop in and see the work when you visit this church.

The **Church of Santa Maria Novella** (tel. 282-187) is a large Dominican edifice built between 1278 and 1350. On the Piazza Santa Maria Novella, its marble inlaid facade was added in the 15th century by Alberti. The church is especially interesting for its frescoes by Masaccio, Ghirlandaio, Orcagna, and Filippo Lippi. The adjoining cloisters, with a 3000-lira ($1.83) admission fee, are also worth a visit, especially the Spanish Chapel with frescoes by Andrea di Bonaiuto and his assistants. They are open daily except Friday from 9 a.m. to 7 p.m.

The **Church of San Lorenzo**, at the Piazza San Lorenzo, was begun in 1442 by Brunelleschi, and the interior completed by Manetti in 1460. Shaped like a Latin cross, the church was the favorite of the Medici (the adjoining "New Sacristy" contains the tombs of the clan), so a great deal of money and artistic effort went into decorating it. The Old Sacristy, at the left of the nave, was partially decorated by Donatello, including some terracotta reliefs. The adjoining **Laurenziana Library** was designed by Michelangelo to contain the huge Medici collection of manuscripts. Open free to the public from 9 a.m. to 5 p.m. on weekdays, it boasts an unusual staircase and an intricately carved and paneled exhibition room.

The **Church of Santa Maria del Carmine**, on the Piazza Santa Maria del Carmine, is a baroque church boasting early frescoes by Masaccio in its Brancacci Chapel. Unfinished at the master's death, the frescoes were completed by Filippo Lippi.

Where to Stay

Florence has a wide range of accommodations in all price ranges. Many hotels and pensions are housed in palaces or old Medici villas. I'll begin with the most expensive, then descend in price level.

THE DELUXE HOTELS: Hotel Excelsior, 3 Piazza Ognissanti (tel. 294-301), is the ultimate in well-ordered luxury during a stopover in Florence. Demand for the elegant bedrooms is so great that during peak season most of the accommodations are reserved weeks in advance. Pending the availability of space, however, the lucky guest is treated to one of the most deluxe hotel experiences in Italy. The hotel has had a long and illustrious history. Once part of the present hotel was owned by Carolina Bonaparte, sister of Napoleon. Kraft, the famous Swiss hotelkeeper, once owned the building. The present hotel was formed in 1927 by the fusion of two other hotels, the De la Ville and the Italie.

Set on a Renaissance square in whose center a naked athlete wrestles with a lion, the yellow-and-white facade of the hotel looks imposing enough to be an embassy. A doorman in front will park your car, and the staff inside will tend to your food and lodging needs. The central panel of the coffered ceiling contains a depiction of a beneficent sun beaming down onto the intricately patterned marble floors, the bouquets of flowers, and the elaborately crafted 19th-century stairwell wide enough (and strong enough) to support a Volkswagen. Several of the bedrooms have terraces, and many offer views of the Arno.

The hotel's roof garden in summer is one of the best places in town for meeting the attractive, the articulate, and the unattached. Hundreds of plants, a piano, and metal tables with pink napery have been installed under a canopy.

The bedrooms have all the luxuries you'd expect, plus lots of comfortably padded chairs, well-appointed space, and opulent bathrooms with heated racks, thick towels, and high-ceilinged comfort. Singles cost from 200,000 lire ($122), with doubles beginning at 280,000 lire ($170.80), going up to 450,000 lire ($274.50). For a description of Il Cestello, the hotel's restaurant, refer to the dining section, and for details on the hotel's popular bar, the Donatello, turn to the nightlife section.

Villa Medici, 42 Via il Prato (tel. 261-331), is a deluxe mansion in a historical center of Florence, near the Congress Hall. It combines old-world distinction with such modern amenities as a rooftop lounge with a panoramic view and a handsome garden with a free-form, heated swimming pool. The Lorenzaccio Restaurant, connected with the hotel, is known for its international and Florentine cuisine. In summer, meals are served by the pool. Its often distinguished clientele books traditionally furnished, large-size rooms (even penthouse suites). Singles begin at 200,000 lire ($122) increasing to 250,000 lire ($152.50). Doubles range in price from 300,000 lire ($183) to 350,000 lire ($213.50).

Grand Hotel Villa Cora, 18–20 Viale Machiavelli (tel. 229-8451), is a grandiose Renaissance neoclassic palace on the hill near Piazzale Michelangelo above the city. Built by Baron Openheim and once lived in by the Italian ambassador to the U.S., the luxury hotel stands in its own formal gardens, with a special recreation area, including an open-air swimming pool. The villa was chosen as a residence for ex-Empress Eugenia, widow of Napoleon III, to whom Florence gave a warm and deferential welcome. The public rooms have architectural splendor, with the drawing rooms opening off the domed circular rotunda. Marble, ornate bronze, white-and-gilt doors, frescoed ceilings, parquet floors, and silk damask walls characterize the decor. Some of the bedrooms, the more expensive ones, are one of a kind, although the others are well furnished with tasteful reproductions and 19th-century pieces. All are air-conditioned, with "frigo-bars." There are no singles, and doubles go for 250,000 lire ($152.50). In the restaurant, Taverna Machiavelli, you can enjoy fine food.

In warm weather meals are also served in the open air near the swimming pool. From the rooftop solarium, a panoramic view of the rooftops of Florence unfolds.

Regency, 3 Piazza Massimo D'Azeglio (tel. 245-247), lies a bit apart from the shopping and sightseeing center of Florence, but happily is only a 15-minute stroll to the cathedral. This spacious mansion, a member of the prestigious international Relais de Campagne organization, has its own garden, across from a park in a residential area of the city. Staying here is quiet and restful. A well-built, old-style villa, the Regency was once known as the Umbria, and, as such, it had many admirers. Now better than ever in its present reincarnation, it offers 29 tasteful, well-furnished rooms. This luxurious hideaway is filled with stained glass and paneled walls, mirrors and cyclamen-toned lacquer chests. Its attractive dining room serves excellent food. In a single, expect to pay from 195,000 lire ($118.95); in a double, 250,000 lire ($152.50)—including a continental breakfast and tax.

THE MODERATE RANGE: **Kraft,**2 Via Solferino (tel. 284-273), features an attractive modern decor, a location near the railway station, and a rooftop swimming pool. It's the creation of the son of one of the greatest hoteliers in Italy (Herman Kraft, of Berne, Switzerland, who launched the deluxe Excelsior in the past century). The Kraft sits on a relatively peaceful square, near the American consulate. Good reproductions of classic furniture are comfortably appointed. A single costs 150,000 lire ($91.50); a double, 220,000 lire ($134.20). The dining room, with superb service and good food, crowns the top. Maestros and singing stars from the nearby opera house often check in, getting a warm greeting from the director, Mario Moschi.

Augustus e dei Congressi, Piazzetta del'Oro (tel. 283-054), is for those who require modern comforts in a setting of historical and monumental Florence. The Ponte Vecchio is just a short stroll away, as is the Uffizi Gallery. The exterior is rather pillbox modern, but the interior seems light, bright, and comfortable. The expansive lounge and drinking area is like an illuminated cave, with a curving ceiling and built-in conversational areas interlocked on several levels. Forest-green couches, white stucco room dividers, and lemon-yellow decorative accents form an inviting backdrop. Some of the bedrooms have forsythia-yellow color accents, and they open onto little private balconies with white garden furniture. Single rooms with shower rent for 140,000 lire ($85.40); doubles with private bath, 175,000 lire ($106.75), with an extra sitting room going for 80,000 lire ($48.80). Included are air conditioning, service, and taxes.

Hotel Principe, 34 Lungarno Vespucci (tel. 284-848), is a converted town house on the Arno. Overlooking the Lungarno Apartments, it has been adapted so that the well-furnished rooms contain private baths. Many guests perfer the front-side upper chambers, where they can have breakfast on a terrace overlooking the river. Others select a quieter nest overlooking a nice little garden in the rear, where they can order drinks on a sunny summer afternoon. Expect to pay 90,000 lire ($54.90) in a single, from 140,000 lire ($85.40) in a double, including taxes and service. The drawing room is home-like and cozy.

Hotel Continental, 2 Lungarno Acciaioli (tel. 282-392), is in the bull's-eye center of everything, right at the Ponte Vecchio. Its rooms are small, but for many the location more than compensates. This second-class hotel is actually modern, most comfortable, with pleasantly styled rooms. In a single with bath or shower, the tariff is 95,000 lire ($57.95). In a double with private plumbing the cost is 140,000 lire ($85.40). Breakfast is included. *Tip:* Ask for the little single room up in the tower, known as the Torre Guelfa dei Consorti. An attractive roof garden has tables set on a terrace overlooking the Arno.

Anglo-American Regina, 9 Via Garibaldi (tel. 282-114), is an old Florentine palace that has been completely redecorated and refurnished. A first-class hotel, it offers 118 rooms, all with bath, direct-dial telephone, radio, and air conditioning. The location is quiet but central, only five minutes from the monumental district and shopping center. The lobby has tent-like draperies covering the sloping skylights, with an elegant dining room with peach-colored walls and fragile Victorian-era chairs. There's also an English club-style bar painted a pleasing shade of blue. Other facilities include a barbershop, a beauty parlor, a sauna, and an inside garden and loggia. In a twin-bedded accommodation with bath or shower, the cost for a room and a continental breakfast peaks at 200,000 lire ($122), dropping to 170,000 lire ($103.70) in a single, also with bath or shower. A table d'hôte dinner at the hotel costs from 45,000 lire ($27.45). The hotel is near the Convention House and American consulate, fronting the back of the opera house.

Grand Hotel Minerva, 16 Piazza Santa Maria Novella (tel. 284-555), bills itself as "the really quietest hotel in town." Only three minutes from the railway station, it is an old palace—entirely renovated and air-conditioned—standing next to one of the most distinguished churches in Florence, Santa Maria Novella with its geometric facade of green-and-white marble. Its best asset is its rooftop swimming pool, with its view of Renaissance domes. The rooms are pristine, but comfortable, all with radios, mini-fridges, and color TV. A single room with bath or shower rents for 125,000 lire ($76.25), a double for 175,000 lire ($106.75). Half board is 40,000 lire ($24.40) per person in addition to the room rate.

Hotel ETAP Astoria, 9 Via del Giglio (tel. 298-095). During the 19th century this hotel housed the offices of a now-defunct newspaper. In the 17th century John Milton wrote parts of *Paradise Lost* in one of the bedrooms. In 1979 ETAP renovated the 14th-century building into one of the most dramatically original hotels in Florence. The stylish lobby is illuminated with a skylight that shines into a copy of a mural by Botticelli and a heroic collection of metallic horses more or less on permanent display. From the freshly upholstered bedrooms on the upper floors you'll have a view over the terracotta rooftops of Florence.

If you choose to stay in one of the stylishly comfortable bedrooms of this hotel, be sure to inspect the conference rooms of what used to be the adjoining Palazzo Gaddi, whose frescoes are filled with chubby cherubs. On the premises is a garden-style restaurant with stylized wall murals, beamed ceilings, and Empire-style lyre-backed chairs. Singles range from 125,000 lire ($76.56) to 155,000 lire ($94.55), while doubles cost between 185,000 lire ($112.85) and 255,000 lire ($155.55), depending on the season. Breakfast is included. Triples are available for between 225,000 lire ($137.25) and 300,000 lire ($183).

MODERATELY PRICED LODGINGS: Helvetia & Bristol, 2 Via De' Pescioni (Piazza Strozzi; (tel. 287-814), is housed in a five-story neoclassical building with lemon-colored walls and gray trim. Near the Piazza della Repubblica, it was built by a Swiss family in 1895 and maintains the same types of exposed paneling, tall ceilings, and marble floors of its original construction. Famous guests have included D'Annunzio, Eleonora Duse, Enrico Fermi (the Italian physicist who participated in the development of the atomic bomb), and Albert Sabin of the oral polio vaccine. Standards of comfort are generally high, and if you arrive in spring the lobby will probably be filled with azaleas. Singles cost about 70,000 lire ($42.70), with doubles going for 115,000 lire ($70.15). An extra bed can be set up for another 21,000 lire ($12.81). All 62 rooms are equipped with bath or shower.

Pensione Monna Lisa (the spelling is correct), 27 Borgo Pinti (tel. 296-213), provides a rare opportunity to live in a privately owned Renaissance palazzo that has been well preserved by its owner, Countess N. D. Oslavia Ciardi-Dupré. Her personal collection of antiques and original oils decorates many of the salons and bedrooms. The exterior, on a narrow street, is foreboding, but once you pass through the heavy entrance door, you'll be instantly attracted to the charm and warmth of the interior. Many bedrooms overlook a rear garden or inner courtyard. Breakfast is included in the price of 120,000 lire ($73.20) for a double, 75,000 lire ($45.75) for a single. No other meals are offered. The Monna Lisa is an easy walk from the Duomo.

Villa Villoresi, 63 Via delle Torri (tel. 449-032), is a rare opportunity for motorists to live in an ancestral villa, dating from the 12th century. It's about two miles from the heart of Florence (exit 19 on the Autostrada del Sole), at Colonnata di Sesto Fiorentino. Contessina Cristina Villoresi de Loche accepts guests in her charming villa, with its gardens and private swimming pool. The front loggia overlooks the garden. An inner gallery must be the longest in the area, and it's decorated with heirloom antiques, as are many of the salons and lounges. Guests dine on an unusually fine cuisine, served in a room with a high, beamed ceiling. Some bedrooms open onto an inner courtyard, some onto the loggia. Accommodations come with and without private bath. It's recommended that you take half-board terms at rates ranging from 100,000 lire ($61) in a single, from 92,000 lire ($56.12) to 120,000 lire ($73.20) per person in a double, the more expensive tariffs for rooms with private baths or showers.

Grand Hotel Cavour, 3 Via del Proconsolo (tel. 287-102), is a remake of a 13th-century palace, retaining its pristine architectural beauty, such as frescoed and coved ceilings. Still intact is a small altar and confessional. Opposite the Bargello Museum, the Cavour is an easy walk from the Piazza della Signoria. However, the furnishings don't match the interior. Nevertheless, accommodations are comfortable and home-like. Private baths have been installed in some of the rooms. Bathless singles go for 42,000 lire ($25.62), rising to 55,000 lire ($33.55) with bath. Bathless doubles cost 62,000 lire ($37.52), peaking at 85,000 lire ($51.85) with private bath. Half-board terms range from 60,000 lire ($36.60) to 75,000 lire ($45.75).

Tornabuoni Beacci, 3 Via Tornabuoni (tel. 212-654), is on the principal shopping street of Florence. Near the Arno and the Piazza S. Trinità, the pension occupies the three top floors of a 14th-century palazzo. All its living rooms have been furnished in a provincial style, with bowls of flowers, parquet floors, a formal fireplace, old paintings, murals, and tasteful rugs. The pension was completely renovated recently, and it bears an air of gentility. The roof terrace, surrounded by potted plants and flowers, is for late-afternoon drinks or breakfast. The view of the nearby churches, towers, and rooftops is worth experiencing. A great deal of the continued popularity of the pension is because of its attractive owner, Signora Lensi-Orlandi-Beacci, who knows how to "mix" her guests. Her books for customers' signatures are numerous, including in days of yore such personalities as John Steinbeck, the Gish sisters, and Frederic March.

The bedrooms are moderately well furnished. Every room of the first-class pension has hot and cold running water, and a number have private baths. The half-board rate ranges from 76,000 lire ($46.36) to 95,000 lire ($57.95) per person, according to plumbing assignment, with tax, service, and heating included. It offers good value, and there's an elevator and air conditioning. The pension has a good restaurant.

Pension Hermitage, 1 Vicolo Marzio (tel. 287-216), is offbeat and intimate, a charming place to stay right at the Ponte Vecchio, on the Arno, with a sun terrace on the roof providing a view of much of Florence, including the nearby Uffizi. Here you can take your breakfast under a leafy arbor, surrounded by potted roses and geraniums. The success of the pension spins around its English-speaking owners, Paolo and Vincenzo Scarcelli, who have made the Hermitage an extension of their home, furnishing it with antiques and well-chosen reproductions. Best of all is their warmth with guests, many of whom keep coming back, enjoying the gatherings in the top-floor living room where they sit around the woodburning fireplace on nippy nights.

The bedrooms are pleasantly furnished, many with Tuscan antiques, rich brocades, and soft beds. The baths are superb, tiled and containing lots of gadgets. For bed and a continental breakfast you'll pay 45,000 lire ($27.45) in a single with bath, 70,000 lire ($42.70) in a double with bath, dropping to just 60,000 lire ($36.60) in a bathless double. Breakfast, served in a dignified, beam-ceilinged dining room, is pleasant and well cooked. Rooms overlooking the Arno have the most scenic position, and they've been fitted with double-glass windows, reducing the traffic noise by 40%.

Porta Rossa, 19 Via Porta Rossa (tel. 287-551), within a few minutes' walk of the Ponte Vecchio and the Signoria, has a history dating from the 13th century, although the present structure is from the 19th. Its original construction was ordered by a silk merchant who offered to house dozens of his competitors here during their visits to Florence. To eliminate their presence at the markets the following day, he drugged their wine, causing them to sleep late into the following afternoon. To this day the symbol of the house is the poppy, whose likeness is carved above the windows and doors.

The lobby, the breakfast room, and the beautiful bar area are outfitted in a 19th-century style the manager calls "decadent romantic." This includes vaulted lunette ceilings, stained-glass inserts, and lavishly carved paneling. Clients who sleep here today are following in a tradition set long ago by such distinguished overnighters as Stendhal and Balzac. True to the origins of the hotel, the clients still include visiting merchants who exhibit their merchandise to wholesalers in the sprawling bedrooms. The labyrinthine interior reveals slightly faded antiques, old jardinières, dingy plaster, and carved stone at virtually every corner.

Your room will probably (that's probably) be high ceilinged and sparsely furnished. The reception is likely to be laconic. Accommodations rent for 38,000 lire ($23.18) in a bathless single, rising to 55,000 lire ($33.86) in a bathless double. Singles with bath go for 48,000 lire ($29.28), rising to 70,000 lire ($42.70) in a double with bath. Breakfast costs another 9000 lire ($5.49).

Pensione Pendini, 2 Via Strozzi (tel. 211-170), off the Piazza della Repubblica, was founded in 1879. It's still family owned and run. Lucia Boldrini, a professor of art, is blonde, charming, and beautiful, offering a homey environment in a colorful and distinguished setting of Florence. Your room may overlook the active piazza or front an inner courtyard (more peaceful). One of the oldest pensions in Florence, it has 42 rooms, and the location is on the fourth floor of an arcaded building. Bathless doubles cost 60,000 lire ($36.91), climbing to 70,000 lire ($42.70) with bath or shower. A single with bath goes for 50,000 lire ($30.50). The all-purpose lounge is furnished family style with a piano and card tables. The breakfast room is pleasantly and modestly provincial, and some of the bedrooms have quite a lot of character, with reproductions of antiques. Only breakfast is served.

Ariele, 11 Via Magenta (tel. 211-509), is an older private villa near the Arno that has been remodeled and turned into a comfortable hotel. Architecturally, it is of generous dimensions, with a homey mixture of traditional and contemporary furnishings. The bedrooms are quite large and comfortable, and private baths or showers have been installed in 28 of the 30 completely remodeled rooms. Outside is a beautiful garden, plus a rustic underground taverna for evening dining and wine-tasting. Depending on the plumbing, singles range in price from 28,000 lire ($17.08) to 36,000 lire ($21.96). Doubles go from 40,000 lire ($24.40) to 52,000 lire ($31.72). These tariffs include a continental breakfast, taxes, and service.

Quisisana e Ponte Vecchio, 4 Lungarno Archibusieri (tel. 216-692), stands directly on the Arno, near the Ponte Vecchio and within an easy walk of the Uffizi Gallery. A late-19th century Florentine pensione, it is serviced by an elevator, which takes you to its 40-room apartment upstairs that has been furnished in a home-like fashion. Bathless singles rent for 44,000 lire ($26.84), increasing to 52,000 lire ($31.72) with private bath. A bathless double goes for 80,000 lire ($48.80), rising to 65,000 lire ($39.65) with private bath. A continental breakfast is included. The pensione's nicest feature is a loggia overlooking the Arno.

Dining in Florence

UPPER BRACKET RESTAURANTS: Enoteca Pinchiorri, 87 Via Ghibellina, near St. Croce (tel. 242-777), is considered by many gourmets as the best restaurant in Italy, with one of the finest wine cellars. Housed on the ground floor of the 15th-century Giacometti-Ciofi Palace in the center of historic Florence, this restaurant might be called a movable feast in more than one sense of the word. Depending on the weather, the service moves from a covered niche at the base of a heroic statue of Apollo to an open-air courtyard with a view of the stars and a pleasing series of vine-covered lattices, to one of two very formal interior rooms where the furnishings include a massive porphyry fireplace, Renaissance antiques, and striking modern paintings. Of course, masses of flowers and silver candelabra are scattered tastefully throughout, but the main feature here is the vibrant personalities of the Nice- and Modena-born owners and chefs, Annie Feolde and Giorgio Pinchiorri.

The establishment began as a wine bar (that's roughly what *enoteca* means in Latin). When Annie began cooking in 1979, she quickly raised the level of cuisine to those high-quality heights that no Florentine restaurant could match. Guests have ranged from Danny Kaye to the Princess of Holland. The representatives of Relais et Châteaux showed up, including the establishment among their prestigious listings. When I first inspected the kitchens here, the phone was almost constantly ringing with calls from the Four Seasons in New York.

The food is an inspired blend of nouvelle French and Italian cuisine, with a fixed-price menu degustatione at around 90,000 lire ($54.90) and a cuisine du marché fixed-price meal at around 105,000 lire ($64.05). The specialties change daily, but notable offerings include cannelloni of salmon with a mousseline of fresh clams, caramelized ricotta with a fondue of fresh peppers, and other equally imaginative recipes. Some of these dishes in the hands of a lesser chef might be an abject failure, but in the hands of that statuesque red-haired queen of the Florentine kitchen, Annie Feolde, they are usually nothing less than sublime. The restaurant is closed all day Sunday, for Monday lunch, and during the entire month of August.

Il Cestello, Hotel Excelsior, 3 Piazza Ognissanti (tel. 294-301), is a deluxe restaurant, attracting an upper-crust clientele who, in summer, come either to drink beside the piano or on the flowered terrace of this hotel's roof garden, or else to eat under a canopy by candlelight. On the sixth floor of what is the finest hotel in Florence, the garden is open only from May to September (in winter it moves back downstairs again). But in summer the hotel closes its downstairs dining room in favor of the gentle breezes and the panoramic views of the Arno that visitors enjoy from this verdant terrace, which is open nightly from 8:30 p.m. to 1:30 a.m. A drink costs from 9000 lire ($5.49) and a dinner around 150,000 lire ($91.50), perhaps less.

The cuisine is Mediterranean with many Tuscan specialties, such as gnocchetti with gorgonzola and veal scaloppine with artichokes. Sea bass is sauteed with herbs, or you can regularly get the famed Florentine T-bone steak. A small part of the menu lists those items that are always "fresh from today's market." These include some of the finest fresh vegetables in Florence. My most recent assorted spring salad and fresh asparagus were a true celebration of the season. The restaurant is open to nonresidents, but reservations are always advised.

At **Ristorante Oliviero,** 51r Via delle Terme (tel. 287-643), the luxurious dining room is small, but smart. You can arrive here any time after 7 p.m. except Sunday and enjoy a drink. From 8 p.m. on, live music entertains guests in the piano bar. The service is elegantly courteous. An excellent beginning to any meal is the chef's crêpes alla Fiorentina. Two top-quality main dishes include sogliola (sole) Oliviero and a veal prepared "in the style of the chef." The featured dessert is crêpes suzette, although I prefer the heavenly, cloud-like soufflé. Expect to spend from 50,000 lire ($30.50) up. Taxes and service are included in the prices quoted. The restaurant closes in August for its annual vacation.

Doney, 48r Via Tornabuoni (tel. 214-308). Everybody now associates this long-enduring establishment with good food. Tuscan, French, even American dishes rarely disappoint here in a setting of quiet dignity, with refined service. Doney's tea room is still the most snobbish and fashionable place in Florence for a good "cuppa." The accompanying pastries are well prepared, although sinfully caloric. I heartily endorse green ravioli Doney. Other chef's specialties include breasts of chicken Doney style and pizzaiola veal escalopes. The chocolate mousse is excellent. A good meal here will cost from 40,000 lire ($24.40) to 50,000 lire ($30.50), plus 15% for service. Closed Monday and in August.

Harry's Bar, 22r Lungarno Vespucci (tel. 296-700), is not only a favorite retreat of expatriate Yanks, but of the Florentines, who know they can get some of the best viands in Tuscany here. The martinis here are superb, and you may want to patronize just the bar—but I'd recommend that you stick around for lunch or dinner as well. The cuisine is international, excellently prepared, and efficiently served by English-speaking waiters. You may start with tortellini "Harry," then follow with one of the specialties, including filet mignon "take it off." If you're stopping by for a light lunch, the chef will prepare a club sandwich. For dessert, the apple tart with fresh cream is good. Crêpes with orange liqueur are outstanding. You'll spend from 40,000 lire ($24.40) and up for a complete meal. Closed Sunday and from December 10 to January 15.

BUDGET TO MODERATE DINING: Otello, 36r Via Orti Oricellari (tel. 215-819). Here's a place to go when you're really hungry; the fine display of antipasto alone tells the story—a glittering array of cold Italian specialties including roast pork tender enough to be sliced with a china plate. The price depends on your actual selection. One woman writes that she was offended by the display of "tordi" (thrushes). However, these small birds, as well as larks, are considered delicacies in Italy. (Because of the new Italian hunting laws, the small birds are only available in winter). For a main course, you can order a special dish, scaloppine vitella Otello. For your opener, I'd suggest taglierini all'Otello. For dessert, why not the Florentine cake, zuccotto? Your tab here is likely to run from 25,000 lire ($15.25) to 35,000 lire ($21.35), plus 12% for service. Closed Tuesday.

Buca Lapi, 1r Via del Trebbio (tel. 213-768), a cellar restaurant founded in 1880, is big on glamor, good food, and the almost *gemütlich* enthusiasm of fellow diners. Its decor alone—under the Palazzo Antinori—makes it fun: vaulted ceilings covered with travel posters from all over the world. There's a long table of interesting fruits, desserts, and vegetables. The cooks know how to turn out the most classic dishes of the Tuscan kitchen with superb finesse. Specialties include pâté di fegato della casa (a liver pâté), cannelloni, scampi giganti alla griglia (a super-size shrimp), and bistecca alla Fiorentina (local beefsteak). In season, the fagioli toscani all'olio (Tuscan beans in the native olive oil) are considered a delicacy by many palates. For dessert, you can order the international favorite, crêpes suzette, or the local choice, zuccotto, a Florentine cake that's "delicato." Meals cost from 25,000 lire ($15.25) to 40,000 lire ($24.40). Evenings can be quite festive, as the singing becomes contagious—a friendly boat. There is music every night except Sunday and Monday, when it is closed. It's also closed from August 1 to August 22.

Caninetta Antinori, 3 Piazza Antinori (tel. 298-298). Hidden behind the severe stone facade of the 15th-century Palazzo Antinori is one of Florence's most popular restaurants and one of the city's few top-notch wine bars. Small wonder that the cellars should be supremely well stocked, since the restaurant is one of the city's showplaces for the vintages of Tuscany and Umbria's largest wine company. It has become the preferred rendezvous point for the well-heeled wine lovers who appreciate an overview of the assembled wines of the region, readily available and cheerfully served.

Vintages can be consumed by the glass at the stand-up bar or by the bottle as an accompaniment for the simple Italian meals served at wooden tables. The room is not especially large, and the overwhelming decorative statement is from the floor-to-ceiling racks of carefully aged and artfully undusted wine bottles set on their sides in innumerable wooden racks. The overflow from the ground floor goes up to the overhead balcony. It is open for lunch at noon and for dinner at 7 p.m. on weekdays only, and is closed in August. Full meals, not counting the wine, range from 35,000 lire ($21.35), but you can eat for less if you want to sample only the snacks, such as salads, sandwiches, and other light dishes.

Buca dell'Orafo, 28 Via dei Girolami (tel. 213619), is a little dive (one of the many cellars or "buca"-type establishments beloved by Florentines). Once part of an old goldsmith's shop, it stands near the Ponte Vecchio, reached via a street under a vaulted arcade right off the Piazza del Pesce. The trattoria is usually stuffed with its habitués, so if you want a seat, go early for either lunch or dinner. Over the years the chef has made little concession to the foreign palate, turning out instead genuine Florentine specialties, including tripe and mixed boiled meats with a green sauce. For a savory beginning, try the fennel-flavored salami or asparagus in the spring. Florentine beefsteaks are the most expensive item on the menu, which is likely to cost from 25,000 lire ($16.25). There's a nice feeling of camaraderie among the diners.

Sostanza, 25r Via del Porcellana (tel. 212-691), is perhaps the best known trattoria in Florence. It's small, with a minimum of decor, but it serves some of the best and most savory Tuscan specialties in the capital. Both the fashionable and the unpretentious make a beeline for its door. On a narrow street, near the Piazza Ognissanti, the restaurant is small and narrow, and sometimes diners share a table. The kitchen in the rear is exposed, and the wafting aroma of Florentine beefsteaks on the charcoal grill fills the air. Typical Florentine dishes include tripe prepared in the Tuscan way—that is, boiled, cut into strips, and baked in a casserole with a sauce of tomatoes, parmesan cheese, and onions. The preferred pasta is tortellini. For dessert, the chef bakes a special cake every day. A typical local meal will cost from 30,000 lire ($18.30). Closed Sunday and in August.

Natale, 80r Lungarno Acciaioli (tel. 213-968), is a good restaurant on the Arno, between the Ponte Vecchio and the Ponte S. Trinità. It's an unassuming place with a reputation for fine Tuscan cuisine. Prices are moderate, and the service is nice too.

You can dine on lasagne or riso alla Fiorentina. Main dishes include grilled trout and petti di pollo (chicken) Natale. Meals begin at 25,000 lire ($15.25), going up. Closed Tuesday.

La Loggia, Piazzale Michelangelo (tel. 287-032), couldn't be more prominent, perched on the most visited panoramic square overlooking the Renaissance rooftops of Florence. In fair weather, statues are placed outside, overlooking the "balcony" with its copy of Michelangelo's *David.* Fortunately, this restaurant doesn't depend on the view alone, but turns out quite good food. In season, it's virtually impossible to get a table, but if you don't mind a long wait, you should chance it. This is not a tourist trap.

Service may be a bit chaotic, but when you get to order, you might like to try the giant porcini and ovoli mushrooms among the favorite antipasti. Florentine steaks are usually tender here, grilled over an open fire. Try also the risotto con fagioli (beans). For a perfect finish for your meal, try a herb drink, Amaro Montenegro. Another specialty of the bartender is a heavenly apéritif of champagne and peaches. Expect to spend from 25,000 lire ($15.25) to 35,000 lire ($21.35) for a complete meal. Closed Wednesday and August 10 to August 25.

Mamma Gina, 37r Borgo S. Iacopo (tel. 296-009), is a Left Bank trattoria, across the Ponte Vecchio, that serves solid food in bounteous portions at reasonable prices. Tuscan fare with a hearty flavor is the rule of the kitchen. Many foreigners like to stop off here for a luncheon date after a visit to the nearby Pitti Palace. The dining room is pleasantly unpretentious, and the service is courteous. To get your taste buds going, try the tortellini verdi. Main dishes, both fish and meat, are excellently prepared. Meals cost 30,000 lire ($18.30) to 45,000 lire ($27.45). Closed Sunday and August 1 to August 20.

Trattoria Cammillo, 57 Borgo S. Iacopo (tel. 212-427), is a celebrated Left Bank choice, on the ground floor of an old Medici palace. Excellent wines and authentic Tuscan specialties draw a never-ending line of habitués plus a large American patronage. Here's a good place at which to try tortellini alla panna. Among the main courses, I'd recommend scaloppa alla parmigiana, although I recently saw a party of eight Florentines dining on tripe. Meals cost from 28,000 lire ($17.08) to 50,000 lire ($30.50). This popular trattoria lies between the Ponte Vecchio and the Ponte S. Trinità. Closed Wednesday and Thursday, and from August 1 to August 20.

Shopping in Florence

Skilled craftsmanship and traditional design unchanged since the days of the Medici have made Florence a goal for the serious shopper. I find its merchandise far superior to that of Venice or Rome. Florence is noted for its hand-tooled leather goods and its various straw merchandise, as well as superbly crafted silver jewelry. Its reputation for fashionable custom-made clothes grows yearly.

The whole city of Florence strikes many visitors as a gigantic department store. Entire neighborhoods on both sides of the Arno offer good shops, although those along the medieval Ponte Vecchio (with some exceptions) strike most people as too touristy. Of course, Florence's Fifth Avenue is the Via dei Tornabuoni, with its flagship Gucci stores for leather and Ferragamo for stylish but costly shoes.

The better shops are, for the most part, along Tornobuoni, but there are many on Via Vigna Nuova, Via Porta Rossa, and Via degli Strozzi. You might also stroll on Lungarno along the Arno.

THE MARKETS: After checking into a hotel, the most intrepid shoppers head for the **Straw Market** of Florence, called Il Porcellino by the Italians because of the bronze reclining pig resting there. The market stands in the monumental heart of Florence, an easy stroll from the Palazzo Vecchio. Open daily from 9 a.m. to 7 p.m., it sells not only straw items but leather goods as well, along with an array of typically Florentine merchandise, such as frames, trays, hand-embroidery, table linens, and hand-sprayed and painted boxes in traditional designs.

However, even better bargains await those who make their way through pushcarts to the stalls of the open-air **Mercato Centrale,** in and around the Borgo S. Lorenzo, in the vicinity of the railway station. If you don't mind bargaining, which is imperative here, you'll find an array of merchandise that includes raffia bags, Florentine leather purses, salt-and-pepper shakers, straw handbags, and art reproductions.

Nearer the Duomo, the covered market called **Piazza del Mercato Nuovo** is a final choice. At Porta Rossa and Santa Maria, the arcaded Renaissance structure is good for casual buyers seeking wooden boxes in traditional Florentine designs, tablecloths, handbags, gold-painted trays, and souvenirs. The true Florentine pats the shiny nose of the bronze boar who guards the entrance.

Warning: In some of these markets you may think you've found Puccis, Guccis, and Louis Vuittons selling for peanuts. You can be sure that such low-priced merchandise is imitation. Most often it is easily recognized as fake.

JEWELRY: Buying jewelry is almost an art in itself, so proceed with caution. Florence, of course, is known for its jewelry. You'll find some stunning antique pieces, and if you know how to buy, some fine bargains.

G. Settepassi & Figli, Ponte Vecchio (tel. 215-506), is one of the most distinguished jewelers of the Renaissance city, drawing a well-heeled patronage.

Away from the Ponte Vecchio, **Mario Buccellati,** 69 Via Tornabuoni (tel. 296-579), specializes in exquisite handcrafted jewelry and silver. A large selection of intriguing pieces at high prices is offered. Buccellati is closed in August.

MOSAICS: **Arte Musiva,** 36–38r Via S. Giuseppe (tel. 241-647), lies in the old quarter of Santa Croce. Florentine mosaics are universally recognized for their distinction. Bruno Lastrucci, the director of Arte Musiva, is one of the most renowned living exponents of this art form. You can visit the shop Monday to Saturday from 9 a.m. to 7 p.m. (on Sunday from 9 a.m. to 1 p.m. and 3 to 6 p.m.). In the workshop you can see artisans plying their craft; some of the major mosaicists of Italy are here. In addition to traditional Florentine, modern mosaic has been developed. A selection of the most significant works is permanently displayed in the gallery. Here, you'll find decorative panels, linings, and tiles, as well as "figures," "landscapes," and "still lifes" of the great masters of the past.

SILVER: There are many charming little antique stores clustered around the Ponte Vecchio that sell silverware. I regard **Peruzzi Brothers,** at 60 Ponte Vecchio, corner 2–4 Borgo S. Jacopo (tel. 292-027), as among the finest silversmiths in the city, specializing in the best chased Florentine silverware as well as handmade jewelry. The firm has been doing business since 1880.

LEATHER: Universally acclaimed, Florentine leather is still the fine product it always was—smooth, well-shaped, and vivid in such colors as green and red. However, it is no longer the "steal" it once was.

S. Luti & Son, 28–32r Via Parione (tel. 287-047), offers hundreds of fine quality articles and has been in the leather-goods business since 1922. It has a large selection of high-fashion women's handbags, as well as many fine gift items and travel articles. Business people can select from a wide range of contemporary attaché cases and well-styled traditional briefcases. The craftsmanship is of top-notch quality. Via Parione is one of the oldest streets in Florence, in the historical center running perpendicular to Via Tornabuoni and parallel to the Arno. In summer, the shop closes on Saturday afternoon.

John F., 2 Lungarno Corsini, near S. Trinità Bridge (tel. 298-985), is a high-fashion house of leather in a Florentine palace. The leather coats and jackets are of exclusive design, and the salon shows models from the crème de la crème of its collection. Although foreign patronage is high, the shop also dresses some of the chicest Florentine women. Accessories, such as handbags and leather articles, made here are well crafted and beautifully styled. The shop is open every day from 9 a.m. to 8 p.m. except Sunday.

Bojola, 25r Via Rondinelli (tel. 211-155), is another leading name in leather. Sergio Bojola has distinguished himself in Florence by his selections for many types and tastes, in both synthetic materials and beautiful leathers. Hundreds of customers are always enthusiastic about the variety of items found here, reflecting first-class quality and craftsmanship.

STRAW: Emilio Paoli, 24–28r Via della Vigna Nuova (tel. 214-596), is a display house for the manufacturers of straw and raffia goods, including women's handbags, hats, skirts, raffia shoes, table mats, baskets, and cane furniture. The exhibits in the showroom are tasteful, and designs show considerable flair. The shop is likely to be closed for three weeks in August.

GIFTS: Menegatti, at the Piazza del Pesce–Ponte Vecchio (tel. 215-202), has a wide collection of souvenirs and gifts. The store sells Cantagalli pottery from the oldest Florentine factory. Pottery from Faenza and Deruta are also offered, along with della Robbia reproductions made in red clay like the originals. Items can be sent home if you arrange it at the time of purchase.

Balatresi Gift Shop, 22r Lungarno Acciaiuoli (tel. 287-851), is presided over by Umberto and Giovanna Balatresi, who have stocked their shop full of treasures, among which are Florentine mosaics created for them by Maestro Marco Tacconi, arguably the greatest mosaicist alive today, as well as original ceramic figurines by the sculptor Giannitrapani, and exclusive Fabergé reproductions. Many Americans come into this store in August to do their Christmas shopping.

PUCCI: The name needs little introduction. Marquis Emilio Pucci's palazzo is at 6 Via Pucci, near the Duomo (tel. 283-061). You'll find a sampling of high-quality fashion in his boutique on the second floor. It is on this same floor that his latest fashions are presented to the world in his much-photographed showroom.

BOOKS: **Libreria BM Book Shop,** 4r Borgognissanti (tel. 294-575), carries a vast array of books. In fact, it is one of the finest such stores in Europe. Browsers are encouraged, aided, and informed. Many customers come here just to look over the collection of art books. The bookshop is near the Excelsior Hotel.

EMBROIDERY: **Rifredi School of Artistic Embroidery,** 29 Via Carlo Bini (tel. 473-575), is unquestionably superior. However, it's a 15-minute ride from the center of town (take bus 14, 28, or 20). Awaiting your inspection is an array of delicate embroidery of artistic design, including tea and breakfast sets, tablecloths, bed linen, handkerchiefs, and women's lingerie.

SHOES: **Lily of Florence,** 2r Via Guicciardini (tel. 294-748), has both women's and men's shoes in American sizes. For women, Lily distributes both her own Lily of Florence designs and Amalfi, another well-known name in shoes. The men's shoes here are by Bally of Switzerland. Color comes in a wide range, and leather texture is of good quality. The styling is refined, the prices reasonable, and the welcome most hospitable.

HANDICRAFTS: **S.E.L.A.N.,** 107r Via Porta Rossa (tel. 212-995), is the society for the exportation of Italian artistic products. Right off the Piazza S. Trinità, it is a star choice for traditional designs in Italian ceramics. A wide assortment or merchandise is offered.

GALLERIES: My personal favorite is the **Arno Art Gallery,** run by Wanda Papini at 73r Via Vigna Nuova (tel. 294-343). If you're a serious collector, Ms. Papini says that September and October are the best months for coming to Florence. All the galleries present their most outstanding artists for the new season at that time. Her own gallery is closed from the end of July until the first of September. She has a policy of presenting young, talented Italian artists at reasonable prices (she drops the ones she considers overpriced). She calls her prices "honest and real," and I concur with her assessment. She also has a large collection of work of the best primitive artists from around the world, and these begin at 300,000 lire ($183), although the price tag may be much, much higher if the artist has the reputation of a great international master. For top artists exhibited here, the average price is 500,000 lire ($305), going up to about 3,000,000 lire ($1830) to 4,000,000 lire ($2440).

Florence After Dark

This is not an exciting prospect, unless you simply like to walk through the narrow streets or head up toward Fiesole for a view of the city at night (truly spectacular). However, for those seeking more organized action, some recommendations follow:

Perhaps nothing could be more unexpected in this city of Donatello and Michelangelo than a club called the **Red Garter,** 33 Via de' Benci (tel. 263-004), right off the Piazza Santa Croce. The American Prohibition era not only lives on, it's been exported. Visitors to the Red Garter can hear a variety of music, ranging from rock to banjo. The club is open nightly from 8:30 p.m. to 1 a.m. throughout the year, attracting young people from all over the world. A mug of Heineken lager on tap goes for 2000 lire ($1.22), and most tall drinks, made from "hijacked hootch," as it's known here, cost from 3000 lire ($1.83).

Space Electronic Discoteque, 37 Via Palazzuolo (tel. 293-082), is a multimedia light-and-sound spectacular on two large floors. On the ground floor—containing a unique aquarium/bar, giant carnival heads, and wall-to-wall mirrors—you can have a quiet drink while seated in one of the comfortable, secluded flower-shaped booths. The floor above offers up-to-date disco music and live music, transmitted via a high-quality sound system. The stainless-steel dance floor is large, and the light show is sophisticated, with lasers and closed-circuit television. The management and employees are friendly and cooperative, creating a relaxing atmosphere. The disco opens nightly at 9 and accommodates a crowd of all ages. The entrance fee is 10,000 lire ($6.10) and includes the price of one drink. Additional drinks cost between 2000 lire ($1.22) and 4000 lire ($2.44).

River Club, 8 Lungarno Corsini (tel. 282-465), was once the baroque Corsini palace, but it has been converted into one of the poshest and most sophisticated nightclubs in Italy, featuring disco, a semi-nude floor show, and a piano bar. You can sit at the bar, with its double-barreled baroque fountain and monumental figures of Adam and Eve. The bar stools opposite the fountain are often adorned with "hostesses." To see the floor show at 12:30 a.m., you must go into the adjoining ornate room. A six-piece orchestra plays until dawn on most nights. At the tables, regular whisky costs around 15,000 lire ($9.15) for your first drink.

Donatello Bar, Hotel Excelsior, 3 Piazza Ognissanti (tel. 294-301), just off the lobby of this grand hotel, offers a buffet lunch at around 45,000 lire ($27.45) per person seven days a week between the hours of 12:30 and 3:30 p.m. The elegant salads and choice of three main courses are lavishly laid out at the feet of a bronze maiden holding harvest symbols. But many of the bar's guests, both residents and nonresidents of the hotel, prefer to visit in the late afternoon or early evening, when the stained-glass windows and baroque sculpture are shown in what might be their best light. This place is the chicest watering hole in Florence. You are likely to see everyone from Milanese industrialists to French movie stars. In any event, the piano music encourages conviviality that makes the 12,000-lira ($7.32) price per drink worth it. In your nightlife prowl of Florence, you might also want to have a drink in the hotel's roof garden (see the dining section), should your visit be during the summer months.

Yab-Yum Club, 5r Via dei Sassetti (tel. 282-018). In Indian dialect, the name of this place means "rendezvous point," and that is precisely what hordes of Florentine disco lovers use it for every night of the week, except Monday. The entrance takes you down an illuminated staircase flanked with Plexiglass columns containing bubbling water and a sort of blend between the electronic age and neoclassicism. As of this writing, the club has been in business for five years, an impressive lifespan in the short duration of many discos. Often live entertainers are presented, occasionally including acrobats and costumed dancers. Banquettes are arranged theater-style around the dance floor, where tunes include American and British music. Near the Piazza della

Repubblica, the club imposes an entrance fee of 14,000 lire ($8.54) on weekdays and 17,000 lire ($10.37) on weekends. The price includes the first drink.

Café Rivoire, 5r Piazza della Signoria (tel. 214-412), offers a classy, amusing, and interesting old-world ambience looking directly onto the statues of one of my favorite squares in the world. You can sit at one of the metal tables set up on the flagstones outside, or at one of the colorful tables in a choice of inner rooms filled with marble detailing and unusual oil renderings of the piazza outside. If you don't want to sit at all, try the mahogany and green marble bar, where many of the more colorful characters making the Grand Tour of Europe talk, flirt, or gossip. A member of the staff will serve you an espresso for 3000 lire ($1.83) or a long drink for 10,000 lire ($6.10). There is also a selection of small sandwiches, omelets, and ice creams. The café is noted for its hot chocolate as well. It is open daily, except Monday, from 8 a.m. to midnight.

Finally, to cap your evening, you may want to do what the Florentines do. Head for **Gelateria Vivoli,** 7r Via Isola delle Stinche (tel. 292-334). This little establishment, run by Piero and Sergio Vivoli, serves the finest ice cream I've tasted in Italy. Buy your ticket first and select your flavor, including such delights as blueberry, fig, melon, and other fruits in season, as well as chocolate mousse, even coffee ice cream flavored with espresso. A special ice cream is made from rice. The gelati range in price from 1500 lire (92¢) to 2500 lire ($1.53), although a smaller size ice cream, popular with families, costs only 1000 lire (61¢). The establishment offers a number of semifreddi concoctions—an Italian ice cream using cream as a base instead of milk. Semifreddi is hardly obtainable outside of Italy, and its most popular flavors are almond, marengo (a type of meringue), and zabaione (eggnog). New flavors include limoncini alla crema (candied lemon peels with vanilla-flavored ice cream) and aranciotti al cioccolato (candied orange peels with chocolate ice cream).

Fiesole

Once a stronghold of the ancient Etruscans, the village of Fiesole is sprawled over the hillside above the city of Florence. Trolley-bus 7 takes you on the 20-minute journey from the Piazza San Marco to the central square of Fiesole. The sights here are a fascinating contrast to the colorful and lavishly decorated buildings of Florence. The ruins of the town's Roman period include the **Roman Theater,** dating from the first century B.C., the restored remains of which may be seen today. Near the theater are the skeleton-like ruins of the baths, which may have been built at the same time. Try to visit the Etruscan-Roman museum, with its many interesting finds dating from the days when Fiesole, not Florence, was supreme (a guide is on hand to show you through). The museum and theater are open March to September from 9 a.m. to 7 p.m., October to February from 10 a.m. to 5 p.m. Admission is 1500 lire (92¢).

The landmark of Fiesole is its **Duomo,** a massive cathedral dating from A.D. 1000, and supported by gray Corinthian columns and Romanesque arches. The adjoining **Bandini Museum** (tel. 59-701) contains della Robbia terracottas and sculptures by Pisano, as well as religious paintings from the 14th-century Tuscan school. Open daily in summer from 9:30 a.m. to 12:30 p.m. and from 2:30 to 7 p.m. (it is closed on Sunday), the museum charges 1500 lire (92¢) for admission. Winter hours are from 9:30 a.m. to 12:30 p.m. and from 2:30 to 4:30 p.m.

FOOD AND LODGING IN FIESOLE: **Hotel Aurora,** 39 Piazza Mino (tel. 59292), on the main square of town in a modernized 1890s building, is concealed behind an ochre facade set with green shutters. This establishment can offer you a bed, a meal, and an entertainment complex a few steps across a series of hillside terraces if you have a mind to disco or to drink above the sparkling lights of Florence. The terrace of the restaurant in back (closed from November to January) offers typical Italian meals and views of hanging vines and city lights. You can also eat inside. The hotel has a high beamed reception area, functional furniture, and bathless singles that rent for 50,000 lire ($30.50), going up to 68,000 lire ($41.48) in a bathless double. Units with private bath cost 68,000 lire ($41.48) in a single, from 110,000 lire ($67.41) in a double with private bath. Breakfast is an additional 12,000 lire ($7.32), with à la carte meals averaging around 35,000 lire ($21.35). Entrance into the adjoining disco and Blu Bar costs 10,000 lire ($6.10), which includes the first drink.

Le Lance at San Domenico (tel. 599-090). The airy and sunny construction of this hillside restaurant could almost be something you'd find in southern California, except for the lights of Florence that stretch below you. The low-lying building has maximum amounts of glass windows and exposed stone, as well as verdant plantings. This restaurant has become increasingly popular with city residents on summer nights. Dining is either indoors on rush-bottomed chairs or on a terrace illuminated with carriage lights and surrounded by shrubbery. Menu specialties include mixed Tuscan hors d'oeuvres from a well-stocked table in the center of the room, fresh mozzarella with fresh tomatoes, fresh spinach parmagiana, beefsteak Florentine (priced by the kilogram), cutlets of lamb with artichokes, risotto with champagne, and sole meunière. Meals range from 30,000 lire ($18.30). The restaurant is closed on Monday and Tuesday and in January.

A carriage ride around Rome

Chapter X

VENICE

VENICE IS a fairytale city of islands and gondolas, where the canals are lined with wedding-cake palaces. The "Serene Republic" of Venice had a turbulent and fascinating history. As Attila the Hun swept through fifth-century Italy toward trembling Rome, he spread proverbial death and destruction in his path. Attila was on his way to claim the emperor's stepsister, Honoria, as his "bride," and although his ultimate sack of Rome was averted, the swath of desolation he left in his wake was real enough. One particularly unfortunate town was razed to the ground, and its terrified inhabitants fled into the marshes on the shores of the Adriatic. The political climate of the times was so insecure that the population deemed it wisest to remain in the swamps and build their houses on stilts in the water, and so Venice got her start. The Venice we know today is from a much later era, however, an era rich with the accumulated spoils of Crusaders and merchantmen. The wizard-like rulers of Renaissance Venice shrewdly—sometimes unscrupulously—parlayed Venice into mistress of the Adriatic, and the many monuments and palaces erected in those days attest to the profit inherent in such a position.

For you, the 20th-century traveler, these mementoes of the past provide one of the richest treasuries of art and architecture anywhere in Europe. The heart of the city is **St. Mark's Square,** awash alternately with pigeons, tourists, and the creeping tides that are slowly sucking Venice into the sea. There is no traffic here, or anywhere in Venice, since all cars must be parked near the railway station on Piazzale Roma, that is, if you're fortunate enough to find garage space.

Actually, it took the efforts of Napoleon to unify the square architecturally. The then emperor ordered the addition of the Fabbrica Nuova, which bridged a gap between the Old and New "Procuratie." Today, before you begin a tour of specific sites, you might want to sit on this square, absorbing the spirit of the "Serenissima," which was Venice in its heyday as a seafaring republic.

The Major Sights

BASILICA OF ST. MARK: Dominating Piazza San Marco is the Basilica of St. Mark (tel. 25-205), named for the patron saint of the city, whose body was carried here from Alexandria in A.D. 828. It is called the "Church of Gold" and is surely one of the most fabulously embellished structures in Europe. A great central dome and satellite cupolas form the silhouette, and inside is a profusion of mosaics depicting biblical scenes—including the story of the Tower of Babel or scenes from the life of Christ.

Walking across an undulating mosaic-patterned floor, you reach the Baptistery. At the aperture over the entrance is one of the best known and most widely reproduced mosaics in the church—the dance of Salome in front of the court of Herod. In her red dress and white fox tails, she is the eternal enchantress.

A 500-lira (31¢) ticket admits you to the Presbytery, said to contain the sarcophagus of St. Mark under a green marble "blanket." Here you'll find the **Pala d'Oro,** a fabulous altar screen made of beaten gold and liberally encrusted with diamonds, rubies, emeralds, pearls, etc. With the same ticket, you're also admitted to the **Treasury,** filled with some of the "loot" the Crusaders brought back from Constantinople. In summer, hours are from 9 a.m. to 5 p.m. (in winter, from 10 a.m. to 4 p.m.).

On leaving the basilica, head up the stairs in the atrium for the **Marciano Museum** and the **Loggia dei Cavalli,** open from 9 a.m. to 5 p.m. in summer and from 10 a.m. to 4 p.m. in winter, charging an admission of 500 lire (31¢). The museum, with its mosaics and tapestries, is especially interesting, but walk out onto the loggia for a view of the Piazza San Marco.

Mounted on the loggia is the replica of St. Mark's horses, known as the **"triumphal quadriga,"** one of the great masterpieces of world art, although of uncertain origin. Perhaps they date from the third or fourth centuries B.C. They were carried to Venice after a sack of Constantinople. Napoleon carted them off to Paris after a sack of Venice, but, happily, they were eventually returned.

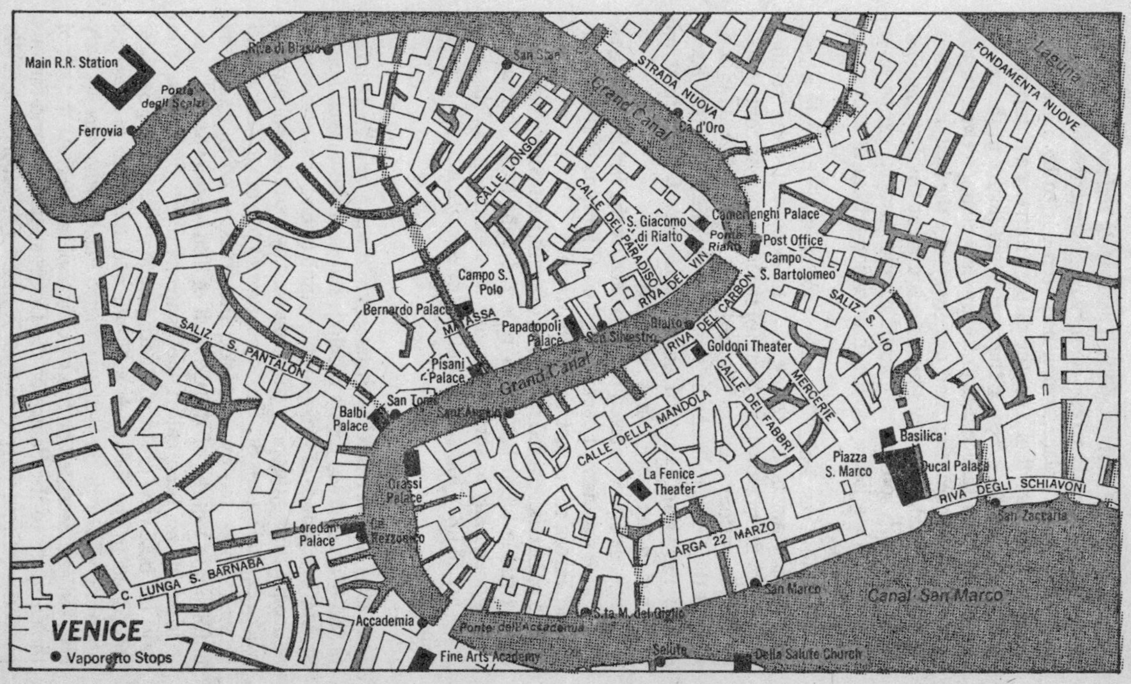
Main R.R. Station
Ponte degli Scalzi
Ferrovia
Riva di Biasio
San Stae
Grand Canal
STRADA NUOVA
Ca d'Oro
FONDAMENTA NUOVE
Laguna
CALLE LONGO
CALLE DEL PARADISO
S. Giacomo di Rialto
Camerlenghi Palace
Ponte Rialto
Post Office
Campo S. Bartolomeo
RIVA DEL VIN
Campo S. Polo
Bernardo Palace
MATASSA
Papadopoli Palace
San Silvestro
Rialto
RIVA DEL CARBON
Goldoni Theater
SALIZ. S. LIO
SALIZ. S. PANTALON
Pisani Palace
Grand Canal
MERCERIE
CALLE DEI FABBRI
CALLE DELLA MANDOLA
San Tomà
Sant'Angelo
Balbi Palace
Basilica
Piazza S. Marco
Ducal Palace
La Fenice Theater
Grassi Palace
RIVA DEGLI SCHIAVONI
San Zaccaria
Loredan Palace
Ca Rezzonico
LARGA 22 MARZO
C. LUNGA S. BARNABA
San Marco
Canal San Marco
S.ta M. del Giglio
Accademia
Ponte dell'Accademia
VENICE
• Vaporetto Stops
Fine Arts Academy
Salute
Della Salute Church

THE PALACE OF THE DOGES: The **Doge's Palace,** practically around the corner, is a 16th-century reconstruction of the original 14th-century palace, which had been gutted by a great fire. Here sat the Council of Ten, the rather arbitrary administrative body of Renaissance Venice that meted out justice at the height of the Republic. Justice was unfortunately characterized largely by torture and execution, and not always for the best of reasons. The room in which the old men sat is a great gloomy chamber, decorated with somber oil paintings, and reached via an antechamber with a lion's mouth, into which letters of accusation were dropped.

The famous resident of the palace was the doge himself, whose **private apartments** are aglow with frescoed walls and ceilings with magnificent paintings. Some of the masters who contributed to the decorations include Veronese (his *Rape of Europa* is considered the finest painting in the gallery); Tintoretto (his *Paradise* in the Grand Council chamber is one of the largest oil paintings in the world) and Sasovino.

Dungeons are connected to the palace by the **Bridge of Sighs.** The bridge was named because of the sad laments of the prisoners led across to torture and even death.

The palace is covered almost entirely in rose-colored stone—unforgettable when bathed in reflected light from the canals.

It is open daily in summer from 8:30 a.m. to 7 p.m., charging 3000 lire ($1.83) for admission. Hours are 9 a.m. to 2 p.m. in winter.

PIAZZETTA SAN MARCO: Adjacent to the palace is the Piazzetta San Marco, noted for its fabulous statue of the winged lion of St. Mark. It stands atop a granite column (which was also ripped off from Constantinople), and is flanked by a similar column, on whose capital stands St. Theodore, former patron of Venice until he was supplanted by St. Mark. Incidentally, on this spot the unfortunate victims of the Council of Ten were executed.

In what has been called the "antechamber" of Venice, you have the best view of the southern facade of St. Mark's Basilica. Imbedded in the facade is a *Virgin and Bambino* in mosaics, honoring a poor baker—that is, Pietro Fasiol, who was unjustly accused and executed on a false charge of murder. At the left of the entrance to the Palace of the Doges stands a world-famous collection of four porphyry figures called *The Moors.* Naturally puce colored, they are huddled together in fear.

THE TWO TOWERS: Two towers in this same area are attractions and familiar landmarks. The first is the **Campanile** or bell-tower (tel. 89-000) of the Basilica San Marco, a reconstruction of the original, which dramatically collapsed into the piazza in the summer of 1902. No one was hurt, since the night before the fall, the tower had emitted a telltale groan that sent everyone within earshot racing to safety. It collapsed the next day when the populace was kept at a safe distance. Today, a modern elevator whisks visitors to the top for a splendid view of the city. The ride costs 1200 lire (73¢) and can be taken from 9:30 a.m. till 10:30 p.m. (from 10 a.m. to 4 p.m. in winter).

The other structure is the **Clock Tower,** Torre dell'Orologio (tel. 31-879), whose sculpted Moors have been striking the same bell for centuries. This too can be climbed—this time on foot—and at the top, a great view unfolds. Notice the signs of the zodiac inscribed on the clock so that astrologers can match the movements of the sun with those of the stars. It's possible to scale the tower from 9 a.m. till noon and 3 to 5 p.m. for a cost of 1500 lire (92¢). Closed Monday.

SCHOOL OF SAN ROCCO: This dark, early 16th-century "school" was richly decorated by the great Tintoretto. "Scuole" were Venetian institutions throughout the various quarters in which the patricians met. The best known one is San Rocco (tel. 34-864), in which Tintoretto won a commission to do 56 canvases, a task that took 18 years. Paintings cover the upper and lower halls, including the well-known *Flight into Egypt.* The school owns what is generally considered Tintoretto's masterpiece, his huge *Crucifixion.* Other scenes also illustrate episodes from the life of Christ. Hours are 10 a.m. to 1 p.m. daily; 10 a.m. to 1 p.m. and 3 to 6 p.m. on Sunday. Admission is 2500 lire ($1.53). Vaporetto stop no. 10.

ALONG THE GRAND CANAL: The main street of town is the Grand Canal, thronged with gondolas and vaporetti (those motorized boat-buses), spanned by graceful bridges and lined with palaces. Many of those palaces house fabulous museums, with collections encompassing art from the Renaissance to the present. Most notable is the **Gallerie dell' Accademia,** (tel. 22-247), with a fine assortment of paintings, mainly of the Venetian school. It's at Campo della Carità (vaporetto stop no. 12). The

Academy is open daily (except Monday) from 9 a.m. to 2 p.m. (holidays, to 1 p.m.), charging 3000 lire ($1.83) for admission.

Of the other galleries, perhaps the grandest is **Ca' d'Oro,** formerly a private palace, donated to the Italian state after the First World War by the owner, Baron Franchetti. The collection ranges from Van Dyck to Carpaccio, and the lush appointments of the palace compete with the works of art on the walls.

The "House of Gold," at vaporetto stop no. 6, was so named because it was once gilded (imagine what that would cost today). In the ogival style, it has a lacy Gothic look, really a candy box. Among the more notable paintings is a version of the suffering of St. Sebastian by Mantegna, as well as one of Titian's voluptuous versions of Venus. Another equally renowned work is Van Dyck's *Portrait of a Gentleman.* You'll also find work by Giorgione. The gallery has reopened after being shut ten years. Check with the tourist office for visiting hours.

As a change of pace from the regular Italian museum, the **Peggy Guggenheim Collection** (tel. 706-288) displays modern art from the private collection of Peggy Guggenheim, who died in 1979. Max Ernst, Picasso, Chagall, Jackson Pollock, and many others are represented here in Ms. Guggenheim's former Venetian palace. It's at Ca' Venier dei Leoni (vaporetto stop no. 14 or on foot from the Academy Gallery). The address is 701 San Gregorio. Open to the public at a 4000-lira ($2.44) admission charge, the collection may be visited daily, except Tuesday, from 2 to 6 p.m., April to October. Since Peggy Guggenheim's death, the collection has been administered by the Solomon R. Guggenheim Foundation, which also operates the Solomon R. Guggenheim Museum in New York. After wandering through the house and seeing the paintings, you can take a leisurely stroll through a sculpture garden.

At **Ca' Rezzonico,** vaporetto stop no. 11 along the Grand Canal, Robert Browning lived as a widower in rooms once occupied by Clement XIII. Nowadays, it's a museum of baroque furnishings and paintings. A Throne Room contains an allegorical ceiling by Tiepolo. Here are all the rich props that characterized Venice in the 18th century, including ebony blacks carrying torches, elaborate chandeliers, gilded furniture, and the inevitable chinoiserie. The best paintings are by Pietro Longhi, including his well-known work, *The Lady and the Hairdresser.* The palace may be visited from 10 a.m. to 4 p.m. for 1000 lire (61¢). On Sunday morning, when no admission is charged, the hours are from 9:30 a.m. to 12:30 p.m.

Where to Stay

GETTING TO A HOTEL: Venice abounds with hotels in all price ranges—but to get to them presents a minor problem. Since there are no cars or taxis, you'll probably be dependent on porters and/or gondoliers (unless you've been smart enough to travel with one light suitcase). How much to pay these people is always a source of confusion to visitors; be advised that the rates are standardized and controlled by the government.

Other than actually renting a gondola, the second most luxurious way to travel is to have a porter carry your luggage aboard a vaporetto (you must pay his fare, however), then escort you, complete with baggage, to your hotel. If you're going on to the Lido, you'll pay more, of course. Vaporetti charge different fares depending on how far you are going and whether you take an express (diretto) or a local (accelerato). The average fare for accelerato is 1200 lire (73¢), going up to 1500 lire (92¢) for diretto, but these prices are subject to change.

DELUXE HOTELS: **Gritti Palace,** 2467 Campo Santa Maria del Giglio (tel. 26-044), is first and foremost. Once the home of Doge Andrea Gritti, it is one of the most sumptuous palaces bordering the Grand Canal. This is a grand hotel in the best European tradition, and former guests have included film stars, royal jet-setters, statesmen, and literary figures (it was "our home in Venice" to Hemingway). There are 100 guest rooms, all done individually and richly, with air conditioning and marble baths. Singles start at 300,000 lire ($183), and doubles are priced at 400,000 lire ($244).

Danieli Royal Excelsior, 4196 Riva degli Schiavoni (tel. 26-480), was built as a grand showcase by the Doge Dandolo in the 14th century. In 1822 it was transformed into a deluxe "hotel for kings." Placed in a most spectacular position, right on the Grand Canal, it has sheltered not only kings but also princes, cardinals, ambassadors, and such celebrated literary figures as George Sand and her 24-year-old lover, Alfred de Musset. In time the palace was to play host to such distinguished men as Charles Dickens, D'Annunzio, and Wagner. A star sapphire in the CIGA chain, the palace fronts the canal with the New Danieli Excelsior, a modern wing. Two neighboring palaces as well have been incorporated into this serenissima ensemble.

"Incredible, breathtaking," said one California visitor. "You enter a four-story-high stairwell, with Venetian arches and balustrades (one almost expects to see Juliet suddenly appear from behind one of the columns)." Throughout, you wander in an atmosphere of silk-flocked walls, gilt mirrors, ornate furnishings, marble walls, decorated ceilings, and Oriental carpeting. Even the balconies opening off the main lounge have been glamorously illuminated by stained-glass skylights. More intimate is the beamed-ceiling drinking lounge, with leather armchairs. The hotel possesses a rooftop dining room, giving you an undisturbed view of the canals and "crowns" of Venice.

The bedrooms, 242 in all, range widely in price, dimension, decor, and vistas, with the ones opening onto the lagoon going for more, of course. The standard accommodations (facing the side) range between 250,000 lire ($152.50) and 350,000 lire ($213.50) in a single; doubles go for 375,000 lire ($228.75). The service charge is included in the price, as is a continental breakfast.

Cipriani, Isola della Giudecca (tel. 707-744), is a select resort villa on a small island across from the Piazza San Marco, which was conceived as a private residence and guest house, emphasizing personal comfort. It's the creation of world-famous Giuseppe Cipriani, the founder of Harry's Bar and the one real-life character in Hemingway's Venetian novel. It's the only hotel in Venice with an Olympic-size swimming pool, plus tennis courts and a sauna. There's even an exclusive Sea Gull Club, reserved for hotel guests. In the evenings, an orchestra plays for informal dancing in the garden, and you dine in elegantly decorated indoor rooms, at poolside, or on terraces overlooking the lagoon. The Cipriani prides itself on serving an authentic Venetian cuisine.

Rooms have different exposures, facilities, and sizes, as reflected by the price scale. A single ranges from 350,000 lire ($213.50). A double goes from 425,000 lire ($259.30) to 500,000 lire ($305). You'll pay even more for a private sitting room or a terrace with a balcony. The rooms have splendid views, either of the lagoon to the south, the Palladian San Giorgio Maggiore to the east and north, or the vineyards and the domed Redentore and La Zitelle to the west. A private launch service ferries guests, at any hour, to and from the hotel's own pier to the Piazza San Marco. The hotel accepts guests from March 2 to November 16.

FIRST-CLASS CHOICES: **Hotel Europa & Regina,** 2159 San Marco (tel. 700-477), was formed by combining two Venetian palaces, both facing the Grand Canal, and joining them together with a low-lying restaurant and a café terrace. Many clients prefer to enter through the side courtyard, which is so quiet you can hear birds singing, rather than through the front door that fronts the canal. The spacious high-ceilinged rooms come in a wide variety of decors, ranging from a monochromatic, tastefully furnished 19th-century style that originally made the hotels so popular, to tastefully renovated rooms in appealing colors that would be perfect for a honeymoon stopover.

A huge drawing room contains a Venetian glass chandelier, unusual reproductions of old maps, and comfortable chairs. The 200 bedrooms are joined by a labyrinthine set of hallways, which a uniformed staff member will easily negotiate for you. On the premises is a terraced restaurant where average meals cost around 70,000 lire ($42.70). Singles range from 155,000 lire ($94.55) to 225,000 lire ($137.25), while doubles cost between 240,000 lire ($146.40) and 340,000 lire ($207.40), breakfast not included. The hotel is a member of the CIGA chain.

Londra Palace, 4171 Riva degli Schiavoni (tel. 700-533), is an elegant first-class hotel that was formed when two palaces were joined together around 80 years ago. President Carter's staff occupied half of the hotel during a summit conference in 1979, and before that Igor Stravinsky stayed in one of the comfortable rooms. Leading off the lobby is an accommodatingly cozy reading room, a velvet-upholstered lobby filled with conservatively modern paintings, an English-style pub and piano bar, and a well-known restaurant, De Leoni. The 90 or so bedrooms rent for 230,000 lire ($140.30) in a single and from 350,000 lire ($213.50) in a double, with a continental breakfast included. Vaporetto stop: Arsenale.

Hotel Luna, 1243 San Marco (tel. 89840), is the oldest hotel in Venice. Founded in 1474 as a monastery by the Congrega di Fratti della Luna, it took in traveling pilgrims on their way through Venice. The tradition of hospitality remains for the thousands of visitors who have found a room at this comfortable hotel on the back side of the Piazza San Marco. Some of the rooms look over the Grand Canal, and most of them have high ceilings, recently renovated interiors, marble floors, air conditioning, and parquet floors. Management places flowers in the hallways of the upper floors, which can be reached by elevator or by a wide marble staircase. Singles range from 120,000 lire

($73.20) to 190,000 lire ($115.90), while doubles cost between 185,000 lire ($112.85) and 330,000 lire ($201.30). Some triple rooms are also available. Vaporetto stop: San Marco.

Saturnia-Internazionale, 2398 Via XXII Marzo (tel. 708-377), is an elaborate old palace dating from the 14th century. If you fancy a profusion of carved woodwork, Venetian glass chandeliers, beamed ceilings, and tapestries, this is the place. Guest rooms are spacious and often furnished with antiques. Many overlook a garden in the rear. All are air-conditioned and have private baths. In high season, March 16 to October 31, singles pay from 170,000 lire ($103.70); doubles from 240,000 lire ($146.40). And there's a choice of dining in a rustic salon or a nautically decorated gallery.

Monaco & Grand Canal, 1325 San Marco (tel. 700-211), occupies a stellar position right on the Grand Canal, across from Harry's Bar. Many of its bedrooms have that remarkable lagoon view. In season, guests take their meals on the canal-bordering terrace. Lounges have been furnished in conservatively traditional modern, with a collection of overscale contemporary paintings. The inner terrace is a cozy rendezvous, with garden furniture and trellises. Try to get one of the French-style accommodations with painted furniture. In high season, a twin-bedded room with bath rents for 320,000 lire ($195.20) to 375,000 lire ($198.25), the higher priced units overlooking the Grand Canal; a single will cost 250,000 lire ($152.50) to 200,000 lire ($122). The completely redecorated, tastefully appointed Grand Canal Restaurant serves à la carte meals.

Gabrielli-Sandwirth, 4110 Riva degli Schiavoni (tel. 31-580), is a Venetian-Gothic palace, with blossom-filled balconies, on the fashionable main street bordering the lagoon. The hotel possesses that rarity: a good-size private garden and courtyard, the center of its life. You'll find a shaded dining terrace and cozy nooks with chairs, swings, and hammocks set out. Inside, its lounges have blue-gray marble, beamed ceilings, modern furnishings, and spaciousness. The bedrooms are well furnished and attractively maintained, reflecting the taste level of the owners, the Perkhofer family of Austria. All of the 110 rooms have private baths or showers, for which singles pay 185,000 lire ($112.85); doubles, 290,000 lire ($176.90). The food—Austrian-Italian meals—is good. The full-board rate in high season ranges from 240,000 lire ($146.40) per person, inclusive.

THE MEDIUM-PRICED RANGE: **La Fenice et des Artistes,** 1936-A San Marco (tel. 32-333), is one of those special one-of-a-kind hotels with a loyal list of habitués. It's hidden away off a little plaza next to the opera house, and is considered "the only" place for visiting groups of singers, conductors, or writers. Its exterior is deliciously mellow, with an intimate entrance garden and an ornate inner staircase. The sitting and breakfast room is richly decorated as well. Breakfast, the only meal served, is also offered on the flagstoned courtyard terrace, surrounded by climbing vines. Each bedroom is unique, differently shaped and furnished with Venetian antiques or reproductions. Singles range from 82,000 lire ($50.02) to 95,000 lire ($57.95), and doubles, from 135,000 lire ($82.35) to 155,000 lire ($94.55). It is open all year.

Giorgione, 4587 SS. Apostoli (tel. 25-810), is a recently glamorized little hotel near the Ca' d'Oro vaporetto stop. In spite of its modernization, its decor is lush and traditionally Venetian. The lounges and dining rooms are equipped with fine furnishings and decorative accessories. Likewise, the bedrooms are designed to coddle guests, being very comfortable as well as stylish. Singles with bath peak at 105,000 lire ($64.05), and doubles go for 175,000 lire ($106.75), including breakfast. Taxes and service are also included. The owner hawkeyes the running of the dining room, seeing that the cuisine is first rate. The hotel also has a typical Venetian garden. It's rated second class by the government, but the Giorgione has a higher standard than many of the first-class establishments.

Flora, 2283-A Via XXII Marzo (tel. 705-844), while not on the Grand Canal, is most central, within walking distance of the Piazza San Marco. It's an old villa, with its own flower-filled courtyard. Many of its bedrooms overlook the so-called Palazzo of Othello. The 36-room hotel is family owned and run in a most personable way by Alessandro Romanelli and his son Ruggero, who is a painter. Each bedroom has its own size, shape, and personality. Some of the rooms are quite small and cramped, and whether or not you like this hotel depends on the room you're assigned. Rates quoted are inclusive. In high season, from March 16 to October 14, a single with bath rents for 100,000 lire ($61). Bathless doubles begin at 130,000 lire ($79.30), going up to 160,000 lire ($97.60) with private bath.

Bonvecchiati, 4488 San Marco (tel. 85-017), is a combination of two villas made into one, bordering a canal, just a short walk from the Piazza San Marco. Its outdoor dining terrace overlooks an arched bridge, where gondoliers row by on their way to the

Grand Canal. The owner, Giovanni Deana, has assembled a superb collection of contemporary paintings that cover many of the walls of the lounges and corridors, occasionally overflowing into one of the bedrooms. For the most part, the bedrooms have been modernized, although they are traditionally furnished. The best way to stay here is on the half-board plan, ranging from 80,000 lire ($48.80) to 95,000 lire ($57.95) per person daily. Rooms come with and without private baths, singles costing from 48,000 lire ($29.28) to 75,000 lire ($45.75); doubles go for 85,000 lire ($51.85) to 120,000 lire ($73.20).

Hotel San Cassiano Ca' Favretto, 2232 Santa Croce (tel. 705-477). This hotel used to be the studio of the 19th-century painter Giacomo Favretto. The views from the hotel's gondola pier and from the four-arched porch of the dining room encompass the lacy facade of the Ca' d'Oro, which is sometimes considered the most beautiful building in Venice. The hotel was constructed in the 14th century as a palace.

Giancarlo Manao, who purchased the property in 1978, worked closely with Venetian authorities to preserve the original details, which include an impressive 20-foot beamed ceiling in the entrance area. Today, the architectural plans from the many renovations hang in gilt frames above the antiques in the lobby. Recent clients have included George McGovern and guests of the American Embassy.

Fifteen of the 35 conservatively decorated rooms look out over one of two canals, and many of them are filled with heirloom antiques or high-quality reproductions. Singles cost from 120,000 lire ($73.20), while doubles go for 180,000 lire ($109.80), with a continental breakfast included. All units contain radio, mini-bar, TV, and air conditioning. Triples are available at 250,000 lire ($152.50) apiece. Vaporetto: San Stae.

Hotel Carpaccio, 2765 San Tomà (tel. 35946). Don't be put off by the narrow winding alleyways leading up to the wrought-iron entrance of this second-class hotel. The building was meant to be approached by gondola. Once you're inside you'll realize that your location in the heart of the oldest part of the city justifies your confusing arrival. This building used to be the Palazzo Barbarigo della Terrazza, and part of it is still reserved for private apartments.

Owner Guido Tassoto, who studied in London, maintains 17 tasteful and spacious rooms filled with serviceable 1960s-style furniture. The salon is decorated with gracious pieces, marble floors, and a big arched window whose exterior is crowned with a bearded head of stone looking, along with you, over the Grand Canal. Bathless units cost 75,000 lire ($45.75) in a single and from 125,000 lire ($76.25) in a double, while accommodations with bath go for 120,000 lire ($73.20) in a single and from 165,000 lire ($100.65) in a double with a continental breakfast included. Vaporetto: San Tomà.

BEST FOR THE BUDGET: **Casa Paganelli,** 4687 Riva degli Schiavoni (tel. 24–324), has been an artist retreat for years. Its sympathetic owner, Signor Paganelli, has accumulated many paintings left by former guests, including one by Ben Nicholson. He's even opened the front wall to allow a better view of his classic picture of the lagoon where gondolas glide by. The reception lounge is furnished with modern simplicity, with large plants and contemporary furniture. The bedrooms, many with water views, are spacious, comfortable, and attractive. Bathless singles cost 50,000 lire ($30.50), increasing to 85,000 lire ($51.85) in a bathless double. With a bath or private shower, singles cost 68,000 lire ($41.48), doubles, 110,000 lire ($67.10)—including continental breakfasts, taxes, and service. The half-board rate begins at 70,000 lire ($42.70) per person daily and goes up to 85,000 lire ($51.85). Take the vaporetto to stop no. 16.

Marconi & Milano, Rialto Bridge, Canal Grande (tel. 22-068), was built in the year 1500 when Venice was at the height of its supremacy on the seas, but now it incorporates a later addition. The older portion, once a wine shop, has been absorbed into the hotel and is bound to titillate lovers of the ornate and dramatic. Drawing room furnishings, for instance, are appropriate for visiting bishops. The hotel lies less than 50 feet from the much-painted Rialto Bridge (vaporetto stop 7). The Savoldi Scherer family operates everything, combining an Italian flair with German efficiency (the German owner married the daughter of the founder). Only four of the lovely old rooms open directly onto the Grand Canal; the others face side and rear streets. The bedrooms are less inspired, with semi-modern furnishings. Bathless doubles rent for 78,000 lire ($47.58); with bath, 94,000 lire ($57.34). Breakfast is included. It's fun to have meals in the L-shaped room, sitting rather formally in Gothic chairs. But in summer, you'll want to dine at a sidewalk table on the Grand Canal.

San Fantin, 1930A Campiello La Fenice (tel. 31-401), is a modest and modernized little hotel with a classic facade in one of the choicest cultural and historical spots of Venice. Its entrance is forbidding, with cannon balls forming part of its decor, but inside you're given a friendlier greeting. The rooms are simply furnished and reasonably comfortable. The most expensive singles rent for 45,000 lire ($27.45), and bathless doubles peak at 75,000 lire ($45.75). A double with bath costs 95,000 lire ($57.95). The hotel shuts down every year around mid-November, reopening its doors in spring.

Pensione Accademia, Fondamente Maravegie (Dorsoduro 1058; tel. 37846), is a slightly run-down but totally charming hotel set in a villa whose garden extends into the angle created by the junction of two canals. Iron fences, twisting vines, and neoclassical sculpture are a part of the setting, as well as Gothic-style paneling, Venetian chandeliers, and Victorian-era furniture. The building served as the Russian Embassy before World War II, and as a private house before that. There's an upstairs sitting room flanked with two large windows and a formal rose garden that is visible from the breakfast room.

When she was in Venice shooting *Summertime,* the Accademia Pensione was the fictional residence of Katherine Hepburn. (Incidentally, it was at this time that she fell into a Venetian canal and got a permanent eye infection!)

The bedrooms are spacious, filled with 1950s-style pieces, and they are kept clean. Depending on the plumbing and the season, singles rent for between 42,000 lire ($25.62) and 60,000 lire ($36.60), while doubles cost between 75,000 lire ($45.75) and 105,000 lire ($64.05), including a continental breakfast. Vaporetto stop: Accademia.

Pensione Seguso, 779 Grand Canal Zattere (tel. 22340), is a terracotta-colored house whose foundation dates from the 15th century. Set at the junction of two canals, this 17-room hotel is off the beaten track, on a less traveled side of Venice, across the Grand Canal from the Piazza San Marco. Its relative isolation made it attractive to such tenants as Ezra Pound and John Julius Norwich and his famous mother, Lady Diana Cooper.

The interior is furnished with the family antiques of the Seguso family, who have maintained the hotel for the past century. Small tables are set up near the hotel entrance, upon which breakfast is served on sunny days. Half board is obligatory in the elegantly upper-crust dining room, where reproduction antiques, real heirlooms, and family cats vie for the attention of the many satisfied guests. Open from March 1 until November 30, the hotel charges half-board rates of around 90,000 lire ($54.90) per person in a room with bath and around 75,000 lire ($45.75) per person in a bathless. Vaporetto stop: Zattere.

Hotel San Moïse, 2058 San Marco (tel. 703-755), is a small hotel on a narrow little canal, the Canale dei Barcaroli, a short walk from the Piazza San Marco, near the theater, La Fenice. The recently renovated hotel has its own private landing stage for gondolas and motorboats. Most of the pleasantly furnished rooms open onto the canal. There is a phone in every room, as well as a frigobar. For a bathless double, the tariff is 80,000 lire ($48.80), rising to 95,000 lire ($57.95) in a double with private bath. Singles without bath cost 55,000 lire ($33.55), going up to 65,000 lire ($39.65) with bath.

Dining in Venice

THE LEADING RESTAURANTS: Antico Martini, 1980 San Marco Campo San Fantin (tel. 37-027), has for a long, long time enjoyed gastronomic stature in Venice. Across from the Teatro della Fenice, it specializes in Venetian dishes, but prepares them with such exceptional flair you'll hardly recognize them. For example, its risotto di frutti di mare, creamy Venetian style, has plenty of fresh seafood (which may vary according to the season). Another excellent main course is sogliola alla murnaia (sole meunière), truly superb. A complete meal will run from 60,000 lire ($36.60) to 85,000 lire ($51.85), depending on what you order. The ambience is in the Venetian-palazzo style, with chandeliers and gilt-framed oil paintings. In summer the guests like to dine in the flower-filled 14th-century courtyard. The restaurant does not serve lunch on Wednesday and is closed all day Tuesday.

Ristorante Club del Doge, Hotel Gritti Palace, 2467 Compo Santa Maria del Giglio (tel. 26044), comes closer than practically any other restaurant in Venice to recreating the setting of a doge's palace, as well as presenting some of the finest cuisine in Venice. Contained within a prestigious deluxe hotel, this restaurant has hosted such luminaries as Hemingway, Somerset Maugham, Princess Grace, Princess Margaret, and numerous show biz figures such as Gregory Peck and Roger Moore.

The restaurant is in an intimate room whose size is more than doubled in summer when tables are placed on an outdoor platform extending over the canal. Indoors, you'll have a view of the beamed ceilings whose gray, beige, and pink patterns subtly match the colors of the marble floors, but outdoors you'll face the stone expanses of Santa Maria della Salute spread out just across the water.

The cuisine is essentially Mediterranean, and the chef always presents a limited selection of regional dishes from the Veneto area, including marinated baby sole in a Venetian sour sauce, Adriatic sea crab, and calf liver with polenta. The menu always includes freshly made antipasti, elegant meats and fish, and other classic Italian dishes with many imaginative touches. Expect to spend from 140,000 lire ($85.71) per person.

Ristorante Terrazza Danieli, Hotel Danieli, 4196 Riva degli Schiavoni. Despite the centuries-old palace that houses it, this terrace-style restaurant on the top floor of this famed deluxe hotel is one of the newest eating places in the city. You can reach it from an elevator near the hotel's reception desk. This will deposit you in an L-shaped room with lots of light-grained paneling, marble accents, delicate copies of 18th-century Venetian chairs, and an almost obsessively panoramic view of the Grand Canal.

The kitchens here were completely ripped out and remade, and the resulting dishes include pasta with onions and anchovies, stewed cuttlefish in a black sauce, green tagliatelle with ham sauce, and a wide range of fresh antipasti. Opened in May 1984, the restaurant charges around 150,000 lire ($91.50) for a full meal. Vaporetto stop: San Zaccaria.

Taverna La Fenice, 1938 San Marco (tel. 23-856), is one of the finest restaurants in Italy. It's most romantic in summer, when guests dine out under a canopy beside the Teatro della Fenice which saw the première of Verdi's *La Traviata.* If you're seeking a pre-opera dinner or a post-opera supper, this is the place. A whole school of Adriatic fish is presented here. You can sample some of them, including gamberetti (small shrimp), squid, and octopi by ordering a seafood antipasto. Main dishes are invariably good. I recently enjoyed a very tender steak Vivaldi. On another night, rigatoni alla Fenice was very good. Desserts are luscious. Expect to spend from 60,000 lire ($36.60) for a complete meal, not including wine. Closed Sunday and from the first of January to the first week of February.

Harry's Bar, 1323 Calle Vallaresso (tel. 36-797), is a former favorite haunt of Hemingway and waterspot for martini-thirsty Americans. Actually, it's a Renaissance palazzo right on the Grand Canal. The martinis are served very, very cold and very dry here. The bloody marys are equally renowned.

But Harry's, the creation of Giuseppe Cipriani, is no mere

saloon. It serves some of the finest food in Venice, although it's hard to get a table. You can dine downstairs in the bar or in a room upstairs. On one recent occasion, my fish soup was among the best I've ever had. The scampi thermidor is expensive but worth every lire. Everything ends well if topped with a chocolate mousse. Meals cost 60,000 lire ($36.60) to 95,000 lire ($57.95), plus 20% service. Closed Monday.

La Caravella, 2398 Calle Larga XXII Marzo (tel. 708-901), next door to the Hotel Saturnia-Internazionale, attracts with its gracious ambience, an elegant pub atmosphere with time-mellowed paneling. Many of the specialties are featured nowhere else in town. For a different beginning, try a smooth gazpacho—the cold "liquid salad" of Andalusia. Standard dishes include chateaubriand for two persons and the spring chicken (cooked in a paper bag). However, the best item to order is one of the poached fish dishes, such as bass—all priced according to weight and served with a tempting sauce. The bouillabaisse in the style of Marseille is also excellent. After all that, the ice cream in champagne is welcome. Meals cost from 55,000 lire ($33.55) to 85,000 lire ($51.85). Closed Wednesday.

Do Leoni, Londra Palace Hotel, 4171 Riva degli Schiavoni (tel. 700-533), offers a big-windowed view of a magnificent 19th-century equestrian statue ringed with heroic women taming lions. On the ground floor of this well-known first-class hotel on the banks of the Grand Canal, the restaurant is filled with colors of scarlet and gold, a motif of lions patterned into the carpeting, and English pub-style furniture. An adjoining piano bar is a popular nightspot. Menu items include both Venetian and international specialties, with overtones of nouvelle cuisine. For example, you might face a selection of sauteed calf liver, spaghetti with clams, a mixed fish fry from the Adriatic, mussel soup au gratin, fettuccine with smoked trout, scampi in a sauce of green peppercorns, and chicken breast stuffed with herbs. Summertime dining is on an outdoor terrace with a view of the pedestrian traffic from the nearby Piazza San Marco. Meals range upward from 72,000 lire ($43.92). The restaurant is closed on Tuesday. Vaporretto stop: Arsenale.

BUDGET TO MODERATE DINING: **"al graspo de ua,"** 5094 Calle dei Bombaseri (tel. 23-647). Don't be surprised if you find a movie star sitting at the next table. This "bunch of grapes" is one of the celebrity favorites of Venice. It has a tavern atmosphere with a series of connecting dining rooms. Few diners fail to succumb to the food-laden antipasto table. A waiter will assist you as you make your selection from this groaning array of food. This feast of hors d'oeuvres is referred to as "self-service mammoth." Later, if you're up to it, you can select the gran fritto dell'Adriatico containing everything from squid to scampi. A complete meal will cost from 35,000 lire ($21.35) to 45,000 lire ($27.45). Take the vaporetto to the Rialto Bridge. The Grapes is only a short walk away. Closed Monday, Tuesday, and from July 20 through the first week in August and from December 20 to January 10.

Archimboldo, 3219 Castello Calle dei Furlani (tel. 86569). The small street containing this exciting restaurant might not be on your map, although most Venetians locate it by walking to the end of the Calle dei Furlani, in the heart of the oldest part of the inner city. Opened in 1982, the restaurant is perfect for devotees of the freshest kinds of vegetables. The chefs present an imaginative array of dishes inspired by nouvelle cuisine and containing the fruits of the Italian harvest.

The sunny decor includes fresh colors of pastel greens and blues, plus an absorbing collection of original paintings by friends of the four owners, and huge baskets of carefully arranged vegetables-as-art that vie for attention with the fresh flowers of the day. The name of the restaurant evokes the Renaissance painter who arranged vegetables into portraits of his contemporaries (a radish for a chin, a carrot for a nose). When four young friends (Silvano, Renato, Flavio, and Luigino) set up their restaurant, they commissioned a copy of one of Guiseppe Archimboldo's most famous works, *Summer,* to hang prominently as a suggestion of the kinds of specialties they would serve.

You might enjoy their fresh asparagus, a variety of eggplant dishes, zucchini in white wine with endive and artichokes, veal liver in butter and sage, veal kidneys with parsley and garlic, beef with pink peppercorns, pork with pineapple, kiwi, lemon, oranges, and grapefruit, spaghetti with melon, chicken with orange, and tagliolini with smoked salmon. Expect to spend around 35,000 lire ($21.35) per person. The restaurant is closed Tuesday. Vaporetto stop: San Zaccaria.

Trattoria alla Colomba, 1665 San Marco-Piscina-Frezzeria (tel. 23-817), is perhaps the best known trattoria in Venice. It's "propriétaire-conducteur" is Giovanni Deana, who also runs the Bonvecchiati Hotel. The restaurant is decorated with a gallery of contemporary paintings, including works by de Chirico,

Picasso, and Chagall. Occupying an entire "alley" near the Piazza San Marco, Colomba serves good food, including such specialties as risotto with mushrooms from the Montello hills; dried cod simmered in milk and seasoned with onions, cinnamon, and anchovies, and granzeola (Adriatic spider crab). Expect to pay anywhere from 35,000 lire ($21.35) to 85,000 lire ($51.85) for a complete meal.

Restaurant da Bruno, 5731 Castello Calle del Paradiso (tel. 21-480), halfway between the Rialto Bridge and the Piazza San Marco, is somewhat of a dining oddity in Venice. The setting is atmospheric, a tavern ambience. Meats grilling on an open-hearth fire create a wafting aroma attracting hungry diners. In season, the proprietor features some of the finest game dishes in the city, including fagiano (pheasant) and capriola (roebuck). These usually expensive dishes are priced surprisingly low here. Of course, you get the classic specialties here as well, including zuppa di pesce (an Adriatic-type bouillabaisse). Expect to pay from 30,000 lire ($18.30) to 40,000 lire ($24.40) for a complete meal, plus 12% for service. Closed Tuesday and from mid-July till the first of August.

Al Teatro, Campo Teatro La Fenice (tel. 37-214), is a restaurant/pizzeria that is romantically and typically Venetian. On a little piazzetta overlooking the opera house, it serves the most scrumptious pizzas in town. On a summer evening, sidewalk tables overflow onto the square. Another special feature of the restaurant is the array of dishes done by the maître d' at your table, including a creamy spaghetti carbonara. For dessert, I'd suggest a macedonia, that is, a fruit salad with ice cream. Meals begin at 25,000 lire ($15.25). Closed Monday.

The Islands

You'll also want to get over to the beach of Venice if you should arrive in summer. It's easily reached by vaporetto. Go to stop no. 6 and buy a round-trip ticket (the boat leaves from a landing stage near the Doge's Palace).

HOTELS ON THE LIDO: Excelsior Palace, 40 Lungomare Marconi (tel. 760-201), is a mammoth establishment that, when it was built, was the biggest resort hotel of its kind in the world. It did much to make the Lido fashionable, luring clients away from the other grande dames nearby and maintaining ever since a position as one of the chicest addresses in the region. At first glance it appears to be a castle—no, a government building; no, a hotel of sweeping magnitude with rooms that range in style and amenities from cozy singles to suites. The most exotic view—encompassing towers that look vaguely Moorish and arches that could even be Indian—is from the hotel's shuttle boat as it brings you up the canal from the lagoon side of the island.

The Excelsior is a monument to *La Dolce Vita.* It's also the preferred hotel of the thousands of film industry spokespersons who book practically every one of the rooms leading off the interminable corridors of the upper floors at festival time.

Most of the social life here takes place around the angular swimming pool, traversed like lines on a Mondrian painting with two bridges, or on the flowered terraces leading up to the cabanas on the sandy beach. Clients can rent boats from a pier extending far into the Adriatic, the entrance to which passes between two guardian sphinxes. One of these, like the original in Cairo, is missing its nose, although the overall effect is undeniably high-style Italian.

All of the rooms—some of them big enough for tennis games—have been modernized, often with vivid colors that look like reminders of summer, regardless of the season. On the premises is one of the most elegant dining rooms on the Adriatic, the Tropicana, with a soaring ceiling, thousands of embellishments, and meals costing around 130,000 lire ($79.30) apiece, not including wine.

The Blue Bar on the ground floor has piano music and views of the beach (drinks here average around 9000 lire, or $5.49). As you register, the bronze monumental fountain in the lobby is worth a second look. On the premises are six tennis courts, and the hotel maintains a private launch for hourly runs to other CIGA hotels on the Grand Canal. Also on the premises is the most popular nightclub/disco on the island. Singles range from 265,000 lire ($161.65) to 380,000 lire ($231.80), while doubles cost from 370,000 lire ($225.70) to 450,000 lire ($274.50), breakfast not included. The hotel is closed from mid-October until mid-April.

Hotel des Bains, 17 Lungomare Marconi (tel. 765-921), is an enormous establishment, built in the grand era of European resort hotels, with its own wooded park and private beach with individual cabanas along with a kind of confectionary facade that could only have been built at the turn of the century. Thomas Mann stayed here several times before making it the setting for his novella *Death in Venice,* and later it was used as a stage for the film of the same name. For delicious comfort, set apart from the intense drama of Venice itself, Des Bains is a good choice.

The renovated interior exudes the flavor of the leisurely life of the aristocratic belle époque era most strongly in its high-ceilinged main salon, whose paneling is a dignified combination of Gothic with art deco. Overlooking the sea, the April to October hotel has 250 well-furnished, fairly large rooms, all with private baths and showers. Room and breakfast rates range from 175,000 lire ($106.75) to 265,000 lire ($161.65) in a single, and from 280,000 lire ($170.80) to 400,000 lire ($244) in a double. Half board ranges from 235,000 lire ($143.35) to 260,000 lire ($158.60) per person, depending on the accommodation.

Guests dine in a large veranda dining room cooled by Adriatic sea breezes. The food is top rate, the service superior. Special features include many resort-type amenities, such as tennis courts, a large swimming pool, a private pier, and a park with shade trees and flowering shrubbery. A motorboat shuttles you back and forth between Venice and the Lido.

In the upper-bracket category, **Quattro Fontane,** 16 Via Quattro Fontane (tel. 760-227), is one of the most charming hotels on the Lido. The trouble is, a lot of people know that, so it's likely to be booked (and it's open only from April to September). Like a chalet from the Dolomites, it's most popular with the discriminating British, who like a homey atmosphere, a garden, friendly management, rooms with superior amenities, and good food served at tables set under shade trees. What a contrast to the sterile modernity of the Casino, a short distance away. The directors are Mr. and Mrs. Bevilacqua (she's Scandinavian). Their hotel was recently enlarged, and it now offers 72 rooms, more than two-thirds with private shower baths. A bathless single rents for 100,000 lire ($61), from 140,000 lire ($85.40) in a single with bath. A double with bath costs from 240,000 lire ($146.40), but only 180,000 lire ($109.80) and up without bath. Full board ranges from 160,000 lire ($97.60) to 220,000 lire ($134.20) per person.

Hotel Helvetia, 4–6 Gran Viale (tel. 768-403), near the commercial center of the Lido, is a four-story, russet-colored, 19th-century building with stone detailing. On a side street near the lagoon side of the island, the hotel is owned by two brothers who acquired it from an earlier Swiss owner who'd named it for his homeland. The quieter rooms face away from the street. The older wing has belle époque high ceilings and attractively comfortable furniture. The newer wing is more streamlined, dating from around 1950, and has been renovated into a style appropriate to the conservative management who maintain this establishment.

Breakfast is served, weather permitting, in a flagstone-covered wall garden behind the hotel. Open from April 1 until October 31, the hotel charges between 80,000 lire ($48.80) and 125,000 lire ($76.25) in a single and between 145,000 lire ($88.45) and 180,000 lire ($109.80) in a double, depending on the plumbing. A continental breakfast is included in the price. The hotel's location is an easy walk from the vaporetto stop from Venice.

DINING ON THE LIDO: If you're a guest in one of the hotels, chances are you are there on the board plan. However, if you're visiting the Lido just for the day, you may want to consider the following dining recommendation.

Restaurant Belvedere, 4 Piazzale S. Maria Elisabetta (tel. 760115). Because of its location at the major boat stop from Venice, you might suspect that this establishment is a tourist trap. That is certainly not the case. Far from it, as exemplified by many well-to-do Venetians who journey over here in spring and summer for a meal on the Lido. The restaurant, attached to a bustling café, is a simple attractive room with cane-backed chairs and big windows on three sides. Care and preparation go into the meals, and as a surprise for Venice, the waiters are actually friendly. Naturally, fish specialties dominate the menu. Try the chef's sea bass or his grilled sole or grilled dorade. The risotto with seafood is a favorite first plate. If you're a tourist on a strict budget, you'll request the set meal at 18,000 lire ($10.98); otherwise, à la carte dinners will cost from 28,000 lire ($17.08). The restaurant is closed on Tuesday.

SIGHTS AND ATTRACTIONS: The lagoon is filled with interesting adventures. Even the most hurried of first-time visitors often head for **Murano,** a center of glassmaking for many hundreds of years. It's here that those characteristic Venetian chandeliers and colored glasses are made. You can stroll into any of the glass factories and observe the activity. Visitors are more than welcome—especially to the little shops selling the factory's handiwork. To reach the island, take vaporetto 5 at Riva degli Schiavoni, a short walk from the Piazzetta San Marco. While on the island you can visit a Renaissance palazzo housing the

Museo Vetrario di Murano, open daily except Wednesday from 10 a.m. to 4 p.m. (on Sunday from 9 to 12:30). The admission is 1000 lire (61¢). Inside is a spectacular collection of antique Venetian glass.

Burano offers a similar type of attraction, although this time the local industry is lace making. The Burrano School of Lace, a late-19th-century institution which sought to preserve the then-dying art, makes an interesting excursion destination. And you can purchase samples of lace in a showroom in the school. The island is charming—it's actually a little fishing village. If time remains, try to visit the Duomo, with its leaning bell tower. Inside is a *Crucifixion* by Tiepolo.

To reach Burano, you can take vaporetto no. 5 (the same one mentioned earlier to Murano) at Riva degli Schiavoni. However, get off at Fondamente Nuova to catch the boat to Burano.

Once on Burano, it's only a short ride to Torcello. This island preserves, more than anyplace else, the sense of isolation and quiet charm that pervades lagoon living. There are open fields and ancient churches. The atmosphere is tranquil and redolent of the past, especially in the old **Church of S. Maria Assunta** (tel. 730-084), dating from the 11th century. For 500 lire ($31¢) you can go inside to view the exceptional Byzantine mosaics.

Nearby, the **Locanda Cipriani** (tel. 730-150) serves the best food of any restaurant in the lagoon. It's owned by the proprietor of the famous Harry's Bar. In the inn so beloved by Hemingway, you can dine in the alfresco loggia in fair weather. Meals range in price from 60,000 lire ($36.60) to 85,000 lire ($51.85), plus a 15% service charge. The locanda is open from March until November 10. It closes in the evening and on Tuesday.

Shopping in Venice

Venetian glass and lace are known throughout the world. But selecting quality products in either craft requires a shrewd eye. There is much that is tawdry and shoddily crafted in Venice. Some of the glassware hawked isn't worth the cost of shipping it home. Yet other pieces represent some of the world's finest artistic and ornamental glass.

Murano is the island where glass is made, and the women on Burano put in painstaking hours turning out lace. If you're interested in some little glass souvenir of your stay, perhaps an animal or a bird, you'll find such items sold in shops all over

Venice. But if you're interested in some more serious purchases, read on.

VENETIAN GLASS: **Salviati & Co.,** 195 San Gregorio (tel. 22532), is perhaps the finest and most reliable dealer in Venetian glass in the city. On St. Mark's Square, it keeps two small shops. If you apply there, you'll be escorted to the main showrooms and museum of antique glass on the Grand Canal. The shops are open not only weekdays from 9 a.m. to 7 p.m. but on Sunday as well (from 9 a.m. to 1 p.m.).

Another premier house of Venetian glass is **Pauly & Co.,** San Marco Ponte Consorzi (tel. 22621). This award-winning house exports all over the world. You can wander through its 21 salons, enjoying an exhibition of artistic glassware, later seeing a furnace in full action. There is no catalog offered; Pauly's production, which is mainly to order, consists of continually renewed patterns, subject to change and alteration based on customer desire.

VENETIAN LACE: **Jesurum,** 4310 Ponte Canonica, behind St. Mark's Basilica (tel. 706-177), is the best place for serious purchases. This elegant shop, a center of noted lacemakers and fashion creators, has been located in a 12th-century church since 1868. Open all year, it may be visited from 9 a.m. to 1 p.m. and from 3 to 7 p.m. You'll find Venetian handmade or machine lace and embroidery on table, bed, and bath linens, hand-printed or embroidered beach clothes, and bathing suits. Quality and originality are guaranteed, and special orders are accepted. The exclusive linens created here are expensive.

JEWELRY: The most highly refined selection of exquisite Venetian jewelry is found at **Nardi Sergio,** 68–71 Piazza San Marco (tel. 25-733). For old pieces, fine silver, antique jewelry, and new and original designs, it is stunning. For that really serious purchase, ask for Signor Sergio to attend you.

LEATHER: **Vogini,** 1291, 1301, and 1305 San Marco Ascensione (tel. 22-573), offers every kind of leatherwork, especially women's handbags, which are exclusive models. There's also a large assortment of handbags in petit-point, and the collection of artistic Venetian leather is of the highest quality. The travel equipment department contains a large assortment of trunks and wardrobe suitcases as well as dressing cases—many of the latest models in luggage.

CHILDREN'S WEAR: **Maricla,** San Marco, 2401 Via XXII Marzo (tel. 32-202), is called in Venice the boutique *per bambini e giovinette,* which means for babies and young girls. It also has a fine collection of lingerie for women, as well as exquisite embroideries. The shop is open in summer from 9 a.m. to 12:30 p.m. and 3:30 to 8 p.m. daily except Sunday.

FOR YOUR DESK NEEDS: **Legatoria Piazzesi,** 2511 San Marco (tel. 21-202), stands near the Gritti Palace. It has beautiful, hand-printed paper and numerous items for your office or study. The shop is open daily except Sunday and on Monday morning.

BARGAINS: If you're seeking some bargain-basement buys, head not for any basement but to one of the little shops that line the **Rialto Bridge.** The shops there branch out to encompass fruit and vegetable markets, as well. The Rialto isn't the Ponte Vecchio in Florence, but what it offers isn't bad, particularly if your lire are running short. You'll find a wide assortment of merchandise here, ranging from angora sweaters to leather gloves. Quality is likely to vary widely, so plunge in with utmost discrimination.

Venice After Dark

Considered the most fashionable and aristocratic rendezvous in Venice, the **Florian,** 56–59 Piazza San Marco (tel. 85338), is romantically and elegantly decorated. Dating from the 18th century, it has pure Venetian salons with red plush banquettes, intricate and elaborate murals under glass, and art nouveau lighting and lamps. The Florian roster of customers, since it opened its doors in 1720, has included such figures as Casanova, Lord Byron, Goethe, Canova, de Musset, and Madame de Stäel. The café is open daily from 9 a.m. to 11:30 p.m. except on Wednesday. An espresso costs from 2500 lire ($1.53); however, if you drink when the orchestra in the square is playing there will be an extra charge of 2000 lire ($1.22). Most long drinks cost from 10,000 lire ($6.10).

Its competitor is the equally famous **Quadri,** 120–124 Piazza San Marco (tel. 22105), which is open from 9:30 a.m. to 11 p.m.

except on Monday. However, in the peak tourist months lasting from July to September, it is open seven days a week. It also retains an old-world elegance in its intimate salons. Wagner used to drop in for a drink when he was working on *Tristan und Isolde.* It was a favorite rendezvous of Austrians during the occupation. It charges about the same drink prices as the Florian and also imposes a cover charge when the orchestra is playing. The Quadri also has one of the best known restaurants in Venice in its rooms upstairs (also one of the most expensive).

Want more in the way of nightlife? All right, but be warned: the Venetian nightclub owners may sock it to you when they present the bill.

The **Antico Martini,** Campo San Fantin, near La Fenice Theater (tel. 24121), is the best choice in the city for a more conventional nightclub visit, in an establishment catering to the post-30 set. But the strippers aren't one-tenth as appetizing as the dishes served in the superb restaurant on the premises. The club is dressy, featuring both a floor show and an orchestra. You'll pay 20,000 lire ($12.20) for the first drink, 16,000 lire ($9.76) thereafter.

From July to September, both residents and nonresidents of the **Bauer Grunwald,** 1459 San Marco (tel. 707022), patronize the club's roof garden, Settimo Cielo or "seventh heaven." Here, under the Venetian moon, you can enjoy piano music every night but Monday from 9:30. Drinks cost from 12,000 lire ($7.32). Off-season, the joint jumps in the tavern downstairs.

Do Leoni, Londra Palace Hotel, 4171 Riva degli Schiavoni (tel. 700-533), has joined the ranks of an increasingly popular kind of establishment throughout Italy—the piano bar. The interior is a rich blend of scarlet and gold carpeting with a motif of lions, English pub-style furniture, and Louis XVI–style chairs, along with plenty of exposed mahogany. An outdoor terrace is more nautical in feeling, with drinks served at canvas director's chairs surrounded with lots of shrubbery. The view is of a 19th-century bronze statue of a collection of Amazonian lion tamers, the lagoon, and the foot traffic along the Grand Canal. The hotel's popular restaurant has already been previewed. However, from 10:30 p.m. (till 1 a.m.), entertainment takes over, the piano adding musical warmth. A whisky costs around 8000 lire ($4.88).

El Souk, 1056A Dorsoduro (tel. 700-371), in the vicinity of the Accademia, is technically a private club and the closest thing to a gay disco in Venice. It is, however, not exclusively gay. You can make a reservation through the concierge of your hotel, although entrance is usually granted to friendly and "unthreatening" visitors. Expect to pay from 12,000 lire ($7.32) to 15,000 lire ($9.15) per drink, and try to go as late as possible. It is open every night except Wednesday from 9:30 p.m., usually remaining so until 2 a.m. or later.

Haig's Bar, 2477 San Marco (Campo del Giglio; tel. 894-456), near the Gritti Palace Hotel, is an English-style bar with taped cassette music and a reputation for being the preferred hangout for visiting gay men, although it also attracts a large straight clientele. Expect to pay from 7000 lire ($4.27) to 10,000 lire ($6.10) for a drink and go as late as possible, preferably between 11 p.m. and 3 a.m. It is closed on Wednesday.

At **Alla Grotta,** 403 San Marco (tel. 31943), performers alternate between operatic arias and old Venetian love ballads, the audience occasionally joining in. And you can drown your blues in purple wine. The grotto is very touristy, but that is a characteristic it shares with nearly every other establishment in Venice. The action with gondolier musicians starts after dinner and usually continues to 1 a.m. or later. However, it is only open in season, usually from April until the end of October. The entrance fee of 15,000 lire ($9.15) includes your first drink.

If you're interested in sampling some of the finest wines of the northeast sector of Italy, you might visit the best enoteca in town, **Al Volto,** 4081 San Marco (Calle Cavalli, lying off Fondamenta del Carbon). It offers excellent French, Hungarian, and even African wines in addition to those of sunny Italy. Snacks are served to accompany your wine drinking. It is closed Sunday, and you should visit in the evening after 5 p.m. and before 9 p.m. A canopy extends over the unobtrusive masonary facade, and the little street where laundry flaps in the wind is somewhat hard to find.

If you'd like merely to stroll through Venice at night but yet need a goal for your wandering, head in the direction of the **Gelateria Paolin,** 2962A San Marco (the Campo Santo Stefano), which lies at the corner of one of the most characteristic squares of Venice. Its ice cream—reputedly the best in Venice—comes in many tempting flavors such as pistacchio. For something different, try the "Málaga." It serves till 11 p.m. in summer but is closed on Friday.

ON THE LIDO: If you want to risk your luck and your lire, you can take a vaporetto ride on Line 28, leaving for the Piazzetta San Marco and delivering you to the landing dock of the **Casino Municipale.** The Italian government wisely forbids that its nationals cross the threshold, unless they work there. The building itself is foreboding, almost as if it could have been inspired by architects for Mussolini, but the action gets hotter once you step inside. Take your passport and be prepared to pay an entrance fee of 15,000 lire ($9.15), perhaps more by the time of your visit. Gambling is usually from 3 p.m. to 2:20 a.m., and it's held on the Lido from April to September. The address is 4 Lungomare G. Marconi (tel. 760626). At the casino, you can play blackjack, roulette, baccarat, or whatever, and you can also dine, drink at the bar, or enjoy a floor show.

However, from October to March, the casino action moves to the **Vendramin-Calergi Palace,** 2040 Cannaregio, Strada Nuova (tel. 710211), which is open from 3 p.m. to 3 a.m. Incidentally, Wagner died in this house opening onto the Grand Canal in 1883.

THE FILM FESTIVAL AND THE REGATTA: Since 1952 Venice has played host to an annual festival of the cinema, usually beginning in the last days of August and running into the first two weeks of September. Steadily mushrooming in popularity, the festival attracts top stars and directors, all accompanied by a glittering assortment of the so-called international set. Motion pictures are most often presented in their original languages, with Italian subtitles. Films are shown at the Palazzo de Cinema on the Lido, near the Casino.

The very fortunate time their visit to Venice to coincide not only with the film festival, but with the spectacular Regatta, usually held on the first Sunday in September. The Grand Canal fills with richly ornamented craft, and spectators from the balconies of the palazzi watch the race of the gondolas. The regatta is an ancient Venetian custom—worth the trip to Venice just to see the period costumes.

THEATER GOING: **La Fenice,** 2549 San Marco (Campo San Fantin; tel. 23954), is one of the most famous theaters in Europe, dating from the 19th century in its present incarnation (an earlier structure was gutted by fire). To cap the perfect visit, try to attend either a concert or an opera at this theater should it be open at the time of your visit.

Chapter XI

THE ABC'S OF ROME

THE EXPERIENCE for the first-time visitor of plunging madly into the traffic of Rome can be maddening. However, armed with some facts of life about how to cope, you will find your adjustment into the capital easier.

Arriving at the airport, transportation, and tipping must be faced even before you check into your hotel. There are any number of situations that might mar your trip. Included in that category is a medical emergency, of course. Although I don't promise to answer all your needs, I can point out a variety of services available in Rome that you need to know about.

The concierge of your hotel, incidentally, is a usually reliable dispenser of information, offering advice about everything—for example, whether you can "bring somebody back" to your room. If the concierge fails you, the following summary of pertinent survival facts may prove helpful.

AIRLINES/AIRPORTS: Chances are your arrival will be at Rome's **Leonardo da Vinci Airport** (popularly known as **Fiumicino**), 18½ miles from the center of the city. Domestic flights arrive at one terminal, international ones at the other. (If you're flying by charter, there is a possibility you might arrive at Ciampino airport.)

The least expensive way into Rome from Fiumicino is to take one of the many **buses** leaving every 15 minutes or so. These buses deliver you to the Air Terminal at 36 Via Giolitti (tel. 464-613), across from the Termini railway station. The one-way cost is about $3 (U.S.) per passenger. Buses are air-conditioned and have ample room for luggage. I once made the trip in from the airport in half an hour, but you'd better count on more than an hour because of heavy traffic.

Taxis are quite expensive and therefore not recommended for the trip from the airport. From the terminal, however, you can take a taxi to your hotel (or walk, if you're staying in the vicinity of the railway station, providing you don't have too much luggage).

If you arrive at Ciampino airport, you're nearer the city of Rome and may reach it in less than half an hour. Because of the shorter distance, you pay the amount shown on the meter if you go by taxi (not double, as some drivers may insist). Suburban buses leaving from the Piazza dei Cinquecento (in front of the Termini railway station) also run to Ciampino, and a train leaves Termini (take the Frascati line).

For air flight information for Fiumicino, telephone 601-541; for Ciampino, 600-251.

Rome is served by many international carriers, but chances are you'll need to consult one of the following about your return flight: **British Airways,** 54 Via Bissolati (tel. 47-171); **Pan American,** 46 Via Bissolati (tel. 47-73); or **TWA,** 59 Via Barberini (tel. 47-21). The national carrier, **Alitalia,** is at 13 Via Bissolati (tel. 46-88).

AMERICAN EXPRESS: The lifeline or pipeline back to America of many visitors, American Express has an office in Rome at 38 Piazza di Spagna (tel. 67-641). There is a branch of American Express in Venice and some other Italian cities.

BABYSITTERS: Most hotel desks in Rome will help you secure a babysitter. You should ask for an English-speaking person if available. If your hotel can't help in this matter, get in touch with **Baby Parking,** 16 Via San Prisca (tel. 572-224).

BANKS: In general, hours are from 9 a.m. to 1 p.m.; then, after a siesta until 3:30 or 4 p.m., many banks reopen until 6 p.m. The **American Express Bank** is at 5 Piazza Mignanelli (tel. 67-271). Two other favorite U.S. banks are **Chase Manhattan,** 27 Piazza Marconi (tel. 54-910), and **Citibank,** 26 Via Boncompagni (tel. 47-13). Banks are closed on Saturday and Sunday.

BOOKSTORES: There are at least two good ones in Rome, selling English-language publications. The **Lion Bookshop,** 181 Via del Babuino (tel. 678-9629), has mainly U.S. and British books, including a section for children. Try also the **Economy Book Center,** 29 Piazza di Spagna (tel. 679-0103), open from 9:30 a.m.

to 7:30 p.m. daily except Sunday, selling American and English paperbacks both new and used. This store is in the heart of Rome, by the Spanish Steps.

BUSES AND TRAMS: For only 600 lire (37¢) you can ride around to most parts of Rome (but not the outlying districts) on quite good bus hookups. Never—but *never*—ride the trams when the Romans are going to or from work, or you'll be mashed flatter than fettucccine.

Buses and trams stop at areas marked *Fermata*, and in general they are in service from 6 a.m. to midnight. After that and until dawn, service, on mainline stations only, is very marginal. It's best to take a taxi in the wee hours if you can find one.

At the bus transport office in front of the Termini station on Via Giolitti, you can purchase a directory complete with maps summarizing the particular routes.

Get on the bus with the exact change. You put your lire coins into a machine in the back of the bus, which will then dispense your ticket.

Roman buses are operated by an organization known as ATAC (Azienda Tramvie e Autobus del Commune di Roma).

CAR RENTALS: Many of the most charming landscapes and villas of Italy lie away from the main cities, far away from the train stations, and for that and for the sheer convenience that train travel cannot match, you'll find that renting a car is usually the best way to travel outside Rome. Renting a car is easy. All drivers in Italy must have nerves of steel, a valid driver's license, a valid passport, and be between the ages of 21 and 70.

Pricewise, it's to your advantage to drive Italian cars with manual transmission, since automatic transmissions in Europe are frequently viewed as a luxury, commanding premium prices. For example, one company rents a Fiat Ritmo with manual transmission for $180 per week, and $24 for each additional day; that same make car with automatic transmission is about $322 per week, and $46 for each additional day.

The longer in advance that you reserve a car, especially in high season, the more likely you'll be to get the model you wanted. It's important to note that all car rental companies in Italy are required to collect an additional 20% of the final charges as tax.

You can get detailed information about car rentals from any of the following companies, all of whom have offices at the airport as well as downtown Rome: Avis (tel. toll free 800/331-1212), at 38A Via Sardegna; Budget (tel. toll free 800/527-0700), in Rome at 24B Via Sistina; and Hertz (tel. toll free 800/654-3131) at 28 Via Sallustiana.

CIGARETTES: Seek out stores called *tabacchi.* Some bars also sell cigarettes. For a package of U.S. smokes in your familiar brand, you'll pay more than for an Italian variety. However, the taste of the cigarettes of the country may be unfamiliar and require some getting used to. American and British contraband cigarettes are sold freely on the streets for much less than you'll pay in the shops. Although purchasing them is illegal, it seems to be the custom.

CLIMATE: It's warm all over Italy in the summertime. The high temperatures (measures in centigrade) begin in Rome in May, often lasting until some time in October. Rome experiences its lowest average 24-hour monthly temperatures (Fahrenheit) in January, 49°; its highest in July, 82°. Here, the temperatures can stay in the 90s for days, but nights are most often comfortably cooler.

CRIME: Purse snatching is commonplace in Rome. Young men on Vespas or whatever ride through the city looking for victims. To avoid trouble, don't walk or stand near the street curb, and hold on tightly to your purse. Likewise, don't lay it on tables or chairs where it can be grabbed up easily.

Luggage is often stolen from airports and terminals. Watch yours with extreme care. Cameras are commonly grabbed as well, and cars with tempting merchandise visible are often broken into (or else the car is stolen altogether). There is much crime in Italy, but if you take discreet precautions, you should have a safe trip. It is unlikely you'll be kidnapped, regardless of what you've read in the paper.

Readers Mr. and Mrs. Clair E. Barnes of Long Beach, Calif., warn of autostrade toll-gate ripoffs. They say they learned to carry a paper that demanded, in Italian, to have the exact fare to their destination written down. The paper also contained the warning that the car could not move until the cost was filled in. "The toll-taker at Pompeii overcharged by 10 times the correct fare," they say, "as did the one at Casserta. If the toll-taker refuses to write the toll fee down, call the police."

CURRENCY: See "Currency Exchange," Chapter I.

CUSTOMS: Most items designed for personal use can be brought to Rome duty free. This includes clothing (new and used), books, camping and household equipment, fishing tackle, a sporting gun and 200 cartridges, a pair of skis, two tennis rackets, a portable typewriter, a record player with ten records, a tape recorder or dictaphone, baby carriage, two ordinary hand cameras with ten rolls of film and 24 slides, one movie camera with ten rolls of film, binoculars, personal jewelry, portable radio set (subject to a small license fee), and 400 cigarettes (two cartons) or a quantity of cigars or pipe tobacco not exceeding 500 grams (1.1 pounds).

A maximum of two bottles of alcoholic beverages per person can be brought in duty free. The bottles must be opened, however. Specifically, overseas tourists arriving in Italy after having visited other countries will be allowed to carry with them, without any special formality except a verbal declaration, travel souvenirs purchased in said countries up to a total lire value equivalent to $500 (U.S.), including fine perfumes up to half a liter.

Upon leaving Italy, citizens of the United States who have been outside their own country for 48 hours or more are allowed to bring back home $400 worth of merchandise duty free—that is, if they have claimed no similar exemption within the past 30 days. If you make purchases in Italy, it's important to keep your receipts.

DENTIST: To secure a dentist who speaks English, call the **American Embassy,** 121 Via Veneto (tel. 46-74). The staff there keeps a list of dentists available for emergency services. You'll probably have to call more than one or two to get an appointment.

DOCTORS: Likewise, call the **American Embassy,** 121 Via Veneto (tel. 46-74), which provides you with a list of doctors who speak English. Of course, all big hospitals in Rome have 24-hour first-aid service (go to the emergency room). You'll find English-speaking doctors at the privately run **Salvator Mundi International Hospital,** 67 Viale Mura Gianicolensis (tel. 580-0141).

DOCUMENTS FOR ENTRY: U.S., Canadian, and British citizens holding a valid passport do not have to have a visa to enter Italy if they do not expect to stay more than 90 days and do not expect to work there. Those who, after entering Italy, find they would like to stay more than 90 days can apply for a permit for an additional stay of 90 days, which as a rule is granted immediately.

DRUGSTORE: In Rome, a pharmacy open 24 hours a day is **Carlo Erba,** 145 Via del Corso (tel. 679-0866). Another all-day and all-night one, most centrally located, is **Farmacia Internazionale,** 49 Piazza Barberini (tel. 462-996). Most pharmacies are open from 8:30 a.m. to 1 p.m. and from 4 to 7:30 p.m. In general, pharmacies follow a rotation system so that several are always open on Sunday.

ELECTRICAL APPLIANCES: Electric current in Italy varies considerably. The current is usually AC, the cycle varying from 42 to 50. The voltage can be from 115 to 220. It is recommended that any visitor carrying electrical appliances obtain a transformer either before leaving the U.S. or Canada or in any electrical appliance shop in Italy. Check the exact local current with the hotel where you are staying. Plugs have prongs that are round, not flat; therefore, an adapter plug is needed.

EMBASSIES: I hope you'll not need such services, but in case of a lost passport or some other emergency, the **U.S. Embassy** in Rome is at 121 Via Veneto (tel. 46-74); the **British Embassy** is at 80a Via Venti Settembre (tel. 475-5441); and the **Canadian Embassy** is at 30 Via Zara (tel. 844-1841). The U.S. has a consulate in Florence also.

EMERGENCY: Rome has a police "hot line"—telephone 212-121. Usually, however, dial 113 for the police and the same number to report a fire or summon an ambulance. If you're on the highway and have an emergency or need immediate repairs, telephone 116.

ETIQUETTE: Forget about politeness when it comes to lining up for anything. For instance, if you want a check cashed or to buy a stamp and you have to line up, you'll learn that the local custom is to push, shove, and elbow your way to the front.

FILM: U.S. brand film is available in Italy, but it's expensive. Take in as much as Customs will allow if you plan to take a lot of pictures. Processing film takes a week or more in Italy, although some of the bigger shops in Rome will have your pictures ready in about four days. I've had very bad luck with getting color film processed. I definitely recommend that you save yours until you return home.

FOOD: You'll find restaurants of international renown here and an indefinite number of *trattorie* and *rosticcerie* where, chances are, good meals may be obtained at moderate prices. The main meals are served between noon and 3 p.m. and between 8 and 11 p.m., but they can also be obtained at other hours. Many restaurants throughout the country offer fixed-price meals that include two courses, a dessert, a house wine, and service.

GAS: It's super-expensive in Italy, about 1320 lire (81¢) per liter (0.264 U.S. gallons) as of this writing—but *subject to change.* Autostrade tolls are also expensive, incidentally, so carry plenty of cash if you're going to be doing extensive motoring (see warning note under "Crime").

HAIRDRESSER: In Rome, the **Sergio Valente Beauty Center,** 11 Via Condotti (tel. 679-1268), offers every cosmetic indulgence—massage, manicure, pedicure, facial, haircut, fashion hair styling, and hair coloring—in luxurious surroundings.

HOLIDAYS AND FESTIVALS: Offices and shops are closed on the following days: January 1 and 6; Feast of St. Joseph (March 19); Easter Monday; Liberation Day (April 25); Labor Day (May 1); Feast of the Ascension of Christ (sixth Thursday after Easter); Corpus Christi (ninth Thursday after Easter); Proclamation of the Republic (June 2); Feast of Saints Peter and Paul (June 29); Feast of the Assumption of the Virgin (August 15); All Saints' Day (November 1); Victory Day, 1918 (November 4); Feast of the Immaculate Conception (December 8); and December 25 (Christmas) as well as December 26.

Local feast days are held in honor of towns' patron saints. Venice observes April 25 (St. Mark), and Florence, June 24 (John the Baptist).

INFORMATION: Tourist information is available at the **Ente Provinciale per il Turismo,** 11 Via Parigi (tel. 461-851). There's another information bureau at the main railroad station (tel. 465-461).

LANGUAGES: Italian, naturally, is the tongue of the land. It bears little resemblance to the Latin that you might have studied in school. If you don't speak Italian, don't be intimidated. English is widely spoken and understood here, especially in facilities catering to tourists.

LAUNDRY: All deluxe, first-class, and second-class hotels have laundry and dry-cleaning facilities. Prices are usually moderate, and a service charge is added to the actual cost. If a hotel doesn't provide these services, the desk clerk can direct you to the nearest shop (tintoria), or you can look in the classified telephone directory under *tintorie* (cleaning and pressing) and *lavanderie* (laundry).

LIBRARIES: In Rome, the **American Library** is at 62 Via Veneto (tel. 46-74), and it's open from 2 to 6 p.m. Monday to Friday. There's also the **British Council Library,** 20 Quattro Fontane (tel. 475-0018), which is open from 10 a.m. to 1 p.m. and 3 to 6:30 p.m. Monday to Friday.

MAIL DELIVERY: General delivery service is available. Correspondence can be addressed c/o the post office by adding *Fermo in Posta* after the name of the city. Delivery will be made at the central post office when you identify yourself as the recipient by showing your passport. The central post office in Rome is at the Piazza San Silvestro, behind the Rinascente Department Store on Piazza Colonna (tel. 672-225). It's open from 8 a.m. to 9 p.m. You can buy stamps from post offices or at little *tabacchi* (tobacco) stores throughout the city. An average letter costs 630 lire (38¢) to mail. Airmail to America begins at 770 lire (47¢) per letter, only 620 lire (37½¢) for a postcard.

In Rome, try to mail your letters and postcards at the central post office at Vatican City. They'll get home much more quickly. Mail delivery in Italy is notoriously bad. One letter from a soldier, postmarked in 1945, arrived at his home village in 1982. Letters sent in, say, November from New York are often delivered the following year—if at all. If you're writing for hotel reservations, it can cause great confusion on both sides. Many visitors arrive in Italy long before their hotel deposits.

OFFICE HOURS: These vary greatly. However, regular business hours are from 9 a.m. (sometimes 9:30 a.m.) to 1 p.m. and from 3:30 or 4 p.m. to 7 or 7:30 p.m. In the white heat of an Italian July or August, offices may not open in the afternoon until 4:30 or 5 p.m.

PETS: A veterinarian's certificate of good health is required for dogs and cats, and should be obtained by owners in advance of entering Italy. Dogs must be on a leash or muzzled at all times. Other animals must undergo examination at the border or port of entry. Certificates for parrots or other birds subject to psittico-sis must state that the country of origin is free of disease. All documents must be certified by a notary public, then by the nearest office of the Italian Consulate.

RELIGIOUS SERVICES: Catholic churches abound in Rome, with some conducting services for English-speaking people, including **San Silvestro,** 1 Piazza San Silvestro (tel. 679-7755), and **Santa Susana,** 14 Via 20 Settembre (tel. 475-1510). The **American Episcopal Church** is St. Pauls, 58 Via Napoli at Via Nazionale (tel. 463-339). The Jewish temple, **Sinagoga Ebraica,** is at Lungotevere dei Cenci (tel. 656-4648).

REST ROOMS: These public conveniences are much improved since I first traveled here. Of course, all airport and railway stations have rest rooms, often with attendants. Bars, nightclubs, restaurants, cafés, and all hotels have facilities as well. Public toilets are also found near many of the major sights in Rome. If you're not checking into a Rome hotel but going on by train elsewhere, you can patronize the Albergo Diurno, a hotel without beds at the Termini Station in Rome, which has baths, showers, and well-kept toilet facilities, for which you pay a small charge.

SHOPPING HOURS: Most stores are open from 9 a.m. to 1 p.m. year round. Shops in Rome in summer reopen at either 3:30 or 4 p.m., doing business until 7:30 or 8 p.m. Grocery stores are likely to reopen at 5 p.m. This siesta is observed in most cities in southern Italy. Most shops are closed on Sunday, except for certain barbershops that open Sunday morning. Most hairdressers are closed on Sunday and Monday. If you visit Rome in summer and the heat is intense, I suggest that you learn the custom of the siesta too.

SUBWAYS: This is the fastest means of transportation in Rome, with two underground lines, called the **Metropolitana,** or **Metro,** for short. Line A goes from Via Ottaviano, near St. Peter's, to Piazza di Cinecittà, stopping at Piazzale Flaminio (near Piazza del Popolo), Piazza Vittorio Emanuele, and Piazza San Giovanni in Laterano. Line B connects the Termini Station with Via Laurentina, stopping at Via Cavour, the Colosseum, Circus Maximus, the Pyramid of C. Cestius, St. Paul's Outside the Walls, the Magliana, and the E.U.R. A big red letter **M** indicates the entrance to the subway. The price anywhere within the walls is 600 lire (37¢), but of course you'll have to pay more to go to the further reaches of the underground.

Tickets are available from vending machines at all stations, but these machines accept only 50-lira and 100-lira coins, not 200-lira coins. Some stations have managers, but they will not make change. Booklets of tickets are available at *tabacchi* (tobacco) shops. Building an underground system for Rome has not been easy, since every time workers start digging, they discover an old temple or other archeological treasure and heavy earthmoving has to cease for a while.

TAXES: As a member of the European Common Market, Italy imposes a tax on most goods and services—currently 8.25%. It is a "value added tax," called I.V.A. in Italy.

TAXIS: Walter Galling, in the *Daily American,* wrote: "Italy's best salesmen are its cab drivers. They even open the door!" Conversely, prices are high—and may well go higher in this edition's lifetime. The meter drops at 1200 lire (73¢), and you'd better watch to be sure you're not paying the previous occupant's bill. There's also a surcharge of 700 lire (43¢) at present. In other words, if you're accustomed to hopping a cab in New York or London, then do so in Rome. If not, take less expensive means of transport. After 10 p.m. and until 7 a.m., there is an additional charge of 1500 lire (92¢). You must also pay 500 lire (31¢) per large suitcase. It's rare for a taxi ride to cost less than 4000 lire ($2.44). If you take a cab from Rome to Fiumicino airport, another surcharge is added to your bill—this one 10,000 lire ($6.10). To come from the airport into Rome, however, the meter reading is simply doubled. Avoid trying to pay your fare with large bills. Invariably, taxi drivers don't have change—but you'd better. Also, the driver will expect a 15% tip.

Tip: Don't count on hailing a taxi driver on the street or even getting one at a stand. Have your hotel call one. At a restaurant, ask the waiter or cashier to dial for you. If you want to do the phoning yourself, you can call 35-70, 38-75, 49-49, or 84-33.

TELEGRAMS: ITALCABLE operates services abroad, transmitting messages by cable or radio. Both internal and foreign telegrams may be dictated over the phone. In Rome, you can send messages day and night at the *Telegrafi* office at the central post office on Piazza San Silvestro, off Via della Mercedes. Call 186 if you want to dictate a cable or express telegram, but you should be proficient in Italian if you do this.

TELEPHONES: A public telephone is always near at hand in Italy, especially if you're in the vicinity of a bar. Local calls from public telephones require the use of a token, which can be purchased at all newsstands, tobacco shops, and bars. Long-distance calls among the major cities can be dialed directly by using the area code numbers.

The token is called a *gettone* and sells for 100 lire (6¢). Deposit it in the slot as you would a coin in the States, then dial your number. When your party answers, press the button near the slot, which allows the *gettone* to drop into the phone box.

In Rome, the central *Telefoni* office stands next to the main post office at Piazza San Silvestro off Via della Mercedes. For information, dial 12. The telephone office is open all night.

Dial 170 if you're placing a transatlantic call to either the U.S. or Canada. An ITALCABLE operator who speaks English will come on. At the telephone office next to the post office, an operator will place your long-distance call at no extra charge. However, at hotels, the cost of a call has been known to be doubled or tripled—so be duly warned.

TELEX: Chances are, your hotel will send one for you.

TIME: In terms of standard time zones, Italy is six hours ahead of Eastern Standard Time in the United States. Daylight Saving Time is in effect in Italy each year from May 22 to September 24.

TIPPING: In hotels, the service charge is already added to a bill. In addition, it is customary to tip the chambermaid 500 lire (31¢) per day; the doorman (for calling a cab), 500 lire; and the bellhop or porter, 1000 lire (61¢) per bag. A concierge expects about 15% over his bill for extra services he may have performed, which is likely to include long-distance calls, newspapers, or stamps.

In restaurants, 15% is added to your bill to cover most charges. An additional tip for good service is almost always expected. Know that it is customary in certain fashionable restaurants in Rome, Florence, Venice, and Milan to leave an additional 10%, which, combined with the assessed service charge, is a very high tip indeed. Checkroom attendants now expect 1000 lire (61¢), although in simple places Italians still hand washroom attendants 200 lire (12¢), more in deluxe and first-class establishments.

In cafés and bars, tip 15% of the bill, and give a theater usher 1000 lire (61¢).

NOW, SAVE MONEY ON ALL YOUR TRAVELS!

Join Arthur Frommer's $25-A-Day Travel Club

Saving money while traveling is never a simple matter, which is why, over 22 years ago, the **$25-A-Day Travel Club** was formed. Actually, the idea came from readers of the Arthur Frommer Publications who felt that such an organization could bring financial benefits, continuing travel information, and a sense of community to economy-minded travelers all over the world.

In keeping with the money-saving concept, the annual membership fee is low—$15 (U.S. residents) or $18 (Canadian, Mexican, and foreign residents)—and is immediately exceeded by the value of your benefits which include:

(1) The latest edition of any TWO of the books listed on the following page.

(2) An annual subscription to an 8-page quarterly newspaper *The Wonderful World of Budget Travel* which keeps you up-to-date on fastbreaking developments in low-cost travel in all parts of the world—bringing you the kind of information you'd have to pay over $25 a year to obtain elsewhere. This consumer-conscious publication also includes the following columns:

Travelers' Directory—members all over the world who are willing to provide hospitality to other members as they pass through their home cities.

Share-a-Trip—requests from members for travel companions who can share costs and help avoid the burdensome single supplement.

Readers Ask . . . Readers Reply—travel questions from members to which other members reply with authentic firsthand information.

(3) A copy of *Arthur Frommer's Guide to New York.*

(4) Your personal membership card which entitles you to purchase through the Club all Arthur Frommer Publications for a third to a half off their regular retail prices during the term of your membership.

So why not join this hardy band of international budgeteers NOW and participate in its exchange of information and hospitality? Simply send $15 (U.S. residents) or $18 U.S. (Canadian, Mexican, and other foreign residents) along with your name and address to: $25-A-Day Travel Club, Inc., 1230 Avenue of the Americas, New York, NY 10020. Remember to specify which *two* of the books in section (1) above you wish to receive in your initial package of members' benefits. Or tear out this page, check off any two books on the opposite side and send it to us with your membership fee.